World War II
Biographies

World War II
Biographies

Kelly King Howes
Edited by Christine Slovey

AN IMPRINT OF THE GALE GROUP

DETROIT · SAN FRANCISCO · LONDON
BOSTON · WOODBRIDGE, CT

Kelly King Howes

Staff

Christine Slovey, *U•X•L Editor*
Carol DeKane Nagel, *U•X•L Managing Editor*
Tom Romig, *U•X•L Publisher*

Rita Wimberley, *Senior Buyer*
Evi Seoud, *Production Manager*
Mary Beth Trimper, *Production Director*

Keasha Jack-Lyles, *Permissions Associate*
Margaret A. Chamberlain, *Permissions Specialist*

Eric Johnson, *Cover Art Director*
Pamela A.E. Galbreath, *Page Art Director*
Cynthia Baldwin, *Product Design Manager*
Barbara J. Yarrow, *Graphic Services Supervisor*

Linda Mahoney, LM Design, *Typesetting*

Library of Congress Cataloging-in-Publication Data

Howes, Kelly King
    World War II: Biographies / Kelly K. Howes
       p. cm.
    Includes biographical references and index.
    ISBN 0-7876-3895-1
    World War, 1939-1945 Biography. I. Title

    D736.H69 1999
    940.53'092'2   99-27166
    [B]–DC21   CIP

Contents

Jacqueline Cochran.
(Archive Photos, Inc.)

Ernie Pyle.
(Archive Photos, Inc.)

Advisory Board

Special thanks are due for the invaluable comments and suggestions provided by U•X•L's World War II Reference Library advisors:

- Sidney Bolkosky, Professor of History, University of Michigan-Dearborn, Dearborn, Michigan

- Sara Brooke, Director of Libraries, The Ellis School, Pittsburgh, Pennsylvania

- Jacquelyn Divers, Librarian, Roanoke County Schools, Roanoke, Virginia

- Elaine Ezell, Library Media Specialist, Bowling Green Junior High School, Bowling Green, Ohio

- Melvin Small, Department of History, Wayne State University, Detroit, Michigan

Reader's Guide

World War II: Biographies presents the life stories of thirty-one individuals who played key roles in World War II. The many noteworthy individuals involved in the war could not all be profiled in a single-volume work. Stories were selected to give readers a wide perspective on the war and the people who played a part in it, including political and military leaders, enlisted men, and civilians. *World War II: Biographies* includes readily recognizable figures such as U.S. President Franklin D. Roosevelt and Nazi leader Adolf Hitler, as well as lesser-known individuals such as Franz Jaggerstatter, an Austrian conscientious objector killed by the Nazis for refusing to serve in the German army, and Dorothy Thompson, an American journalist who wrote against Hitler's political and social policies in the years before the war.

Other Features

World War II: Biographies begins with a "Words to Know" section and a timeline of events and achievements in the lives of the profilees. The volume has more than sixty black-and-white photos. Entries contain sidebars of related, interesting information and additional short biographies of people who are in some way connected with the main biographee. Sources for further reading or research are cited at the end of each entry. Cross-references are made to other individuals profiled in the volume. The volume concludes with a subject index so students can easily find the people, places, and events discussed throughout *World War II: Biographies*.

Comments and Suggestions

We welcome your comments on *World War II: Biographies*, as well as your suggestions for persons to be features in future editions. Please write, Editors, *World War II: Biographies*, U•X•L, 27500 Drake Rd., Farmington Hills, Michigan 48331-3535; call toll-free: 1-800-877-4253; fax to (248) 699-8097; or send e-mail via http://www.gale.com.

Words to Know

A

Allies: The countries who fought against Germany, Italy, and Japan during World War II. The makeup of the Allied powers changed over the course of the war. The first Allied countries were Great Britain and France. Germany defeated France in 1940 but some Free French forces continued to fight with the Allies until the end of the war. The Soviet Union and the United States joined the Allies in 1941.

Afrika Korps: The experienced, effective German troops who fought under German field marshal Erwin Rommel in the North African desert.

Anschloss: The 1938 agreement that made Austria a part of Nazi Germany.

Antisemitism: The hatred of Jews, who are sometimes called Semites.

Appeasement: Making compromises in order to stay on neutral terms with another party or country.

Atlantic Charter: An agreement signed in 1941 by President Franklin D. Roosevelt and British Prime Minister Winston Churchill in which the United States and Great Britain stated their commitment to worldwide peace and democracy.

Atomic bomb: A weapon of mass destruction in which a radioactive element such as uranium is bombarded with neutrons to create a chain reaction called nuclear fission, which splits atoms, releasing a huge amount of energy.

Axis: During World War II, Germany, Italy, and Japan formed a coalition called the Axis powers.

B

Blitzkrieg: Meaning "lightning war" in German, this is the name given the German's military strategy of sending troops in land vehicles to make quick, surprise attacks while airplanes provide support from above. This method was especially effective against Poland and France.

C

Chancellor: In some European countries, including Germany, the chief minister of the government.

Communism: An economic system that promotes the ownership of all property and means of production by the community as a whole.

Concentration camps: Places where the Germans confined people they considered "enemies of the state." These included Jews, Roma (commonly called Gypsies), homosexuals, and political opponents.

Conscientious objector: A person who refuses to fight in a war for moral, religious, or philosophical reasons.

D

D-Day: Usually refers to June 6, 1944, the day the Normandy Invasion began with a massive landing of Allied troops on the beaches of northern France, which was occupied by Germany; also called Operation Overlord. D-Day is also a military term designating the date and time of an attack.

Depression: An economic downturn. The United States experienced the worst depression in its history from 1929 to 1939, referred to as the Great Depression.

Dictator: A ruler who holds absolute power.

Draft: The system by which able young men are required by law to perform a term of military service for their country.

Il Duce: The Italian phrase meaning "the leader" by which dictator Benito Mussolini was known.

E

Executive Order 9066: President Franklin D. Roosevelt's order directing all Japanese Americans living on the West Coast to be sent to internment camps.

F

Fascism: A political system in which power rests not with citizens but with the central government, which is often run by the military and/or a dictator.

Final Solution: The code name given to the Nazi plan to eliminate all the Jews of Europe.

Free French Movement: The movement led by Charles de Gaulle, who, from a position outside France, tried to organize and encourage the French people to resist the German occupation.

Führer: The German word meaning "leader"; the title Adolf Hitler took as dictator of Germany.

G

G.I.: Stands for government issue, G.I. has become a nickname for enlisted soldiers, or former members of the U.S. armed forces.

Gestapo: An abbreviation for Germany's *Geheime Staats Politzei* or Secret State Police.

H

Hitler Youth: An organization that trained German boys to idolize and obey German leader Adolf Hitler and to become Nazi soldiers.

Holocaust: The period between 1933 and 1945 when Nazi Germany systematically persecuted and murdered millions of Jews, Roma (commonly called Gypsies), homosexuals, and other innocent people.

I

Internment camps: Ten camps located throughout the western United States to which about 120,000 Japanese Americans were forced to move due to ungrounded suspicion that they were not loyal to the United States.

Isolationism: A country's policy of keeping out of other countries' affairs.

L

Lend-Lease Program: A program that allowed the United States to send countries fighting the Germans (such as Great Britain and the Soviet Union) supplies needed for the war effort in exchange for payment to be made after the war.

Luftwaffe: The German air force.

M

Manhattan Project: The project funded by the U.S. government that gathered scientists together at Los Alamos, New Mexico, to work on the development of an atomic bomb.

Mein Kampf (My Struggle): The 1924 autobiography of Adolf Hitler, in which he explains his racial and political philosophies, including his hatred of Jews.

N

Nazi: The abbreviation for the National Socialist German Workers' Party, the political party led by Adolf Hitler, who became dictator of Germany. Hitler's Nazi Party controlled Germany from 1933 to 1945. The Nazis promoted racist and anti-Semitic (anti-Jewish) ideas and enforced complete obedience to Hitler and the party.

Noncombatant: A job in the military that is not directly involved with combat or fighting; such a job may be given to a conscientious objector during a war.

O

Occupation: Control of a country by a foreign military power.

Operation Overlord: The code name for the Normandy Invasion, a massive Allied attack on German-occupied France; also called D-Day.

P

Pacifist: A person who does not believe in hurting or killing others for any reason.

Pact of Steel: An agreement signed in 1939 that established the military alliance between Italy's Benito Mussolini and Germany's Adolf Hitler.

Propaganda: Material such as literature, images, or speeches that is designed to influence public opinion toward a certain doctrine. The content of the material may be true or false.

Purge: Removing (often by killing) all those who are seen as enemies.

R

Reich: The German word meaning "empire." Hitler's term as Germany's leader was called the Third Reich.

Reichstag: Germany's parliament or lawmaking body.

Resistance: Working against an occupying army.

S

Segregation: The forced separation of black and white people, not only in public places and schools but also in the U.S. military. The opposite of segregation is integration.

Socialism: A political system in which the means of producing and distributing goods are shared or owned by the government.

SS: An abbreviation for *Schutzstaffel,* or Security Squad, the unit that provided German leader Adolf Hitler's personal bodyguards as well as guards for the various concentration camps.

Swastika: The Nazi symbol of a black, bent-armed cross that always appeared within a white circle set on a red background.

T

Tripartite Pact: An agreement signed in September 1940 that established an alliance among Germany, Italy, and Japan. The countries promised to aid each other should any one of them face an attack.

Tuskegee Airmen: A group of African Americans who became the first black Army Air Corps pilots, and who performed excellently in combat in Europe.

V

Versailles Treaty: The agreement signed by the countries who had fought in World War I that required Germany to claim responsibility for the war and pay money to other countries for damage from the war.

Vichy Government: The government set up in France after the Germans invaded the country; headed by Henri Petain, it was really under German control.

W

WACs: The Women's Army Corps, an organization that allowed American women to serve in a variety of noncombat roles.

WASPs: The Women's Airforce Service Pilots, an organization that recruited and trained women pilots to perform noncombat flying duties.

War crimes: Violations of the laws or customs of war.

Timeline

1916   **Jeanette Rankin** becomes the first woman elected to the U.S. Congress; she immediately causes controversy by voting against the country's entry into World War I.

1923   **Adolf Hitler,** leader of the National Socialist German Worker's Party (Nazis), is in charge of the Munich Beer Hall Putsch, a failed attempt to take over the German government, for which Hitler serves a short prison term.

1926   Fascist leader **Benito Mussolini** becomes dictator of Italy.

Benito Mussolini and Adolf Hitler.
(National Archives and Records Administration.)

1914 World War I begins	1918 World War I ends	1920 League of Nations formed

1912   1918   1924

1926 Following the death of his father, **Hirohito** becomes emperor of Japan, giving his reign the name Showa (enlightened peace).

1927 **Chiang Kai-Shek** establishes the Kuomintang or Nationalist government at Nanking, China.

1927 American journalist **Dorothy Thompson** interviews Adolf Hitler, now a rising German politician, for *Cosmopolitan* magazine.

1932 **Franklin D. Roosevelt** begins the first of four terms as president of the United States.

1933 Adolf Hitler becomes chancellor of Germany. Within a few months he and his National Socialist German Workers' Party (the Nazis) have taken control of the country.

1934 **Harry S. Truman** is elected to the U.S. Senate and begins to build a reputation as a very effective leader.

1934 Adolf Hitler orders American journalist Dorothy Thompson out of Germany, giving her twenty-four hours to leave the country.

1938 British prime minister **Neville Chamberlain** signs the Munich Pact with Adolf Hitler, who will soon break his promise not to invade Czechoslovakia.

1938 Austrians vote in favor of the *Anschloss,* an agreement that makes their country part of Nazi Germany.

1938 The Nazis stage Kristallnacht ("night of broken glass"), in which the homes, businesses, and synagogues of German Jews are destroyed and tens of thousands of people are sent to concentration camps.

1939 Soviet leader **Joseph Stalin** and German dictator Adolf Hitler sign an agreement promising that neither will

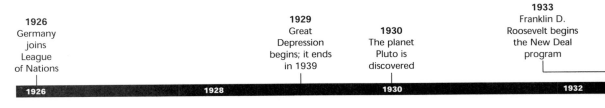

1926
Germany joins League of Nations

1929
Great Depression begins; it ends in 1939

1930
The planet Pluto is discovered

1933
Franklin D. Roosevelt begins the New Deal program

| 1926 | 1928 | 1930 | 1932 |

invade the other's country; Hitler will break the agreement two years later.

1939 General **George C. Marshall** is sworn in as chief of staff, the highest office in the U.S. Army.

1939 Germany invades Poland, and World War II officially begins when Great Britain and France respond by declaring war on Germany.

1940 **Winston Churchill** becomes prime minister of Great Britain.

1940 German tanks roll into France, and soon the French government signs an agreement allowing Germany to control the country.

1940 The Germans begin bombing England in a long air campaign that is fiercely resisted by the British.

1940 American journalist **Ernie Pyle** arrives in London to report on the war there.

1940 **Benjamin O. Davis, Sr.,** becomes the first African American general in the United States Army.

1941 American president Franklin D. Roosevelt and British prime minister Winston Churchill sign the Atlantic Charter, in which they agree to promote peace and democracy around the world.

1941 Germany invades the Soviet Union and quickly takes control of much of the country.

1941 **Oveta Culp Hobby** is named director of the new Women's Auxiliary Army Corps (WAAC), which will eventually be made part of the U.S. Army and renamed the Women's Army Corps (WAC).

1941 German general **Erwin Rommel,** the "Desert Fox," leads the Afrika Korps in several victorious battles against the British army.

Oveta Culp Hobby with Dwight D. Eisenhower.
(AP/Wide World Photos.)

1933
The United States and Soviet Union establish diplomatic relations

1935
Italy invades Ethiopia

1936
Spanish Civil War begins

1938
First nuclear fission of uranium is produced

1934   1936   1938   1940

Benjamin O. Davis, Jr., receives the Distinguished Flying Cross medal.
(U.S. Army.)

1941 American pilot **Jacqueline Cochran** flies a Hudson V bomber plane from Canada to Great Britain, becoming the first woman to fly a military aircraft over the Atlantic Ocean.

1941 **Hideki Tojo** becomes prime minister of Japan.

1941 Japan launches a devastating surprise attack on the U.S. naval base at Pearl Harbor, and the United States soon declares war against Japan.

1942 African American sailor Dorie Miller receives the Navy Cross for his heroic performance during the Pearl Harbor bombing.

1942 President Roosevelt signs Executive Order 9066, directing all Japanese Americans living on the West Coast to be sent to internment camps.

1942 Twenty-nine Navajos are inducted into the U.S. Marine Corps to begin training as "Code Talkers"; the men will use the Navajo language to provide secure communications during battles in the Pacific.

1942 Commanded by **Benjamin O. Davis, Jr.**, and trained at the Tuskegee Institute in Alabama, the Tuskegee Airmen become the first African American pilots to enter the U.S. Army Air Corps.

1942 Hollywood movie director **Frank Capra** arrives in Washington, D.C., to begin work on *Why We Fight,* a series of documentary films designed to educate soldiers about the causes of World War II and why the United States is involved.

1942 **General Dwight D. Eisenhower** takes command of all U.S. forces in Europe.

1942 **Edith Stein**, who was born a Jew but converted to Catholicism and became a nun, is killed at a concentration camp in Auschwitz, Poland.

1940
Tripartite Pact signed by Germany, Italy, and Japan

March 1941
President Franklin Roosevelt signs the Lend-Lease Act

June 1941
Germany attacks the Soviet Union

December 1941
Germany declares war on the United States

1942
Penicillin is discovered

1941   1942

1942   Erwin Rommel becomes the youngest German officer to be named a field marshal, the highest rank in the German military.

1942   The Allies launch Operation Torch, an invasion of German-occupied North Africa that ends with the Germans being chased out of the region.

1942   U.S. general **George S. Patton** takes command of the First Armored Corps (a tank division) and leads them to victory during Operation Torch, the Allied invasion of North Africa.

1942   In the Battle of El Alamein, British field marshal **Bernard Montgomery** leads the British 8th Army in an important victory against German field marshal Erwin Rommel's Afrika Korps.

1942   Physicist Enrico Fermi achieves the first self-sustaining nuclear reaction in his laboratory at New York's Columbia University.

1943   Russian troops defeat the Germans at the Battle of Stalingrad, but at a terrible cost in lives lost.

1943   *Prelude to War,* the first film in the *Why We Fight* film series directed by Frank Capra, wins the Oscar for best documentary.

1943   Italian dictator Benito Mussolini is removed from office by the Fascist Grand Council; with German leader Adolf Hitler's help, Mussolini tries to establish a separate government in northern Italy.

1943   General George S. Patton arrives in Sicily, the large island off the coast of Italy, to begin the Allied invasion that will continue on the Italian mainland.

1943   General Dwight D. Eisenhower goes to England to take command of the Supreme Headquarters Allied Expeditionary Force (SHAEF).

George S. Patton.
(The Library of Congress.)

June 1942
The United States defeats Japan at the Battle of Midway

September 1943
Italy surrenders unconditionally to the Allies

June 1944
Allied forces enter Rome

1943   1944

1943 Allied leaders meet at Casablanca, Morocco, and Cairo, Egypt, to discuss the progress of the war. At another meeting in Quebec, Canada, they plan Operation Overlord (or D-Day), an invasion of Europe that will take place six months later.

1943 Austrian farmer **Franz Jaggerstatter** is executed for refusing to serve in Hitler's army.

1943 Jacqueline Cochran becomes director of the Women's Air Service Pilots (WASPs).

1944 D-Day—hundreds of thousands of Allied troops take part in the Normandy Invasion, which begins with a massive landing on the beaches of northern France on June 6.

1944 German army officer Nicholas Stauffenberg leads an unsuccessful attempt to kill Adolf Hitler.

1944 Allied troops liberate the city of Paris from its German occupiers.

1944 The 761st Battalion, an African American tank unit, arrives in France to take part in the Allied drive toward Germany.

1944 General **Douglas MacArthur** returns to liberate the Philippines from Japanese control, just as he had promised nearly three years earlier.

1944 In a bloody struggle known as the Battle of the Bulge, the Germans fight back against the Allies with one last, fierce counter-offensive in the Ardennes region of France.

1945 Allied leaders meet in Yalta in the Soviet Union to discuss how to end the war and what will happen to Germany and the rest of Europe when the war is over.

1945 President Franklin D. Roosevelt dies of a cerebral hemorrhage in Warm Springs, Georgia; Vice President

1944
G.I. Bill signed
into law

1945
Auschwitz
liberated by
Soviet troops

1946
First session of the United
Nations General Assembly
opens in London

1945   1946

Harry S. Truman takes the oath of office and will lead the nation into peacetime.

1945   Soon after German leader Adolf Hitler commits suicide in his underground bunker in Berlin, Germany surrenders to the Allies.

1945   Nazi leader **Hermann Göring** surrenders to American troops; a year later, he will commit suicide after being condemned to death for war crimes.

1945   While reporting on the Allied invasion of Okinawa, Ernie Pyle is killed by a Japanese sniper.

1945   President Harry S. Truman and other world leaders sign the charter establishing the United Nations as an international peacekeeping organization.

1945   **J. Robert Oppenheimer**, leader of a group of scientists working to develop an atomic bomb, oversees a successful test of the bomb at the Alamogordo Bombing Range near Los Alamos, New Mexico.

1945   The Allies drop atomic bombs on the Japanese cities of Hiroshima and Nagasaki in a devastating attack that leads to Japan's surrender to the Allies.

1945   Japanese leaders sign an official surrender document aboard the USS *Missouri*.

1947   Secretary of State George C. Marshall introduces the European Recovery Act, a plan for helping the European countries recover from the effects of the war.

1948   President Harry S. Truman signs Executive Order 9981, which calls for the integration of the U.S. armed forces.

1948   Defeated by the Communists, Chiang Kai-Shek flees China with others loyal to his Nationalist Party, taking refuge on the island of Formosa (now Taiwan).

General Douglas MacArthur accepts Japan's surrender.
(UPI/Corbis-Bettmann.)

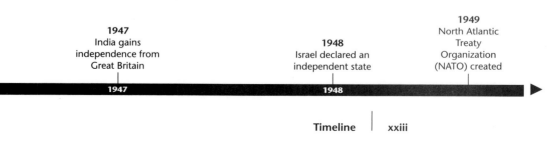

1947
India gains independence from Great Britain

1948
Israel declared an independent state

1949
North Atlantic Treaty Organization (NATO) created

1947

1948

Hideki Tojo at his war crimes trial.
(National Archives and Records Administration.)

1948 Prime minister of Japan Hideki Tojo is executed for war crimes.

1952 Dwight D. Eisenhower is elected president of the United States.

1953 George C. Marshall wins the Nobel Peace Prize.

1983 The judgment against **Fred Korematsu**, who tried in 1944 to claim that the internment of Japanese Americans was unconstitutional, is finally overturned.

1998 Edith Stein becomes the first Jewish person in modern times to be made a saint by the Roman Catholic church.

1998 Fred Korematsu is awarded the Presidential Medal of Freedom, the highest civilian honor in the United States.

1954
Vietnam War begins;
it ends in 1973

1969
American astronauts
land on the moon

1989
The Berlin Wall
is destroyed

1999
NATO forces
bomb Serbia

1950　　　　　　　　　　1970　　　　　　　　　　1990　　　　　　　　　　2010

World War II
Biographies

Frank Capra

Born May 18, 1897
Bisaquino, Sicily
Died September 3, 1991
La Quinta, California

American film director

A t the peak of his career as a Hollywood film director, Frank Capra was beloved by the moviegoing public and acclaimed by critics for his films portraying honest, hardworking "little guys" who triumph over seemingly unbeatable obstacles and more powerful and deceitful opponents. Capra's background as a film director made him an ideal choice to produce a series of inspirational documentary films that aimed to help American troops understand why the United States had entered the war.

A strong desire to succeed

Born in Bisaquino, Sicily (an island off the coast of Italy), Capra moved to the United States with his family when he was six years old. They settled in East Los Angeles, California, and his father worked picking oranges. One of seven children, Capra took a variety of jobs to help support his family (and eventually to pay for college), including selling newspapers and playing the banjo in local bars. He later wrote in his autobiography, "My goal was to leap across the tracks—to rise above the muck and meanness of peasant poverty. I wanted

"My goal was to leap across the tracks—to rise above the muck and meanness of peasant poverty. I wanted freedom from established caste systems, and ... freedom could only be won by success."

Portrait: Frank Capra.
(Reproduced by permission of AP/Wide World Photos.)

freedom from established caste systems, and ... freedom could only be won by success."

Capra graduated from the California Institute of Technology with a degree in engineering—but the year was 1918 and the United States had entered World War I (1914–18). He immediately enlisted in the army. When the war was over, Capra couldn't find any work as an engineer, so he began to drift around the West, earning money by playing poker and selling books.

Capra was living in San Francisco in 1922. Down on his luck, he met some filmmakers who had formed a small film production company. Even though he didn't know anything about making movies, Capra convinced them to let him direct a film. Capra received $75 for his work on the film, which was an adaptation of a poem by English poet Rudyard Kipling, called *Fultah Fisher's Boarding House*.

A film industry apprentice

Enjoying his experience as a director, Capra became interested in the film industry. He was hired as an apprentice at a film laboratory, where he worked in exchange for food and lodging. Next he got a job with a Hollywood director, Bob Eddy, as a propman and editor. Then he was hired to write jokes for a studio run by Hal Roach, but his new employers didn't find him very funny and he was fired after six months. Nevertheless, Capra got another job writing jokes, this time for director Mack Sennett. He was assigned to work with Harry Langdon, a comic actor who was popular in silent movies. When Langdon moved over to the First National studio in 1926, he took Capra with him as his director. It was at First National that Capra co-wrote and co-directed Langdon's hit movie *Tramp Tramp Tramp* (1926) and directed two subsequent hits, *The Strong Man* (1926) and *Long Pants* (1927).

A successful career is launched

After being fired by Harry Langdon over a dispute about who deserved the most credit for the partners' success, Capra worked for Mack Sennett again. The turning point in Capra's career came in 1928, when he was hired as a director for Columbia Pictures. The executives at Columbia gave Capra complete freedom to make the kind of films he liked, and it also paired him with a talented screenwriter, Robert Riskin, who had formerly worked as a journalist and playwright. With Riskin's help, Capra put out a long series of highly successful films during the 1930s and early 1940s.

The typical Capra film is a comedic fable (a story intended to teach a lesson) featuring an idealistic central character. This unlikely hero overcomes tremendous odds and triumphs over the forces of cynicism and materialism. The film may touch on darker themes but invariably ends in a mood of rosy optimism. Praised for his skill in handling actors, staging complex scenes, and recreating authentically American dialogue onscreen, Capra received best director Oscars (the awards given each year by the Academy of Motion Pictures) for *It Happened One Night* (1934), *Mr. Deeds Goes to Town* (1936), and *You Can't Take It With You* (1938). Another acclaimed film, *Mr. Smith Goes to Washington* (1939), starred James Stewart as an idealistic freshman senator who finds himself immersed in political corruption.

Capra's outlook was essentially optimistic, and the world he created in his films was one in which the good and pure of heart won out over evil and corruption. Presented with a mixture of sentiment and screwball comedy (later known as "Capracorn"), these themes played very well with audiences beaten down by the Great Depression (a period of economic decline and hardship that lasted from 1929 to 1939), who flocked to Capra's films in great numbers.

The U.S. Army recruits Capra

One of Capra's highest-ranking fans was General George Marshall (1880–1959; see entry), the army's chief of staff (top officer). Soon after the United States entered World War II in December 1941, General Marshall decided it would be a good idea to make some films for the troops to educate them about why the United States was fighting. These films would be a form a propaganda, which is material put out by a government or other group that is intended to persuade people to adopt a certain viewpoint; propaganda may be based on either facts or opinion.

Marshall felt it was important that the producer be someone who knew how to make entertaining films, and that

Hollywood Goes to War

Director Frank Capra was not the only member of Hollywood's entertainment community who contributed to the war effort. Most of them stayed at home, using their status as celebrities to help sell war bonds (a way to raise money needed for weapons and other war expenses) and appearing at fund-raising events. Some stars went overseas to entertain the troops, or served in the Hollywood Canteen, one of the entertainment clubs set up for soldiers on leave. Photographs—called "pin-ups"—of female actresses and singers like Betty Grable, Jane Russell, and Marlene Dietrich decorated the bunks of countless soldiers, reminding them of the world they'd left behind.

A few celebrities were among those who actually served in the military and saw action. Others created a soldierly, macho image on the screen but never actually fought (such as John Wayne, who appeared in many war movies but was exempted from military service because he was too old, married, and a father), while a few stayed out of the fighting altogether as conscientious objectors (those who object to war for moral or religious reasons).

Some Who Fought

James Stewart was a popular young actor who had appeared to critical acclaim in *Mr. Smith Goes to Washington*, among other films, when the war started. He enlisted in the Air Corps and became a pilot. First assigned to do a radio show to amuse the forces, Stewart begged to be allowed to go into combat, and finally his wish was granted. Promoted to the rank of captain in July 1943, Stewart went to England to join the 445th Bombing Group,

the best person for the job was Frank Capra. For his part, Capra was eager to contribute to his country's war effort, and he especially wanted to counter the mood of pessimism and despair he felt had overtaken many people. Capra was made a major in the Signal Corps, the branch of the military that handled training films. He arrived in Washington on February 15, 1942, and immediately faced a power struggle with other officers in the Signal Corps who felt Capra was ill equipped to educate soldiers.

This conflict was resolved by June through the creation of a special unit, the 834th Signal Services Photographic Detachment, which included eight officers and thirty-five enlisted men under Capra's command (by 1943 the staff had which was flying bombing raids all over Europe. He flew twenty missions and won a number of medals, including a Distinguished Flying Cross.

Movie idol Clark Gable had recently lost his beloved wife Carole Lombard in a plane crash when he joined the army, making some of his admirers wonder if he was so griefstricken that he hoped he'd be killed in the war. After attending officers' training school in Miami Beach, Florida, Gable was recruited by General Hap Arnold to make a film about aerial gunners. He joined the 351st Heavy Bombardment Group, planning to make a movie showing the unit's day-to-day operations. In April 1943, the group was assigned to an air base in England, and Gable began flying on combat missions, earning the respect of the men who flew with him. Gable returned to the United States in December, only to learn that the gunner film had been cancelled.

Audie Murphy's path to wartime fame was the reverse of Stewart's and Gable's. He was a Texas farm boy who enlisted in the army in 1942, when he was eighteen and went on to become the most decorated American soldier of the war. Among Murphy's thirty-seven medals and other decorations was the Medal of Honor, which he earned for fighting off a German infantry company by himself in January 1945. He was said to have killed 241 Germans. After the war, the good-looking Murphy was recruited to become an actor. He appeared in forty-five films, including *The Red Badge of Courage* (1951) and *To Hell and Back* (1955), which was based on his own life story. He died in a plane crash in 1971.

grown to 150). Because he did not have a very big budget to work with (the total cost of Capra's films came to only $400,000, which was less than 1 percent of the $50 million the War Department spent on films during the war), Capra realized he was going to have to rely on "found footage." This term referred to film that already had been shot and could be reused, whether it came from newsreels, Allied or enemy propaganda, combat films, or even entertainment films.

Thus Capra was not really the director of these films, because very little new footage was shot. It is more accurate to call him the "executive producer" (the title he used to describe his role), and to give him credit for shaping the films through his expert editing and his choice of content—which was based on guidance from the army and subject to approval by Marshall, the secretary of war, and other high-level officials.

Getting started on *Why We Fight*

Homesick for his family—wife Lucille, two sons, and a daughter—Capra moved them to the Washington, D.C., area, and he recruited a group of skilled screenwriters from Hollywood to work as "expert consultants" in putting together an effective script (which would be narrated by actor Walter Huston, who had appeared in one of Capra's hit movies). Some of these writers were later dismissed due to fears that they might slip a pro-Communist message into the films. During the Depression, some Americans had turned toward communism as an answer to the nation's problems, but now the tide was turning amid fears that communism threatened the American political system and way of life.

Looking for ideas to inspire him, Capra visited New York's Museum of Modern Art (MOMA), along with Russian-born director Anatole Litvak who had directed films in Germany from 1927 to 1933 and who would work closely with Capra on his war films. They watched all of the Nazi propaganda films in MOMA's collection (the Nazis were Germany's ruling National Socialist Party, headed by Adolf Hitler). The most impressive of these propaganda films was director Leni Riefenstahl's *Triumph des Willens* (*Triumph of the Will*). This film of the Nazis' 1934 Nuremberg Party Congress presented the event as a grandiose spectacle with music that powerfully underscored all the marching soldiers, speeches, and waving flags.

As quoted in Joseph McBride's biography of the director, Capra emerged with a feeling of dread: "It scared the hell out of me. My first reaction was that we were dead, we couldn't win the war.... I sat there and I was a very unhappy man. How can I possibly top *this?*"

Capra's response was to use these Nazi films to beat them at their own game. In preparing the first film of the *Why We Fight* series, which would be titled *Prelude to War,* Capra explained the events leading up to the war in Europe by using parts of *Triumph of the Will* itself. He also included footage from several other German propaganda films and newsreels. The narration was simply but strongly worded, describing the war as "a common man's life-and-death struggle against those who would put him back into slavery. We lose it—and we lose everything. Our homes, the jobs we go back to, the books we read, the very food we eat, the hopes we have for our kids, the kids themselves—they won't be ours anymore. That's what's at stake. It's us or them. The chips are down."

Prelude to War is a success

Realizing that about 37 percent of the U.S. troops had less than a high school education, Capra felt that he needed to make complex issues simple. Thus the *Why We Fight* series does not provide much historical analysis of the causes of the war. It also features some stereotypical and insulting references and portrayals (such as saying that Germans were born with a love for harsh discipline and that the Japanese were "blood-crazed") that troubled some critics.

Asked about this issue while speaking to an Ohio film association in 1979, Capra is quoted in McBride's biography as saying that these were not meant to be "hate films," but that some hatred did creep into the dialogue. "At the time there was a need for these films," he said. "I'm glad and I'm proud that I was able to satisfy that need, but now I don't like to see these films because of the memories they bring back."

In July 1942 Capra moved his unit to Hollywood, both to be close to movie industry resources and to avoid the political scene in Washington. In August, he was promoted to the rank of lieutenant colonel. *Prelude to War* was shown to the troops in October. General Marshall and President Franklin D. Roosevelt (1882–1945; see entry) wanted the public to see the film, so it was shown in commercial theaters. In March 1943, *Prelude to War* received an Oscar for best documentary (along with three other war films). The award was given to the army and accepted by Capra.

Despite the acclaim the *Why We Fight* films received when they were released, there is some question as to whether they really accomplished what they set out to do. A postwar

James Stewart (second from right) and Donna Reed (third from right) in a scene from Capra's *It's a Wonderful Life.* *(Reproduced by permission of The Kobal Collection.)*

study conducted by the military, based on surveys of soldiers taken during the war, showed that the films did increase the knowledge of events leading up to the war. But they seemed to have little or no effect on the troops' motivation to fight; in some cases they may have even hurt motivation by making the enemy look stronger than previously suspected.

Other war films made by the 834th

In addition to the *Why We Fight* series, the 834th made ten other propaganda films (including such titles as *The Negro Soldier, Your Job In Germany,* and *Know Your Enemy—Japan*). They also produced fifty issues of the *Army-Navy Screen Magazine* and forty-six installments of the weekly *Staff Film Report,* which collected classified battle film and other footage to be shown to the president, Joint Chiefs of Staff, and other high-level commanders. In August 1943 Capra turned over the command of the 834th to Litvak and became commanding officer of the Signal Corps' Special Coverage Section. His duties included supervising combat photography. Capra received the Distinguished Service Medal on June 14, 1945.

A creative slowdown after the war

After the war, Capra joined with fellow directors George Stevens and William Wyler to form a new production company, Liberty Films. The company produced only one film, *It's a Wonderful Life* (1946), starring James Stewart as an extraordinary but profoundly discouraged man who around Christmas is allowed to see what the world would have been like if he had never been born. Although Capra felt that this was his best film yet—and it is probably the Capra film best known to contemporary audiences, due to its widespread Christmas-season appearances on television—it was not popular with the audiences of the period.

By 1950 Capra's most creative years were behind him. His last film was *Pocketful of Miracles* (1961), a remake of his 1931 film, *Lady for a Day*. Capra died in 1991, and was succeeded in the film industry by his son, Frank Capra Jr., a film producer, and grandson, Frank Capra III, a director.

Where to Learn More

Books

Bohn, Thomas. *An Historical and Descriptive Analysis of the "Why We Fight" Series*. New York: Ayer, 1977.

Capra, Frank. *The Name above the Title: An Autobiography*. New York: Macmillan, 1971.

Carney, Raymond. *American Vision: The Films of Frank Capra*. Cambridge: Cambridge University Press, 1986.

Glatzer, Richard and John Raeburn. *Frank Capra: The Man and His Films*. Ann Arbor, MI: University of Michigan Press, 1974.

McBride, Joseph. *Frank Capra: The Catastrophe of Success*. New York: Simon and Schuster, 1992.

Poague, Leland. *The Cinema of Frank Capra: An Approach to Film Comedy*. Cranbury, NJ: A. S. Barnes, 1974.

Scherle, Victor and William Levy. *The Films of Frank Capra*. Secaucus, NJ: Carol Publishing Group, 1977.

Periodicals

Arnold, Gary. "Though More than 60 Years Old, Films of Frank Capra Stay Fresh." *Insight on the News* (February 9, 1998): 38.

Neville Chamberlain

Born March 18, 1869
Birmingham, England
Died November 9, 1940
Hampshire, England

English statesman who was
prime minister from 1937 to 1940

Neville Chamberlain
unsuccessfully tried to
prevent World War II
through a policy of
compromise with
Germany.

Neville Camberlain is best known for his failure to fend off war with dictators Benito Mussolini of Italy and Adolf Hitler of Germany. For many years his policy of compromise with these leaders—known as appeasement—was criticized and condemned, but recently some historians have suggested that it actually allowed England time to arm itself for the later conflict. Although those who didn't like Chamberlain's policies called him weak and blind to reality, others have claimed that he was really a man of integrity who had devoted his life to public service.

The son of a politician

The Chamberlain family had been shoemakers in the eighteenth century, and over the next 100 years or so they rose steadily to become businessmen of the upper middle class. Joseph Chamberlain, Neville's father, gave up business to pursue politics, becoming a radical member of England's Liberal Party with a deep concern for social welfare. Neville's mother, Florence Kenrick, was his father's second wife; tragically, she died in childbirth when Neville was six years old.

Portrait: Neville Chamberlain.
(Reproduced by permission of USHMM Photo Archives.)

After Florence's death, Joseph Chamberlain spent less time at home and grew rather distant from his children. As a result, Neville grew up without the affection of either a mother or a father; fortunately, he was the eldest in a large troupe of younger siblings and cousins whose company he greatly enjoyed. He went away to school at Rugby (a famous private school), where he did well academically but was unhappy due to his poor relationship with the school's headmaster (principal) and because he missed his large family.

A business venture in the Bahamas

Chamberlain left Rugby in 1886 and attended Mason College in Birmingham, where he studied (again unhappily) science and engineering design. He was working in an accounting firm when, in 1890, his father suddenly announced that the family was going to start a business growing and processing sisal (a plant with strong fibers that can be used to make rope and other products) in the Bahamas. Neville and his brother Austen were put in charge of the operation and moved to the Bahamas to search for a suitable piece of land.

They settled on Andros Island (about twenty miles from Nassau, the biggest city in the Bahamas) and established the Andros Fibre Company. Austen soon returned to England, and Neville became the company's managing director. He worked long days of hard labor, clearing the land and putting up buildings. Although the plantation seemed promising at first, it eventually failed. Chamberlain returned to England, extremely disappointed but wiser and more self-reliant after his experiences.

Business, marriage, and politics

Chamberlain went into business in Birmingham, buying a company called Hoskins and Son, a manufacturer of berths (beds) for ships. He also got involved in local politics, sharing his father's interest—though he was neither as passionate nor as liberal as his father—in social issues. He was elected to the Birmingham City Council in 1911.

By the time Chamberlain was in his early forties he was still unmarried, and his friends and relatives were beginning to think he might always remain a bachelor. Then he met and fell in love with Anne Cole, and the two were married in January

1911. Their daughter Dorothy was born that December, and son Frank two years later. Throughout their life together Chamberlain was known to say about his accomplishments (including becoming prime minister), "I'd never have done it without Annie."

Chamberlain served as lord mayor of Birmingham from 1915 to 1916. His career in national politics began during World War I (1914–18), when he became director of National Service, overseeing the drafting of soldiers into the armed forces. He was elected to the House of Commons (England's legislative body) in 1918 as a member of the Conservative Party.

Rising to the top position

Chamberlain rose rapidly into the upper levels of the government, serving as minister of health (responsible for administering social services, especially public health care) from 1923 to 1929 (and again in 1931) and as chancellor of the exchequer (in charge of deciding how the government should spend its money) from 1923 to 1924 and from 1931 to 1937. He gained a reputation as a skilled, orderly administrator with the ability to push through needed reforms; Winston Churchill (who would succeed Chamberlain as prime minister) described him as "alert, businesslike, opinionated, and self-confident in a very high degree."

At the end of the 1930s, Germany and Italy were taking aggressive actions against other countries and threatening world peace. This was the most dominant concern when Chamberlain was elected to the position of prime minister (the chief executive and top leader of the government) in 1937. His first priority was to avoid war, and he decided that the best way to do so was through appeasement, which meant remaining on neutral terms and making compromises with Hitler and Mussolini.

Chamberlain's appeasement policy has been judged negatively over the years, but at the time there were many leaders other than Chamberlain who supported it. On the other hand, Foreign Minister Anthony Eden strongly disagreed and warned Chamberlain about the dangers of negotiating with dictators. He felt that England needed to stand up to Hitler and Mussolini.

From left are Neville Chamberlain, Edouard Daladier, Adolf Hitler, and Benito Mussolini at the Munich Peace Parley in September 1938.
(Reproduced by permission of AP/Wide World Photos.)

"Peace in our time"

Chamberlain's first step was to make a treaty with Mussolini that accepted Italy's recent conquest of the East African country of Ethiopia, on the condition that Italy would stay out of the Spanish Civil War. Meanwhile, Germany was eager to reclaim some territory in Czechoslovakia, which it had lost in World War I, where many Germans still lived. Hitler claimed that he did not want war and would not try to gain any more of Czechoslovakia.

Chamberlain told Parliament that this was not an issue worth fighting about—that it was "a quarrel in a far away country, between people of whom we know nothing." After three meetings with Hitler (whom Chamberlain once described as "a gentleman"), both leaders signed the Munich Pact on September 30, 1938. In this agreement Germany promised to occupy only specified Czech territories and to leave the rest of the country alone.

Chamberlain made a triumphant return to London and was photographed waving the signed agreement in his hand, proclaiming that he had secured "peace in our time." He was praised as a superb peacemaker by the press, public, and other statesmen. But the glory was short-lived, for on March 14, 1939, Germany broke its promise and invaded all of Czechoslovakia .

A sad end to a career and life

Meanwhile, England had agreed to take action if Germany went even further and invaded Poland, so when the invasion occurred on September 1, 1939, Chamberlain had no choice but to try to protect Poland and the rest of Europe from Hitler. Two days later, England declared war on Germany.

The complete failure of Chamberlain's efforts to keep peace led to discontent in his own party and the refusal of the opposition, the Labour Party, to work with him. Many critics felt that he had completely misjudged Hitler and his intentions. After he invaded Poland Hitler began to act on his plan to conquer all of western Europe. England's failure to stop the German invasion of Norway and Denmark was the final blow, and Chamberlain resigned in May 1940. He stayed on in the government of the new prime minister, Winston Churchill, serving as lord president of the council, but by the end of the summer he had become ill with cancer.

Chamberlain resigned from his post in October and died a month later. Like many other famous public figures he was buried at Westminster Abbey in London, but in his village church in the town of Hampshire was placed a memorial that reads, "Neville Chamberlain. Prime Minister of Great Britain 1937–1940. Write me as one that loves his fellow-men."

Where to Learn More
Books

Charmley, John. *Chamberlain and the Lost Peace*. Chicago: I. R. Dee, 1990.

Dilks, David. *Neville Chamberlain*. Cambridge: Cambridge University Press, 1984.

Macleod, Iain. *Neville Chamberlain*. New York: Atheneum, 1962.

Periodicals

Bartlett, J. W. "Munich Agreement Is Signed: September 30th, 1938." *History Today* (September 1998): 40.

Web sites

Beattie, A.J. *Neville Chamberlain*. [Online] Available: http://www.grolier.com/wwii/wwii_chamber.html (January 8, 1999).

Chiang Kai-Shek

Born October 31, 1887
Zhejiang, China
Died April 5, 1975
Taipei, Taiwan

Chinese general and leader of the Kuomintang or Nationalist Party

As a young man Chiang Kai-Shek fought with the revolutionary leader Sun Yat-Sen, who successfully ended the reign of the Manchus, a minority ethnic group that had controlled the government of China for three hundred years. Even after Chiang had gained great power as head of the Kuomintang or Nationalist Party, he continued to battle—this time against Japanese invaders as well as warlords, rival politicians, and Communists from within his own country. During World War II, Chiang and his wife tried to influence public opinion in the United States to raise money for China's war against Japan. Although they were successful for a while, Chiang was unable to stop the tide of change that swept over China when Communists led by Mao Zedong took power.

Chiang Kai-Shek fought both the Japanese and Chinese Communists for control of China, finally retreating to Taiwan.

Finding a home in the military

Chiang's father, Chiang Su-an, was a village leader and manager of a government-owned salt company. When he died, his nine-year-old son was left to the care of his mother, Wang Tsai-yu, and grandfather, who sent him to work for some relatives who owned a shop. Chiang was mistreated and

Portrait: Chiang Kai-Shek.
(Reproduced by permission of Archive Photos.)

unhappy, so he ran away and joined the army. There he found a new home, and he was to remain devoted to the military for the rest of his life.

When he was eighteen, Chiang passed the entrance examination for the Baoding Military Academy. Although young, Chaing was already married—he had wed a young woman named Miss Dao in a traditional wedding ceremony—and his son, Chiang Ching-kuo, was born before he entered the academy. He would eventually divorce his first wife.

Sun Yat-Sen's revolutionary movement

In 1907 Chiang went to Tokyo to attend the Japanese Army Military State College. At this time he, like many other Chinese students living in Japan, became involved with the revolutionary movement led by Sun Yat-Sen. The movement aimed to overthrow China's Manchu government. Chiang returned to China in 1911 and took part in fighting near the city of Shanghai. The Manchus were defeated, and a republican government (in which power is held by citizens entitled to vote for elected officials, who rule or govern by law) was formed. Sun was the first president but he resigned one year later and General Yuan Shikai, a strong military leader, took over.

Sun Yat-Sen was disappointed in Yuan's rule, which was repressive, and withdrew to Japan. After taking part in an unsuccessful counter-revolution to remove Yuan from power, Chiang and other members of Sun's T'ung-meng Hui ("Revolutionary Alliance") party, which later became the Kuomintang party, also fled to Japan. Chiang returned to Shanghai in 1915 and spent a few years moving in a shady world of business and organized crime as part of a secret organization called the "Green Society."

A new government

The death of President Yuan Shikai in 1916 led to disorder in China, and power was divided among about 200 warlords (military leaders not connected to a central government). In 1918, Sun Yat-Sen formed another government ruled by the Kuomintang. Its capital was established at Guangzhou (located in southern China) and Chiang became Sun's military advisor.

Meanwhile, most of the warlords supported a rival government that had been established in the northern part of the country at Beijing.

In setting up his government, Sun had relied on supplies and advice from the Soviet Union and he had strong ties to that country's ruling Communist Party. Chiang was sent to Moscow in 1923 to study the Soviet military and political systems, but he did not become a convert to communism—in fact, he decided that he hated communism. He returned to China in 1924 to become the director of the Whampoa Military Academy, where his job was to train young men to be loyal, capable members of the military.

Leading the Kuomintang to power

When Sun Yat-Sen died in 1925, China was still a divided country. Taking charge of the Kuomintang, which still controlled only two southern regions, Chiang set out to unify China by force. In a military campaign called the Northern Expedition, he moved his army into northern China and captured the city of Hankou. Chiang's army defeated many warlord armies and absorbed them into the Nationalist army. In March 1927 the Nationalist Party established a new, central government at Nanjing. Chiang's distrust of communism led him to order a purge or cleansing of all Communists from the Kuomintang, many of whom were executed. Despite his efforts to oust the Communists, the movement continued to grow in China.

On December 1, 1927, Chiang—having divorced both his first wife and his second, Chen Chieh-ju, whom he had wed six years earlier—married the polished, charming, and attractive Soong Mei-Ling, the younger sister of Sun Yat-Sen's wife. Madame Chiang had been educated in the United States and would prove an effective spokesperson for her husband when he later sought aid from the West. The majority of Chinese follow Buddhism or other Eastern religions, but Madame Chiang was a Christian, and on October 23, 1930, Chiang too was baptized into the Christian faith.

From 1927 to 1931, Chiang ruled the Kuomintang government, while trouble brewed in the form of rebellious warlords, devious political leaders, and the Communist movement.

How Madame Chiang Kai-Shek Helped Her Husband

In 1927, Chiang Kai-Shek married a woman from a famous Shanghai family. Soong Mei-ling was the daughter of Soong Yao-ju or Charles Jones Soong, who had gone to college in the United States and returned to serve as a Methodist missionary before becoming a businessman. Mei-Ling's brother, T.V. Soong, attended Harvard and held several important positions in the Kuomintang government; one of her sisters was married to Sun Yat-Sen.

Like her father and all of her siblings, the new Madame Chiang Kai-Shek had reached young adulthood in the United States, graduating from Wellesley College in Massachusetts. She was intelligent and charming, and she found several ways to help her husband in his quest to keep China free from both foreign aggression and Communist influence.

In the years just before World War II, she tried to help China's orphans and homeless people, find work for poor women, and promote children's education, but her efforts did little to ease the great suffering of her people.

Madame Chiang played her most important role during the war, when she served as her husband's voice in pleading for help from the rest of the world. When General Claire L. Chennault arrived with his Flying Tigers—a small but effective group of American fighter pilots who battled the Japanese in China and Burma— she helped him communicate with her husband, and she was made honorary commander of the group.

The high point of Madame Chiang's wartime career was her visit to the United States from November 1942 to May 1943. She spoke to crowds at rallies and addressed Congress, describing how the war had affected her country and asking for help in the form of money and supplies. Her face even appeared on the cover of *Time* magazine.

After the Communists took over China in 1949, Madame Chiang fled with her husband to Taiwan, where she remained until his death in 1975. Since then she has spent most of her time living quietly in New York City.

In 1931, Japan occupied Manchuria, a region in northeast China, but Chiang decided not to try to regain the region. He felt it was necessary first to attack China's growing Communist movement. Public opinion turned against him for not resisting the Japanese invasion of Manchuria and Chiang retired from public life. Within a year, however, he was called back to lead the government. It had become clear that no one else could do a better job of bringing the hostile groups together—even though Chaing was still unable to control the Communists, who had gained control of some regions of China.

Fighting the Japanese

The Japanese remained a threat throughout the early 1930s, and some Chinese thought that the Kuomintang and the Communists should put aside their differences in order to fight their common enemy. One of these was a former military officer named Chang Hsueh-Liang, who managed to kidnap Chiang in 1936. He tried to persuade Chiang to cooperate with the Communists in resisting Japanese aggression.

When he was released, Chiang claimed that he had not agreed to anything; nevertheless, his party and the Communists soon formed a "United Front" against the Japanese. War broke out in July 1937 when Chinese and Japanese forces clashed at the Marco Polo Bridge near Beijing. By the fall of 1938, the Japanese had conquered all of eastern China. They had control of the most fertile farmland in the country, which resulted in starvation for millions of Chinese peasants.

A plea for help from the United States

In 1941, with World War II raging, the Allied countries (the United States, Great Britain, the Soviet Union and and the other countries fighting against Germany, Italy, and Japan) joined China's fight against Japan, which was expanding its empire throughout the eastern Pacific region. Chiang had been serving as commander in chief of China's army, and now the Allies put him in command of the entire Chinese theater (area of action in the war). Chiang and his wife traveled to the United States to request help with their war effort through the Lend-Lease Program, which allowed those on the Allied side to borrow money and weapons with the promise of paying for them after the war.

Although Chiang was portrayed by both Chinese and American propaganda (printed or other material designed to persuade people to support a certain viewpoint) as a courageous leader struggling against a brutal enemy, some American leaders felt that precious war supplies and funds were being wasted on China, when they could be put to better use else-where in the world. General Joseph W. Stilwell, the leading military advisor on China, claimed that the Chinese leaders were incompetent and corrupt. He criticized Chiang for refusing to modernize his army and for not taking more aggressive action against the Japanese. It seemed that Chiang wanted to conserve his troops for a future struggle with the Communists, and that he was more concerned about keeping his own power than helping the Chinese people.

Nevertheless, President Franklin Roosevelt (1882–1945; see entry) hoped that perhaps Chiang could lead China to greatness. In November 1943, Chiang represented his country at the Cairo Conference , a meeting between world leaders (including Roosevelt and Winston Churchill, the prime minister of Great Britain) where the Allies mapped out their plans for the war in Asia. But by 1944, the Japanese had conquered much Chinese territory, while the Kuomintang government and military grew weaker and weaker. Meanwhile, the Communists worked behind the Japanese lines in northern China to strengthen their own troops and to win over more Chinese to their ideas.

Civil War with the Communists

The war in Asia ended when Japan, devastated by a long series of defeats in battles as well as the atomic bombs that had been dropped on the Japanese cities of Hiroshima and Nagasaki, surrendered to the Allies in August 1945. For about a year after the end of the war, the chief of staff of the U.S. Army, General George Marshall (1880–1959; see entry), and other leaders tried to get Chiang to form a coalition government with the Communist Party. These efforts did not succeed, and the Communists began a full-scale civil war against the Kuomintang.

The Nationalist government had been greatly weakened by the many years of fighting against Japan. The Chinese people suffered from famine, inflation, crime, high taxes, and forced conscription (involuntary enrollment) into the army. Many of them were attracted to the Communist message of equality between people and the sharing of both resources and power. The Communist fighters made steady gains against Chiang's forces, so that by the end of 1948 they controlled most of northern China.

Chiang Kai-Shek in China in 1949, shortly before his retreat to Taiwan.
(Reproduced by permission of AP/Wide World Photos.)

Retreat to Taiwan

Chiang appealed desperately to the United States for help, but the American government did not want to get involved in the civil war. On December 10, 1949, Chiang fled to Taiwan (formerly called Formosa), an island located about one hundred miles off the eastern coast of China. He made a brief return to China and tried to reorganize his exhausted soldiers, but finally brought them back with him to Taiwan.

Over the next two decades, Chiang vowed that he would return to China and vanquish the Communists, but he never did. When Communist North Korea invaded South Korea in 1950, the United States began to worry about the spread of communism through Asia. Since Taiwan was not Communist, it was seen as worth strengthening, so Taiwan received more U.S. aid. Chiang continued to portray himself as a fighter against tyranny, yet he ruled Taiwan as a dictator. Taiwan's economy did very well, but the country became more and more isolated as mainland China's relations with other countries—especially the United States—improved.

In 1971, the United Nations voted to recognize the People's Republic of China (the name the Communists had given their country) as the true China, and the delegates from Taiwan were expelled. Chiang, who had been elected president in every election since his arrival in Taiwan, died on April 5, 1975. His son from his first marriage became the ruler of Taiwan.

Where to Learn More

Books

Chang, Chun-ming. *Chiang Kai-Shek, His Life and Times*. New York: St. John's University, 1981.

Crozier, Brian. *The Man Who Lost China: The First Full Biography of Chiang Kai-Shek*. New York: Scribner, 1976.

Curtis, Richard. *Chiang Kai-Shek*. New York: Hawthorn Books, 1969.

Dolan, Sean. *Chiang Kai-Shek*. New York: Chelsea House, 1988.

Loh, P.P.Y. *The Early Chiang Kai-shek*. New York: Columbia University E. Asian Institute Occasional Papers, Books on Demand, 1971.

Winston Churchill

Born November 30, 1874
Oxfordshire, England
Died January 24, 1965
London, England

British statesman, soldier, and writer

One of the greatest British leaders of all time, Winston Churchill became a figure of monumental importance during World War II, when he led his country through some of its darkest days. Churchill's career was long and rich and featured many ups and downs—times when many of his fellow politicians scorned him as well as times when he was considered a hero. Some of his varied accomplishments include helping to establish a welfare system in Britain, preparing the British navy for World War I (1914–18; a war that started as a conflict between Austria-Hungary and Serbia and escalated into a global war involving thirty-two nations), and earning the Nobel Prize for literature. But it is for his role in World War II that he is most remembered and admired. His powerful speeches, his two-fingered "V for Victory" wave, his ever-present cigar, and his tenacious refusal to give in to tyranny inspired hope and courage in people around the world.

Prime Minister Winston Churchill led his country to victory in World War II and inspired others to fight tyranny.

An aristocratic background

Churchill was the son of an English aristocrat, Lord Randolph Churchill, and a descendant of John Churchill, the

First Duke of Marlborough, who led a great military victory against the French in 1702. His mother was Jennie Jerome, an American from New York whose own mother was one-quarter Iroquois. Although Lord Randolph Churchill had once been a respected political figure, his career eventually collapsed and he died a failure at forty-six. Some observers have speculated that the younger Churchill was determined to succeed where his father had failed—or perhaps he wanted to prove his worth to his father, who once wrote that Winston lacked "cleverness, knowledge, and any capacity for settled work."

Indeed, Churchill's younger years do not reflect the achievements of his later life. He entered Harrow (a famous private school), but was not admitted to the upper (secondary) school because he refused to study Greek and Latin, preferring to read and write in English. Churchill got into the Royal Military College at Sandhurst only on his third attempt.

Enjoying life as a soldier

After leaving Sandhurst, Churchill joined the British army as a cavalry officer, and he seemed to thoroughly enjoy life as a soldier. In 1895, he took a break from his military duties to travel to Cuba, where he served as a correspondent for London's *Daily Graphic,* reporting on the clash between the island's Spanish colonizers and guerrilla soldiers fighting for independence.

Rejoining his army regiment, Churchill was sent to India, which was then a British colony. In 1897, he served with the Indian army on the Malakand expedition, in which they put down a rebellion of people living in the northwestern part of the country; he also wrote a book about this experience: *The Story of the Malakand Field Force* (1898).

The next year, Churchill went to Sudan in northern Africa and took part as both an army officer and a reporter in the Battle of Omdurman, which featured what was probably the British army's last cavalry charge. About this experience he wrote to his mother that he "never felt the slightest nervousness. [I] felt as cool as I do now." Again, Churchill recorded his adventures in a book, *The River War* (2 vols., 1899).

A South African adventure

In 1899, Churchill traveled to South Africa to report for the London *Morning Post* on the war between that country's English colonizers and the Boers, Dutch settlers who had arrived in South Africa several centuries earlier. Caught up in some fighting near the town of Ladysmith, Churchill was captured by a Boer officer named Louis Botha, who many years later would become South Africa's prime minister and Churchill's good friend. Churchill made a daring escape from a prison camp and returned to the front, an experience he chronicled in *London to Ladysmith via Pretoria* (1900). This book made Churchill world famous.

Political career begins

Churchill's political career began when he was only twenty-six years old. On January 23, 1901, he became a member of Parliament for Oldham (located in England's Lancashire region). At that time he belonged to the Conservative Party, but by 1904 he had joined the Liberals and become undersecretary of state for the colonies. Churchill also found time to write a biography of his father, which was published in 1906.

Churchill claimed that following his 1908 marriage to Clementine Hozier the couple "lived happily ever afterwards." They had four children: a son named Randolph and daughters Diana, Sarah, and Mary (as well as one child who died in infancy). Meanwhile, his political career was thriving.

From 1908 to 1910 he served as president of the Board of Trade, then from 1910 to 1911 as home secretary. In this position he oversaw the early legislation setting up a welfare system. He also helped to create innovative labor exchanges, and introduced benefits for workers such as old-age pension acts.

In charge of the navy

In 1911, Churchill was named First Lord of the Admiralty, which put him at the head of Britain's navy. Concerned about Germany's rapid buildup of naval power and convinced that peace could only be maintained by preparing for war, Churchill resolved to improve the British navy through such measures as switching from coal-burning to fuel-burning ships and setting up a naval air service.

During the early years of World War I (1914–18), Churchill planned aggressive military campaigns. But when these attacks failed, Churchill lost his job. For a few years he took up painting (a hobby he pursued for the rest of his life), but in 1916, he volunteered to serve in the army. He went to the western front as commander of the 6th Royal Scots Fusiliers. This didn't last long, though, because Prime Minister (the chief executive or top leader of the government) Lloyd George soon called on Churchill to rejoin the government.

Some frustrating years

As secretary of state for war and air (and later for air and colonies), Churchill spent the first few years after World War I working to reform the army and develop Britain's air power—he even became a pilot himself. He also spoke out against the Bolshevik revolution in Russia (in which Russia's traditional monarchy was toppled by a Communist regime) and participated in the establishment of the Irish Free State.

Churchill failed to be elected to Parliament in 1922, and he turned to writing for a few years. He returned briefly to government service when he became chancellor of the exchequer (in charge of deciding how the government spends its money) for a short, unhappy stint, but by the beginning of the 1930s he had gone back to private life.

This was a difficult decade for Churchill. He warily watched Germany rebuild its power and worried about the danger posed by Adolf Hitler. He strongly opposed the policy of appeasement (to compromise or conciliate in order to avoid a conflict) pushed by Prime Minister Neville Chamberlain (1869–1940; see entry). In 1935, Churchill made a speech to the House of Commons warning against the "ever-advancing sources of authority and despotism."

World War II changes Churchill's fortunes

When war with Germany began in 1939, Churchill was made First Lord of the Admiralty—more than twenty-five years after he had first held this post. Meanwhile, Chamberlain's government was quickly losing favor. By now, everyone realized that it had been wrong to go along with Hitler for so long, and that Churchill was one of the few who had warned

against it. Now the Germans had overrun Poland, northwestern Europe, and France. They were attacking Britain by air and could invade at any time.

It was under these frightening circumstances that Churchill was chosen to lead his country. He became prime minister on May 10, 1940, and he immediately expressed his determination to keep Britain safe and, eventually, to free the rest of the world from Nazi tyranny. In a fiery speech to the House of Commons on May 13, he said, "I have nothing to offer but blood, toil, sweat, and tears. You ask, what is our policy? I will say: it is to wage war, by sea, land, and air, with all our might. You ask, what is our aim? I can answer in one word: Victory."

Waging war from Britain and abroad

Churchill planned war strategy from the cabinet war rooms, seated in front of a huge map of the world, with his aides and advisors around him. He spoke often before Parliament and on the radio, urging the British people to stand firm, and he traveled around the world trying to gain support for the war effort and visiting battle fronts. Two of the trips he made were to the United States, where he addressed Congress in December of 1941 and May of 1942, and met with U.S. president Franklin Delano Roosevelt (1882–1945; see entry).

Churchill considered his ties with Roosevelt crucial to England's success in beating Hitler. Although the United States did not initially want to enter the war, Churchill and Roosevelt worked out deals allowing Britain to borrow weapons, destroyers, and personnel. (This agreement was called the Lend-Lease Program.) With the Japanese attack on Pearl Harbor (December 7, 1941) and America's entrance into the war, Churchill's hopes of a closer alliance were fulfilled.

Churchill gained another unlikely ally when the Soviet Union got into the war. The Soviets were unexpected allies because Churchill had always been strongly opposed to communism and the Soviet Union was a Communist country. But he recognized the value of having such a powerful friend, and he told the House of Commons, "If Hitler were to launch an attack on Hell itself, I would at least continue to make a favourable reference to the Devil in the House of Commons."

The Allies on the road to victory

So now the "Grand Alliance" was in place—Britain, the United States, and the Soviet Union were united in their efforts to defeat Germany, Italy, and Japan—the Axis powers. The first joint British-U.S. campaigns were the "Operation Torch" landings in North Africa and the invasion of Italy and Sicily, which forced the Nazis to fight on two fronts instead of one. As a result, the Nazi forces were spread too thin to attack England. The Americans were also eager to regain France and the rest of northwestern Europe, but it was too risky to try this until the armies were better prepared.

That time finally came on D-Day in June 1944 when the Allied forces landed on the beaches of Normandy in France. Churchill was so enthusiastic about this campaign that he wanted to land with the troops, and only a special order from King George VI prevented him from doing so. D-Day was the beginning of the end of the war in Europe, as hundreds of thousands of Allied troops moved into France and swept their way east, pushing the Germans back into their pre-World War II borders and finally reaching the Nazi capital of Berlin. The Germans surrendered to the Allies in May 1945. The Americans were still fighting the Japanese in the Pacific region.

Voted out of office

During the last year of the war, Churchill had played a less prominent role. First, his strong relationship with Roosevelt began to weaken due to their difference of opinion about Joseph Stalin (1879–1953; see entry), the leader of Russia: Churchill felt that the United States and England should be suspicious of Stalin; Roosevelt thought they could work cooperatively with the Soviet leader. In addition, the focus of the war had shifted away from Britain as the Russians drove back the Germans on the eastern front and the Americans concentrated on defeating the Japanese.

When the war was over, Churchill took part in the victory celebrations, but he did so with a sense of anxiety about the future. In the election of 1945, he was voted out of office. This was a sign not that the people did not respect him, but that they considered him a prime minister for *war* time and wanted someone else to lead them through their postwar reconstruction.

Postwar pursuits

In the years following the end of World War II, Churchill turned to his favorite pursuits: writing (his book *The Second World War* was published in six volumes between 1948 and 1953), painting (he exhibited his works at the Royal Academy of Art), and public speaking. Churchill continued to warn against the spread of communism and urged all English-speaking people to band together to defeat it. In a famous speech delivered at Westminster College in Fulton, Missouri, he used the words "Iron Curtain" to describe the secrecy behind which the Soviet Union operated, and that term that would be used by many others for years to come.

In 1951, when he was seventy-seven years old, Churchill again became prime minister of Britain. He was made a Knight of the Garter (a high honor granted by the Queen of England which meant that he gained the title " Sir" in front of his name) a few weeks before the 1953 coronation of the young Queen Elizabeth. That year he also received the Nobel Prize for literature, in recognition of his many accomplished works of history, biography, politics, and memoirs. Churchill resigned as prime minister in 1955, although he continued to hold his seat in the House of Commons until 1964. He received the unusual honor of being made an honorary American citizen in 1963.

Honoring a world hero

Churchill died in January 1965. His impressive state funeral service at St. Paul's Cathedral in London reflected his stature as a hero to the people of Britain and much of the rest of the world. A man of incredible vitality, intellect, courage, and wit, he was admired for his ability to inspire greatness in those who heard his words, such as these he delivered at his old school, Harrow, in 1941: "Never give in, never give in, never, never, never, never—in nothing, great or small, large or petty—never give in except to convictions of honor and good sense."

Where to Learn More
Books

Bradley, John. *Churchill.* New York: Gloucester Press, 1990.

Charmley, John. *Churchill, The End of Glory: A Political Biography.* San Diego, CA: Harcourt Brace, 1993.

Driemen, J. E. *Winston Churchill: An Unbreakable Spirit.* Minneapolis, MN: Dillon Press, 1990.

Lace, William W. *Winston Churchill*. San Diego, CA: Lucent Books, 1995.

Manchester, William. *The Last Lion: Winston Spencer Churchill*. Boston: Little, Brown 1988.

Robbins, Keith. *Churchill*. Longman, 1992.

Rodgers, Judith. *Winston Churchill*. New York: Chelsea House, 1986.

Severance, John B. *Winston Churchill: Soldier, Statesman, Artist*. New York: Clarion Books, 1996.

Periodicals

Keegan, John. *Time* (April 13, 1998): 114.

Web sites

"Winston Churchill" in Grolier's *World War II Commemoration* [Online] Available http://www.grolier.com/wwii/wwii_churchill.html (November 16, 1998).

Jacqueline Cochran

Born c. 1906
Muskogee, Florida
Died August 9, 1980
Indio, California

American pilot

Jacqueline Cochran served as director of the WASPs (Women's Airforce Service Pilots), whose members transported airplanes and performed other noncombat duties during World War II.

Portrait: Jacqueline Cochran. *(Reproduced by permission of Archive Photos.)*

Jacqueline Cochran overcame a difficult childhood to achieve many of the goals she set for herself. She was already an experienced, fearless pilot who had set many flying records when the United States entered World War II (December 7, 1941), and she quickly saw a way in which women could help the war effort. Cochran suggested that the U.S. government set up an organization of women pilots to perform various non-combat duties, an experiment that was already working well in Great Britain. Thus the Women's Airforce Service Pilots (WASPs) were born, and Cochran became their director in August 1943. Although the program was canceled in 1944 and its members left with no veterans benefits and little recognition, Cochran and other female pilots had demonstrated both women's eagerness to serve their country and their abilities in the air.

A rough, tough childhood

Cochran celebrated her birthday on May 11 and estimated that she had been born around 1906, but she never knew who her parents were; when she was a teenager, she chose her last name from a phone book. Raised by a foster family in northern Florida, Cochran spent her early years traveling with them as they worked in different sawmills. The family was desperately poor, and Cochran often slept on the floor, went without shoes, and wore clothing made from discarded flour sacks. As recounted in *Women Aviators* by Lisa Yount, Cochran later wrote that this rough background gave her "a kind of cocky confidence...I could never have so little that I hadn't had less. It took away my fear."

Cochran began working at a cotton mill in Columbus, Georgia, when she was only eight years old, and as soon as she earned enough money she bought herself two pairs of shoes. By the time she was ten, Cochran was supervising fifteen other child workers at the mill. She told them that she was destined for a life of wealth and adventure. A strike (work stoppage staged by workers as a way to win more benefits, better pay, or more rights) forced Cochran out of her job, but she was soon working as an assistant in a beauty salon in Columbus.

An aviator is born

Throughout her teenage years, Cochran worked in beauty salons in different cities, and after she bought herself a Model T Ford car (one of the earliest and most affordable automobiles) in Montgomery, Alabama, she was able to move even faster and further. By 1929 she was in New York City, working at a popular salon called Antoine's. Cochran's wealthy clients often invited her to their parties, and at one of these she met an older man named Floyd Odlum whom she liked immediately. The two became friends, and Cochran later learned that Odlum was a multimillionaire businessman.

Cochran told Odlum that she would like to become a traveling cosmetics salesperson. Odlum's casual comment that she would need wings for that job inspired Cochran to sign up for flying lessons. In the summer of 1932, she arranged to spend part of her vacation at the Roosevelt Flying School on Long Island. Odlum bet her the cost of the lessons that she would not get her pilot's license in six weeks, but Cochran won the bet by earning her license in only three weeks. The first time she took to the air, Cochran later said (as quoted in Yount's book), "A beauty operator ceased to exist and an aviator was born."

A career in business *and* flying

Cochran took more lessons and even worked as an unpaid flight attendant on an airline in exchange for occasional time at the controls of airplanes. By the end of 1933 she had enough skill and flying hours to earn her commercial pilot's license. Still interested in the cosmetics business, and backed by money provided by Odlum, Cochran started the Jacqueline Cochran Cosmetics Company. She designed and sold hair dyes, moisturizing lotions, and other products. This company remained in business for the next fifty years, even though Cochran sold her interest in 1964.

On May 11, 1936, Cochran married Odlum, who was to remain until his death in 1976, a devoted husband who supported his adventurous wife in everything she did. The two bought a ranch near the town of Indio in the southern California desert and spent most of their time there.

Cochran started entering air races in 1934 and soon began setting records, so that within a few years she was ranked among such top women pilots as Amelia Earhart, Anne Lindbergh, and Edna Whyte. In 1937, for example (the same year Earhart disappeared while flying over the Pacific Ocean), Cochran set three speed records, including one for flying from New York to Miami. In 1938, she won the Harmon Trophy, an award given each year by the International League of Aviators to the top woman pilot.

"To go faster or farther..."

Cochran's main goal was to work as a test pilot. According to Yount, Cochran wrote that she always wanted "to go faster or farther through the atmosphere or higher into it than anyone else and to bring back some new information about plane, engine, fuel, instruments, air, or pilot that would be helpful in the conquest of the atmosphere."

Cochran remained well informed about advances in research and new technology that could benefit aviation, and in 1937 she learned about a young surgeon named Randolph Lovelace who had developed a special oxygen tank and mask for pilots who flew at high altitudes. This was an important development because pilots who flew above 20,000 feet over the earth often experienced nosebleeds and could even pass

out. Cochran believed Lovelace's invention could prove even more valuable if the United States should have to go to war against Germany, which was then beginning to stir up trouble in Europe. She convinced a committee to award Lovelace the Collier Trophy, which honored people who had made major contributions to aviation.

It was not just her strong competitive spirit that led Cochran to enter air races, but also her interest in testing new airplanes. One of her favorite yearly events was the Bendix cross-country air race, when pilots flew from Los Angeles, California, to Cleveland, Ohio. Cochran had entered the race in 1935 but had to drop out after a treacherous takeoff, and in 1938 she decided to try again. This time she would fly in a new military pursuit plane, the P-35, which was considered fast but not too reliable.

During the flight, Cochran avoided a major catastrophe when she figured out how to correct a gas tank problem,

Jacqueline Cochran in 1937 waving from the cockpit of her plane after setting the speed record for flying from New York to Miami.
(Reproduced by permission of AP/Wide World Photos.)

and she went on to win the race. After picking up her trophy in Cleveland, she immediately took off again and flew to New York City, setting a new women's record for west-to-east transcontinental flight in a propeller-driven plane.

War brings a need for women pilots

In 1939 World War II began when Great Britain and France declared war on Germany after the German invasion of Poland. Through a special "Lend-Lease" program, the United States sent supplies and equipment to England, including airplanes. On June 17, 1941, Cochran joined this effort by flying a Hudson V-bomber from Canada (since the United States was officially a neutral country, the flight had to take off from Canada) to Great Britain, becoming the first woman to fly a military plane over the Atlantic Ocean. The U.S. government insisted, however, that a male pilot fly with her to perform the takeoff and landing.

In addition to publicizing Great Britain's need for airplanes and pilots, Cochran felt that the historic flight had shown that women were capable of noncombat military flying. If they could perform some duties other than those that would put them into battle, she reasoned, more male pilots would be available for combat. In fact, Great Britain had already put this idea into action by setting up the Air Transport Authority (ATA), through which women pilots flew planes from manufacturers to airports near fighting units. Cochran thought the United States should do something similar. Meanwhile, Cochran recruited twenty-five American women to serve in the British program and took them to England for training. These women performed well, and some stayed for the rest of the war.

The WAFS and the WASPs

Meanwhile, another American pilot, Nancy Love (1914–1976), did convince the U.S. government to establish the Women's Auxiliary Ferrying Squadron (WAFS). This was a small group made up of experienced women pilots to ferry aircraft to Canada so that it could be sent on to England. Cochran got another chance to help women get involved in the war effort when her friend General A.H. "Hap" Arnold suggested she set up a program to train more women to fly the military aircraft.

German Aviator Hanna Reitsch

While Jacqueline Cochran was proving what women could achieve in the service of the Allies (Great Britain, the United States, the Soviet Union, and the other countries fighting against Germany, Italy, and Japan), Hanna Reitsch was doing something similiar in Germany.

Born in 1912 in Hirschberg, located in a part of Germany that is now part of Poland, Reitsch was a young woman of small stature but incredible bravery when she became a stunt pilot known for her skill and daring. A devoted follower of Nazi dictator Adolf Hitler (1889–1945; see entry), Reitsch was chosen in 1937 to test military aircraft for the Luftwaffe (the German air force). After a terrible crash that left her hospitalized for months and afraid of flying, Reitsch recovered her health, conquered her fear, and went continued flying.

In 1944, Reitsch took part in an experiment to test whether the new V-1 buzz bomb could be carried in a manned aircraft that would then become a suicide weapon (the pilot would sacrifice his or her own life by intentionally crashing the plane with the bomb aboard). The experiment was banned after two pilots crashed while trying to land, but Reitsch defied the ban and made a successful flight. She later said, "Those other two did not know how to bring down fast planes."

Reitsch made a dramatic visit to Hitler when, in April 1945, he had been forced to hide in an underground bunker while the Soviet Union's Red Army kept up a steady attack on Berlin. Assigned to carry General Ritter von Greim to see Hitler, she landed on a shell-battered Berlin street, flying out safely several days later through Russian anti-aircraft fire. Reitsch was the first woman to earn Germany's highest military honor, the Iron Cross, and was the only civilian (nonmilitary person) so honored.

Reitsch was eventually captured by the Allies and held for fifteen months before being released without trial. She resumed her flying career, winning many glider championships and establishing a gliding school in the West African country of Ghana in 1962. She died in 1979.

Twenty-five thousand women applied to Cochran's program. She accepted 1,830 women; 1,074 completed the difficult twenty-three-week training (the same success rate for men who joined the Army Air Corps). When Cochran's first class of trainees graduated in the spring of 1943, she told them they were being given "the greatest opportunity ever offered women pilots anywhere in the world."

The WAFS and Cochran's group merged in August 1943 and were named the Women's Airforce Service Pilots (WASPs). Cochran was assigned to direct the organization, with Love still managing her own group but serving under Cochran. The WASPs learned how to fly almost every plane the air force used, including the gigantic B-29 Superfortresses and the Mustang and Thunderbolt fighter planes. They not only ferried airplanes between airports but transported cargo, weapons, and troops as well as tested new airplanes for safety. They towed targets for anti-aircraft gunnery practice and made low-altitude flights so that radar and searchlight operators could practice spotting them. By the end of the war the WASPs had flown 60,000 hours and sixty million miles, delivering 12,650 planes and performing just as well as male pilots (but with fewer hours lost due to illness or accidents).

The end of the WASPs

Cochran and most of the WASPs were disappointed and angered when Congress canceled their organization in December 1944. Because the organization had never been made an official part of the military, the women were not eligible for the veterans' benefits (such as continuing pay and medical care) that male members of the armed forces received. Three decades later, some WASP veterans who had been angered by the air force's announcement that it would soon start to train its "first women military pilots" started a campaign to publicize their accomplishments and gain recognition as the first women U.S. military pilots. On September 20, 1977, Congress voted to allow the WASPs or their families to receive benefits.

Breaking the sound barrier

Cochran received the Distinguished Service Medal (the second-highest honor an American civilian [nonmilitary person] can receive) for her contributions during World War II. Then she went back to testing new airplanes, which had been her first love. In 1947 test pilot Chuck Yeager became the first person to fly faster than the speed of sound (this means that the plane is flying so fast that the sound waves carrying the noise it makes cannot keep up with the plane). Cochran was a friend of Yeager's, and she longed to join him in testing military jets. Only air force members on active status were allowed to do so, though, and neither Cochran nor any other woman was a member of this group.

Cochran found a way to break this barrier with her husband's help. He owned the company that made the F-86 Sabre, one of the air force's newest jets and used his connections to make Cochran a pilot for Air Canada. Cochran could then borrow a Sabre from the Canadian Air Force, which also owned some of the planes, bring it back to the United States, and test-fly it.

In May 1953 Cochran made a historic flight. With Chuck Yeager following in a chase plane and ready to help her if she got into trouble, Cochran took the Sabre up to 45,000 feet, then went into a nosedive that soon put her at a speed of 500 to 600 miles per hour. Suddenly the noise of the plane died, proving that Cochran had reached Mach 1, the speed of sound. Then she heard the voice of Chuck Yeager over her radio, saying, "Congratulations, Jackie, you've made it." Cochran said that becoming the first woman to fly faster than the speed of sound was the most thrilling event of her life.

Setting more records

Cochran made twelve more flights in the Sabre, breaking three men's records and flying faster than the speed of sound three times. She went on to set even more records, including sixty-nine inter-city and straight line distance records in 1962 alone, and becoming the first woman to fly jet airplanes over the Atlantic Ocean. During the 1960s, the National Aeronautics and Space Administration (NASA) was developing its manned space program, and Cochran wrote (as quoted in Yount's book), "I'd have given my right eye to be an astronaut." Instead, she helped other women undergo tests to show that they too could qualify for space travel.

A heart attack in 1971 put an end to Cochran's flying career. She had once commented that life without risk would be the same as death to her, so it is not surprising that her health declined even more when she could no longer fly. Cochran died in August 1980, leaving behind an incredible record: she had set about 250 speed, altitude, and distance records (more than any other male or female pilot), earned the

Distinguished Flying Cross and Order of Merit from the U.S. government, received the Harmon Trophy fifteen times, been named "Pilot of the Decade" for 1940-49 by the Harmon trophy committee, and served as the only woman president of the Federation Aeronautique Internationale (which also made her the only woman to receive its gold medal).

In 1971, Cochran became the first living woman to enter the Aviation Hall of Fame, and she was featured as part of the U.S. Postal Service's Great Aviators stamp series, issued in 1996.

Where to Learn More

Books

Fisher, Marquita O. *Jacqueline Cochran: First Lady of Flight.* Champaign, IL: Garrard, 1973.

Mondey, David. *Women of the Air.* Morristown, NJ: Silver Burdett, 1981.

Smith, Elizabeth Simpson. *Coming Out Right: The Story of Jacqueline Cochran, the First Woman Aviator to Break the Sound Barrier.* New York: Walker, 1991.

Schraff, Anne E. *American Heroes of Exploration and Flight.* Springfield, NJ: Enslow Publishers, 1996.

Yount, Lisa. *Women Aviators.* New York: Facts on File, 1995.

Web sites

"Fact Sheet: Women's Airforce Service Pilots." Secretary of the Air Force Public Affairs.[Online] Available http://www.af.mil/50th/library/wasp.html (March 28, 1999).

"Jacqueline Cochran." U.S. Stamps Alive Archive. [Online] Available http://www.usps.gov/kids/stompfeature23.html (March 28, 1999).

Benjamin O. Davis, Jr.

Born December 12, 1912
Washington, D.C.

United States Air Force general

Overcoming obstacles and achieving great things was a longstanding tradition in the family of Benjamin O. Davis, Jr. His father, Benjamin O. Davis, Sr. was the U.S. Army's first African American general. And even as Davis, Sr. spent the years during World War II advising the U.S. government on race-related matters, his son, Davis, Jr., was leading the Tuskegee Airmen as they showed what black servicemen could achieve. Only the fourth African American to attend the U.S. Military Academy at West Point, New York, Davis, Jr. endured harsh treatment at the academy and was told he would never realize his dream of becoming a military pilot. He not only became a pilot but led hundreds of other black pilots as they trained at Tuskegee Army Air Field in Alabama and went on to combat duty in Europe. Under Davis's command, the Tuskegee Airmen became a highly skilled, disciplined unit that, among other accomplishments, never lost any of the bombers they escorted. Davis went on to become the first African American air force officer to reach the rank of general.

Benjamin O. Davis, Jr. commanded the Tuskegee Airmen, a group of African American pilots whose excellent performance during World War II helped break down barriers for blacks in the armed forces.

Portrait: Benjamin O. Davis, Jr.
(Reproduced by permission of the U.S. Air Force.)

A tradition of pride and determination

Davis was born in Washington, D.C., at the home of his grandparents, Louis and Henrietta Davis. His mother, Elnora, died in 1916 and his father soon left Washington to serve with the U.S. Army in the Philippines. Surrounded by aunts, uncles, and cousins, Davis and his sisters, Olive and Elnora, were part of a large, supportive family. A calm, serious boy, Davis always felt deep pride when he saw his father dressed in his army uniform.

In 1919, Benjamin Davis, Sr. married an old family friend named Sadie Overton. Assigned to teach military science and tactics at Tuskegee Institute (the school for African Americans founded in 1881 by Booker T. Washington), he moved his family to Alabama. Even though he had seen how his ambitious, dedicated father experienced many career setbacks because of his race, Davis, Jr. felt his father had also given the Davis children an example of determination to follow.

As soon as they left the grounds of the Tuskegee Institute, the Davis family experienced the racial prejudice that dominated the South at that time. The "Jim Crow" segregation laws required separate schools, restaurants, movie theaters, rest rooms, and even drinking fountains for black and white people. Although forced to endure this inequality, Davis, Sr. was not about to show any fear of the Ku Klux Klan, a group that expressed their hatred for blacks in many ways, including violence. When the Klan rode past Tuskegee, Davis, Sr. stood under his front porch light in his white dress uniform, his family seated behind him.

Dreaming of flying

When he was thirteen and back in Washington, D.C., for the summer, Davis, Jr.'s uncle took him to see some barnstormers (pilots who performed daring stunts in the air to entertain audiences) at nearby Bolling Air Field. Davis was awestruck, and when his father later paid for him to take a ride with a barnstormer, he decided he loved airplanes and wanted to be a pilot.

The Davis family moved to Cleveland when Davis, Sr. was assigned as an instructor to a black National Guard unit. Davis, Jr. graduated—with the highest grades in his class—

from Cleveland's Central High School in 1929. He entered Western Reserve University in Cleveland but was not happy there. He still wanted to fly planes, but there were no training programs available for black pilots. Prejudices against blacks led many people to believe that blacks did not have the ability to fly airplanes.

Shunned at West Point

Davis's father suggested that he apply to West Point, even though no other African Americans had attended the academy in the twentieth century (there had been three black graduates in the nineteenth century). All applicants had to be appointed by an official of the U.S. government, such as the president or a member of Congress, so Davis got an appointment from the only black member of the House of Representatives, Oscar DePriest of Illinois. Davis took the school's entrance exam in March 1931 and, to his deep shame, failed. The next year, he studied hard for the exam and passed it easily.

When Davis arrived at West Point in July 1932, he was told that he would be rooming alone—no white cadet would be asked to share a room with him. He also quickly learned that he would be given the "silent treatment." In a practice that was usually given only to those who had broken the school's honor code (by, for example, cheating on a test). Other students would speak to him only in the line of duty. Davis was to spend the next four years shunned by his fellow cadets, eating his meals in silence and studying and attending activities by himself.

Discouraging words from a general

Determined to succeed in spite of the discrimination, Davis grew accustomed to life at West Point, settling into a routine of academic study, military training, and drills. At a New Year's Eve dance in New York during his second year, Davis met a Connecticut schoolteacher named Agatha Scott. He saw her again a year later, and the two fell in love.

As graduation approached, Davis expressed an interest in applying to the Army Air Corps (at that time, the air force was still part of the army). But West Point's superintendent, General William Connor, told him he should give up

The 761st Tank Battalion

While African American aviators were proving their courage and loyalty in the skies above Italy, black soldiers on the ground were also making a name for themselves. Made up of the U.S. Army's first black tankers (soldiers who operate armed tanks), the 761st Tank Battalion was praised for its performance in France as the Allies fought their way across several European countries in pursuit of the Germans.

Although widespread racism and discrimination kept African Americans from climbing the ranks of the U.S. Army, there were some white army officers who wanted to offer them more opportunities. One of these was Lieutenant Lesley James McNair, who as commanding general of army ground forces is credited with having allowed the 761st Tank Battalion to come into existence.

General McNair (who would later lose his life in the war) first visited the battalion at their training camp in Louisiana, and when they arrived for duty in France on October 31, 1944, he told them, "I am damned glad to have you with us. We have been expecting you for a long time, and I am sure you are going to give a good account of yourselves." General George S. Patton (1885–1945; see entry) also visited and welcomed the men of the 761st.

Having joined the army's 26th Division, the 761st Battalion entered battle on November 8, 1944, at Athaniville, France. For the next 183 days they would fight without stopping, advancing through six European countries, killing 6,266 enemy soldiers, and capturing 15,818.

One especially brave member of the battalion was Staff Sergeant Ruben Rivers of Tecumseh, Oklahoma. Severely wounded in the leg when his tank ran over two mines, Rivers refused to leave the battle and stayed for three more days of combat, even though he had a bone protruding from his wound. During a later exchange of gunfire with German troops, Rivers was killed when his tank was hit by an armor-piercing shell. Veterans of the 761st are still pursuing a Medal of Honor for Rivers.

It was not until January 24, 1978, that the 761st Battalion's excellent combat record was recognized. On that day, they received a Presidential Unit Citation.

that dream because the Air Corps would never train black pilots and white troops would never serve under black officers. Despite these discouraging words, Davis did not give up his dream.

Prejudice at Fort Benning

In June 1936, Davis graduated from West Point, ranked 35th in a class of 276. Two weeks later, he married Agatha in the West Point chapel. Now a second lieutenant, Davis was assigned to the army base at Fort Benning, Georgia, where he and Agatha quickly learned that they were not to be treated like other new arrivals. Instead, white officers and their families avoided the Davises.

At Fort Benning, Davis worked with Company F, a black unit commanded by white officers. In the segregated army, African American soldiers were being trained not for combat but to perform service jobs, such as keeping equipment clean, groundskeeping, and cleaning stables.

In September 1937, Davis attended the army's Infantry School, studying war tactics and military history. His next assignment was the same one his father had been given several years earlier: teacher of military science and tactics at Tuskegee Institute. Now a captain, Davis knew he deserved a more challenging, responsible position and considered quitting, but jobs were hard to come by and he decided to stay in the army.

More opportunities open up

Davis's prospects began to change for the better in September 1940 when President Franklin D. Roosevelt—responding to pressure from the African American community, which had helped him get elected—made his father a brigadier general. Davis, Sr. was given command of the 9th and 10th Cavalries at Fort Riley, Kansas, and he requested that his son serve as his aide.

As the 1930s drew to a close, it appeared that the United States might eventually become involved in World War II, which began in September 1939 with Germany's invasion of Poland. The U.S. government began preparing its armed forces for possible war, an effort that included—again due to the pressure applied by civil rights groups—the formation of a black flying unit to be called the 99th Pursuit Squadron.

Davis was overjoyed when, in 1941, he received orders to serve as the commander of the 99th, and to report to the Tuskegee Army Air Field for flight training. This facility had been created just to train black pilots; the army's rules about segregation wouldn't allow black and white pilots to be trained together. And even *this* air field was segregated, with white instructors having separate housing and other facilities . The nearly 1,000 black pilots were angry about this, but Davis told them to let it go, and to focus on their own achievements.

The Tuskegee Airmen prepare for combat

After completing their classroom studies, the Tuskegee Airmen began their flight training, learning in bulky BT-13 airplanes how to perform the many maneuvers they would need as fighter pilots. When the Japanese bombed the American naval base at Pearl Harbor, Hawaii (December 7, 1941), the United States entered World War II. The airmen knew they would soon have a chance to test their skills. They earned their "wings" (became pilots) on March 7, 1942, becoming the first African Americans to enter the U.S. Army Air Corps. They all knew that future opportunities for others might depend on their performance in the war.

Performing well in Italy

One year later, the Tuskegee Airmen finally received their combat orders. The 99th Squadron was sent to North Africa, where Allied troops (mostly from the United States and Great Britain) had been fighting the German army in Algeria, Morocco, and Tunisia. The Germans surrendered just before the 99th Pursuit Squadron arrived, but the Allies were also getting ready to invade Italy so the Tuskegee Airman would still have their chance in battle.

Their first combat mission took place on June 22, 1943, with a successful attack on Pantelleria Island off the coast of Tunisia. The squadron performed strafing missions (flying low and raining bullets onto the enemy) and escorted the heavy bombers, protecting them from enemy aircraft.

During the later invasion of Sicily (an island off the southern coast of Italy), they protected troops landing on the beaches and chased enemy planes away from navy ships. Lieutenant Charles B. Hall became the first member of the 99th Pursuit Squadron to shoot down an enemy plane. Soon they were flying up to twelve missions per day, bombing air fields, railroad yards, bridges, and factories.

A false report

On September 3, Davis was called back to the United States to command the new 332nd Fighter Group, which was made up of three squadrons of African American pilots who were training for duty. Davis soon learned that the 99th Squadron had been criticized by Colonel William Momyer who had submitted a report stating that they were poorly disciplined, didn't work together as a team, and tended to panic under fire. The report concluded: "The Negro type has not the proper reflexes to make a first-class fighter pilot." Momyer suggested that the 332nd be assigned to noncombat duty and that plans to train more black pilots be cancelled.

Knowing that the report was based not on the 99th Squadron's performance record but on racism, Davis was furious. But when he met with a committee from the War Department, he did not talk about racism. He simply showed the committee the proof of what the squadron had accomplished in Italy. The government then conducted its own study of the black pilots' performance, which revealed no difference between this and any other combat unit.

The 332nd gets its chance

The 332nd arrived in Italy in January 1944 and immediately learned that the 99th Squadron had just played a key role in the Allied victory at Anzio (a town on Italy's seacoast). They had shot down twelve enemy planes. News of what the 99th had accomplished reached the U.S. newspapers.

Davis was disappointed when the 332nd Squadron's first assignment was to patrol the coast (guarding harbors and escorting supply ships) instead of entering combat. In his autobiography, Davis wrote that he felt this was "a betrayal of everything we had been working for and an intentional insult to me and my men." Nevertheless, Davis behaved as if the squadron were performing an important role.

In March 1944 the 332nd was assigned to escort bombers. Davis was promoted to colonel, and the squadron moved to a new base at Ramitelli on Italy's east coast. From there they accomplished a successful mission to Munich, Germany, where only thirty-nine pilots managed to hold off one hundred German fighter planes and even shot down five of

Benjamin O. Davis, Jr. receives the Distinguished Flying Cross medal, which was pinned onto his uniform by his father.
(Reproduced by permission of the U.S. Army.)

them. Nicknamed the "Red Tails" because of the distinctive red paint on their planes, the Tuskegee Airmen gained a reputation for staying with bombers over the target (the most dangerous part of a bombing mission) and for always safely escorting the bombers back to base.

Davis had personally led the mission to Munich, and in honor of his performance he received the Distinguished Flying Cross, which was pinned onto his uniform by his father.

A long list of accomplishments

Those who had hoped that the Tuskegee Airmen would perform well and thus prove that African American servicemen were as capable as whites were thrilled at their performance record. Among them they earned more than a hundred Distinguished Flying Crosses as well as three Distinguished Unit Citations.

"The best-managed base ..."

The Germans surrendered in May 1945, ending the war in Europe. Davis was assigned to command the 477th Bombardment Group, which was preparing to fight the Japanese when they too surrendered in August. The following March, Davis moved the 477th to Lockbourne Air Base near Columbus, Ohio, which became the first black air base that was not under the control of white officers. Under Davis's command, Lockbourne became—according to an inspection report—"the best-managed base in the Air Corps." In fact, white troops and white civilian employees worked under African American officers with no problems.

Tuskegee Airmen's Record

- 111 enemy aircraft shot down
- 150 enemy aircraft destroyed on the ground
- 1 German navy ship destroyed (an unusual feat for an air squadron)
- 40 other enemy boats and barges destroyed
- 200 escort missions completed without ever losing a bomber (the only fighter group to do so)

In September 1947 the U. S. Air Force became a separate branch of the armed forces. An even bigger change occurred the following year, when President Harry S. Truman (1884–1975; see entry) signed Executive Order 9981, which called for integration of the armed forces. All-black units were to be abolished and black troops fully integrated with white troops. Many felt that the Tuskegee Airmen had had a huge effect on the change of attitude that allowed this step to occur.

Commanding at home and overseas

In 1949 Davis became the first black officer to attend the Air War College. Throughout the 1950s and 1960s, he commanded pilots both at U.S. bases and overseas. He worked at the Pentagon (the headquarters of the Department of Defense) as head of the Fighter Branch, commanded pilots fighting in the Korean War, and served in Korea, Japan, Taiwan, and Germany. During the Vietnam War, Davis commanded the 13th Air Force, based in the Philippines.

By the time of the Vietnam War, 50,000 African Americans were serving in the armed forces in all capacities and there were twelve black army generals, three black air force generals, and one black admiral. African Americans earned twenty of the 277 Medals of Honor awarded during the war.

A busy retirement

Having reached the rank of major general (three stars) and after serving thirty-three years in the military, Davis decided in 1971 that it was time to retire. He became director of public safety for the city of Cleveland, then went to work for U.S. Secretary of Transportation John Volpe to help with the problem of "skyjacking" (armed hijacking of passenger planes), which was then a frequent occurrence. New security systems suggested by Davis resolved the problem in nine months.

In 1989 Davis proudly witnessed the elevation of an African American to the most important post in the military when General Colin Powell became the Chairman of the Joint Chiefs of Staff (a group made up of the heads of all the branches of the armed forces). Davis received his own high honor on December 9, 1998, when he was made a four-star general by President Bill Clinton, who said, "He earned this a long time ago."

Where to Learn More

Books

Applegate, Katherine. *The Story of Two Generals, Benjamin O. Davis, Jr. and Colin L. Powell.* New York: Dell, 1992.

Davis, Benjamin O. *Benjamin O. Davis, Jr.: An Autobiography.* Washington, D.C.: Smith's Press, 1991.

Reef, Catherine. *Benjamin Davis, Jr.* Frederick, MD: Twenty-First Century Books, 1992.

Web sites

Gropman, Alan L. "Benjamin Davis, American." [Online] Available http://www.afa.org/magazine/897benja.html.

Benjamin O. Davis, Sr.

Born May 28, 1877
Washington, D.C.
Died November 26, 1970
Chicago, Illinois

The first African American general in the United States Army

For most of Benjamin Davis's military career, which spanned more than fifty years, the United States armed forces (including the army, navy, marines, and air force) were segregated. Even though African Americans had taken part in every military conflict in American history, it was thought that black and white soldiers should not fight side by side—that, in fact, black soldiers should not fight at all but should perform such jobs as cleaning and cooking meals. In addition, there was little opportunity for African Americans to advance in their military careers. Despite this discrimination, Davis rose slowly through the ranks to become a general. During World War II, he advised military leaders on ways to integrate the forces, and he worked to resolve racial conflicts. Thus he helped to lay a foundation for the changes that would later come, when blacks finally achieved equal status with whites in the military.

A hard-working family

Davis was born into a family whose ancestors were freed blacks (former slaves who had either earned or been granted their freedom). His parents, Louis and Henrietta Davis,

Benjamin O. Davis, Sr. took part in early efforts to desegregate the armed forces and served as an advisor and mediator on racial issues during World War II.

Portrait: Benjamin O. Davis, Sr. *(Reproduced by permission of AP/Wide World Photos.)*

were hardworking people and respected members of the African American community in Washington, D.C. Louis worked as a government messenger, and Henrietta was a nurse. They taught their children that a good education was the best way to advance in life.

Benjamin attended a grammar school named for abolitionist (someone who fought to abolish slavery) Lucretia Mott. It was an integrated school and he had both black and white friends; later, he said that he did not encounter racial discrimination until later in his life.

Interested in history, Davis saw the famous Native American leader Sitting Bull when he visited Washington. He also learned about the role of African American cavalry soldiers in America and the exploits of black soldiers during the Civil War. Despite his father's desire that he make a government career his goal and his mother's wish that he someday become a Baptist minister, Davis wished for a career in the military.

Eager to join the military

When he was a high school student, Davis joined the Cadet Corps, a group that practiced military drills and learned about weapons. Although he took some courses at Howard University (a predominantly black school in Washington, D.C.) during his last year of high school, Davis chose to pursue a military career after graduation rather than attend college.

In 1898, war broke out in Cuba when revolutionary soldiers fought Spanish forces to win Cuba's independence from Spain. The United States entered the conflict—called the Spanish-American War—on the side of the Cuban revolutionaries. Many young American men, both black and white, were eager to join the fighting, and Davis was no exception. He became a member of a volunteer company and was given the temporary rank of lieutenant.

Davis spent his first months as a soldier in various training camps. He visited the southern United States for the first time in his life when he was posted to Fort Thomas, Kentucky, and Chickamauga Park, Georgia. There he was shocked by the rigid separation between blacks and whites and the poor way in which African Americans were treated.

Rising ambitions

When the Spanish-American War ended, Davis entered the regular army as a private in the 9th Cavalry. His ability to write well, take dictation, and type as well as his obvious dedication to the military and enthusiasm for military life made him popular with superior officers and helped him to advance through the lower ranks. He was assigned to serve at Samar, an island in the Philippines, where he became a sergeant major—the highest rank available for an enlisted man.

Ultimately, Davis wanted to become an army officer. This meant that he would have to take special examinations testing his knowledge of military history and other subjects. Davis's black colleagues told him that even if he passed the exams, which seemed unlikely, other obstacles would surely be put in his way to prevent him from moving ahead. Nevertheless, Davis took the exams and passed, becoming a second lieutenant in the 10th Cavalry.

In October 1902 Davis married Elnora Dickerson, and she accompanied him to his new post, Fort Washakie, Wyoming. There they were the only African American people on the base, and they felt socially isolated.

Unhappy with his assignment

In 1905, Davis was assigned to teach military history at Wilberforce University, an all-black, Christian school in Ohio. He was not happy about the assignment, because he was not a particularly religious person and felt his military background set him apart from the other staff and students. He got into disputes with Wilberforce's president over discipline, which he did not think was strict enough. Most important, it seemed to Davis that the army could have put his skills and training to better use elsewhere.

Davis was released from his unhappy term at Wilberforce when he was named military attaché (a technical expert who serves on an ambassador's diplomatic staff) to Liberia, a West African country that had been settled in the nineteenth century by former slaves from the United States. Davis moved his growing family (he now had a five-year-old daughter, Olive) to Liberia's capital city, Monrovia, and spent the next two years reporting back to the U.S. government on Liberia's military activities. He found that the Liberian army was very poorly trained and inefficient, and he came up with many ideas on how to reorganize and strengthen it. Davis volunteered to stay in Liberia as a military advisor, but U.S. law required that he complete his term of service and then return home, which he did in 1911.

Next Davis served a tour of duty on Arizona's border with Mexico. In 1915, he was made a captain, but instead of assigning this ambitious and accomplished officer to a responsible and challenging position, the U.S. Army sent him to Wilberforce University again. Tragedy struck the Davis family the next year when Elnora died after giving birth to her third child, also named Elnora (Benjamin, Jr. had been born three years earlier). For the next few years Davis relied on his parents and his deceased wife's parents for help in raising his children.

World War I and beyond

During World War I (1914–1918; a war that started as a conflict between Austria-Hungary and Serbia and escalated into a global war involving thirty-two nations), Davis was posted to the Philippines, where he served as commanding officer of a supply troop. His successful tour was stymied in 1920 when a high-ranking officer who disapproved of black officers interacting with white officers and soldiers demanded that Davis be replaced.

In 1919, Davis married Sadie Overton, a family friend who had impressed him and his children through her kindness at the time of Elnora's death. Davis was now assigned to teach at Tuskegee Institute , the famous all-black school established by Booker T. Washington in Tuskegee, Alabama. Although he enjoyed this position, Davis felt that it was not equivalent to his rank, especially after he was made a lieutenant colonel. Living in the South again, he encountered racism. He once protested a Ku Klux Klan (KKK) rally (the Klan is an organization promoting white supremacy and segregation, often through violent means) by standing on his front porch, attired in his white dress uniform and with his family seated behind him while Klan members marched by.

Davis became an instructor to the Ohio National Guard, based in Cleveland, in 1924. After he was made a colonel in 1929, the army again assigned him—against his own wishes—to Tuskegee Institute. This also outraged much of the African American community. The black newspapers lamented that an army officer with so many years of experience and dedication was being pushed to the sidelines.

Reaching the highest ranks

It had long been the desire of many African Americans that black officers be assigned to command black soldiers. In 1938 this hope was fulfilled when Davis was made commander of the 369th Cavalry New York National Guard (known as the "Harlem Regiment"). At this time Davis was also involved in the Gold Star Mothers' Pilgrimage program, which gave the mothers of slain servicemen the opportunity to visit the World War I battlefields and gravesites where their sons had fought and were buried. Davis and his wife accompanied several groups of African American mothers on tours to Europe.

By 1940, President Franklin D. Roosevelt (1882–1945; see entry) was under pressure to do something about discrimination against blacks in the armed forces. After all, African American voters had played an important role in his election victory in 1936. Yet there were still restrictions on the number of blacks who could enlist, the navy accepted blacks only for mess (kitchen) duty, and African Americans were routinely denied promotions.

In a gesture that acknowledged Davis's long and distinguished career in the military, Roosevelt overrode a military law limiting promotions to those age fifty-eight or younger (Davis was now sixty-three), and made Davis a brigadier general. He was given command of the Fourth Cavalry Brigade at Fort Riley, Kansas. Davis retired from the army in the summer of 1941, but then World War II came along and changed his future.

Called back to aid the war effort

After the United States entered World War II in December 1941, Davis was called back from retirement and assigned to work in Washington, D.C., helping the army's inspector general coordinate the induction of about 100,000 African American soldiers into the army. His job involved inspecting

Pearl Harbor Hero: Dorie Miller

Through his heroic actions during the bombing of the U.S. naval base at Pearl Harbor, Hawaii, a sailor named Dorie Miller showed the world how much talent and courage were being wasted by the military's discrimination against African Americans.

Like so many other black men who would have preferred to serve their country as frontline fighters, Miller's opportunity had been limited to serving as a U.S. Navy mess (kitchen) attendant aboard the USS *West Virginia*. On the morning of December 7, 1941, the *West Virginia* was anchored in the peaceful bay at Pearl Harbor when, totally unexpectedly, Japanese fighter planes filled the sky and began raining down bombs on the ships and men below.

When the attack began, Miller had been gathering laundry below decks. He ran up on deck and was first assigned to carry wounded men to safety. Later he took over an anti-aircraft machine gun whose operator had been killed, shooting down at least one Japanese plane before the battle was over. Miller had not been trained in the use of the gun, but later said, "It wasn't hard. I just pulled the trigger and she worked fine. I had watched the others with these guns."

News of Miller's heroism soon reached the African American community. He was celebrated as a symbol of black black units around the country and helping to solve the racial problems that were cropping up as black soldiers intermingled both with white soldiers and with segregated communities near their bases. He also helped to produce a film called *The Negro Soldier* designed to educate white soldiers about their black counterparts.

Many racial conflicts were caused by the segregation that was built into the U.S. Army, which required, for example, that black and white soldiers eat, see movies, and have their hair cut at separate facilities on the same base. But other problems developed when white officers used derogatory and belittling terms when speaking to black soldiers, or when white townspeople harassed them. Davis's approach to resolving these problems quiet and evenhanded. Some civil rights advocates at the time were urging a quick end to segregation; Davis advocated patience.

Dorie Miller. *(Reproduced by permission of the Schomburg Center.)*

patriotism (loyalty to one's country) and pride, and his admirers asked President Roosevelt to admit him to the Naval Academy. Miller never did attend the Naval Academy, but he was decorated for his bravery. On May 27, 1942, Miller received the Navy Cross from Admiral Chester Nimitz, who noted that this was the first time the medal had been given to an African American; he added, "I'm sure that the future will see others similarly honored for brave acts."

Miller continued to serve in the navy until he was killed in the South Pacific when his ship, the USS *Liscome Bay*, was attacked and sunk by a Japanese submarine on November 24, 1943.

As World War II progressed and troops spread out around the world to fight in the various theaters (areas of action), more racial conflicts erupted overseas. For example, in England some white officers and soldiers from the United States resented the way that the British seemed to make a point of interacting socially with blacks. In 1944, Davis toured the European war zone in an effort to ease this racial tension. He asserted that "[if] the people of the U.S. cannot evolve some kind of platform so that various groups can get along in harmony, they cannot make a world peace."

Advice for General Eisenhower

In addition, Davis made several strong recommendations to General Dwight D. Eisenhower (1890–1970; see entry), the commander of all U.S. troops in Europe. He said

Brigadier General Benjamin O. Davis, Sr. in England in 1942. Davis came out of retirement to help with the war effort during World War II.
(Reproduced by permission of AP/Wide World Photos.)

that in view of the profound shortage of infantrymen (especially after the bloody Battle of the Bulge in late 1944), African American soldiers—many of whom were weary of endless training and eager to get into combat—should be allowed to volunteer for the normally all-white combat replacement program. Davis's plan called for black soldiers to be assigned to any units that needed them, rather than to all-black units.

But it seemed that the U.S. Army was still not ready for such a change. Eisenhower did, however, modify Davis's idea by allowing black platoons (a subdivision of a company, usually made up of two squadrons) to be fitted into white companies (infantry units with two or more platoons, usually commanded by a captain) as needed.

Major change comes after the war

Discrimination and segregation in the armed forces existed throughout World War II, but the experiences and contributions of both black and white soldiers during the war—as well as the input of Davis and other advisors—opened up many eyes to the injustice in the American military. Six days after Davis's July 20, 1948, retirement from the army (which was marked by a special ceremony in the White House Rose Garden), President Truman issued Executive Order 9981. The order stated: "There shall be equality of treatment and opportunity for all persons in the armed services without regard to race, color, religion, or national origin."

Davis lived for another twenty years after his retirement. In 1951 he returned to Liberia to represent the United States at that country's centennial celebration. He made many other public appearances until 1960, when his health began to decline. Davis died of leukemia on November 26, 1970, at Great Lakes Naval Hospital in Illinois.

Where to Learn More

Books

Astor, Gerald. *The Right to Fight: A History of African Americans in the Military.* Novato, CA: Presidio Press, 1998.

Fletcher, Marvin E. *America's First Black General: Benjamin O. Davis, Sr., 1880–1970.* Lawrence: University Press of Kansas, 1989.

Greene, Robert Ewell. *Black Defenders of America, 1775–1973.* Chicago: Johnson Publishing Company, 1974.

Web sites

"New Roles: Gen. Benjamin O. Davis." *National Archives and Record Administration: A People at War.* [Online] Available http://www.nara.gov/exhall/people/newroles.html (November 16, 1998).

Charles de Gaulle

Born November 22, 1890
Lille, France
Died November 9, 1970
Colombey-les-Deux-Eglises, France

French general, political leader, and president of the Fifth Republic

Portrait: Charles de Gaulle.
(Reproduced by permission of AP/Wide World Photos.)

After Adolf Hitler's forces invaded France in 1940, many French people worked to free their country from the Nazis. The head of the resistance movement working from outside France during the World War II, Charles de Gaulle proved a bold and courageous leader. He also led the first French government established after the war, and helped to define France's postwar identity. His critics said that he was arrogant and never willing to compromise, but not even they could deny that he loved his country deeply. In fact, de Gaulle's personal ambitions and his desire for a strong, independent France were closely intertwined; at one point he even said, "Je suis la France" (I am France).

An early dedication to France

De Gaulle was born in the northern town of Lille, located near France's border with Belgium. His father was a teacher and headmaster of a Jesuit school. Although Charles was not an excellent student, he had a very good memory and did well in the subjects that interested him, especially history. As a boy, he liked to pretend he was a soldier, and even when he was very young he imagined himself growing up to serve his country in some way.

It's not surprising that the young de Gaulle decided to pursue a career in the army, a choice that required him to spend his first year after graduating from preparatory (high) school serving as a soldier. When his year in the army was over, de Gaulle entered a military academy called Saint-Cyr, graduating in 1912.

Fighting in World War I

De Gaulle enlisted in the 33rd Infantry Regiment. His commanding officer, Colonel Philippe Petain (1856–1951), was so impressed by the young man's performance that he quickly promoted him from sublieutenant to lieutenant. When World War I (1914–1918) began, de Gaulle fought in Belgium. He was wounded twice, in 1914 and 1915, before taking part in the Battle of Verdun, in which he was again wounded and finally captured by the Germans. During his thirty-two months as a prisoner of war, de Gaulle made five escape attempts.

His army career advances

After the war, Poland and Russia got into a dispute over their borders. Poland was fighting Russia's Bolshevik army (the Bolsheviks were the party, led by Vladimir Lenin, that took control of Russia after its 1917 revolution). De Gaulle joined a Polish cavalry unit to gain valuable military experience and move ahead in his military career. While on leave, he married a girl named Yvonne, the daughter of a Paris biscuit manufacturer.

When Poland and the Soviet Union finally made peace, de Gaulle returned to France and lectured on military history at his old school, Saint-Cyr. He also attended the Ecole Superieure de Guerre (Higher Military School) in order to qualify for a higher rank. There he was known as a brilliant but arrogant student who didn't like to be criticized. His instructors were ready to give him a failing grade, but his old friend Petain—who was now a field marshal—made sure he received the high grade that would allow him to earn a promotion.

While rising through the ranks of the army, de Gaulle published a number of articles and books on military topics. In one of these, *The Army of the Future* (1934), de Gaulle recommended that the French army be reformed through the use of mechanized, mobile warfare and especially armored tanks. Few of his superiors, however, were ready to listen. They still believed in using a system of fixed fortifications to defend their country. Only a few years later de Gaulle was proved correct when the German army successfully invaded France.

The Germans invade France

In the fall of 1939, Germany invaded Poland. France and Great Britain responded to Hitler's aggression by declaring war on Germany. Fighting didn't start between the countries until May 10, 1940, when the Germans attacked France. The German army, which had made the change to mechanized, mobile warfare, rolled its tanks easily over France's fixed fortifications. On the same day, Germany also invaded Holland, Belgium, and Luxembourg in order to extend its European empire.

Before the invasion de Gaulle had been assigned to a tank unit in Alsace, France. On May 11, de Gaulle was to lead an armored division that had been very quickly assembled and that was not very well prepared to fight against the Germans. Nevertheless, his forces made a good showing in several battles, and he was promoted to the rank of brigadier general. On June 5, de Gaulle was called to Paris, where French premier Paul Reynaud named him undersecretary of state for national defense.

Making the call to resistance

At this time, the prospects for a French victory looked bleak, and many French leaders wanted to make peace with Germany. De Gaulle was among the few who thought France should keep fighting, even if the government had to move to a safe spot in North Africa, where France had control of the colonies of Morocco, Algeria, Tunisia, and Equatorial West Africa.

On June 16, the government of France was taken over by the Nazis, who established a new French government headed by Petain, de Gaulle's old patron. Petain's government

agreed to move to the southern city of Vichy and to cooperate with the Nazis, who would have control of northern France, including Paris. Throughout the war, the French leaders who were working with the Nazis would be known as the "Vichy Government."

Meanwhile, de Gaulle had flown to London aboard a British aircraft. He had made a good impression on Britain's

As leader of the Free French Movement, Charles de Gaulle urged the French people to continue resisting the Nazis. *(Reproduced by permission of AP/Wide World Photos.)*

prime minister, Winston Churchill (1874–1965; see entry), who allowed de Gaulle to use the BBC (British Broadcasting System) to make a four-minute "Call to Honor," in which he urged all French people to resist the Nazis. "Believe me!" de Gaulle exclaimed. "Nothing is lost for France! The same methods which have defeated us may one day bring us victory."

The Free French movement grows

Unfortunately, de Gaulle was not very well known, and at first it didn't seem that his radio messages were having any effect. Gradually, though, he gathered some supporters from among his fellow refugees. De Gaulle called his movement the Provisional French National Committee, but it came to be known as the Free French movement.

With the help of the British Navy, de Gaulle's forces gained enough strength to attack the pro-Vichy forces at Dakar, French West Africa (now Senegal). Although de Gaulle and his followers lost this battle, they continued to gain popular support, and by November 1940 they had about 35,000 troops and twenty warships. De Gaulle moved his headquarters to Brazzaville in French Equatorial Africa (now Congo), and from there he declared that since no true French government now existed, "it is necessary that a new authority should assume the task of directing the French effort in the war. Events impose this sacred duty upon me. I shall not fail to carry it out."

Another turning point came in the spring of 1941, when the British and Free French overpowered the Vichy forces in Syria and Lebanon. After a small power struggle with the British over what should be done with the captured Vichy troops, de Gaulle convinced the British to allow him to try to persuade the soldiers to join the Free French. About 6,000 of the 25,000 Vichy soldiers did join de Gaulle. In June, the Free French won their first victory against the Germans at Bir Hakeim, Libya.

De Gaulle's power increases

Things did not always go smoothly between de Gaulle and the British, but his relationship with the United States was even stormier. The United States had maintained ties with the

Vichy government, which was still the official government of France, and President Franklin D. Roosevelt distrusted de Gaulle, fearing that he had the potential to become a dictator. When the United States and Britain launched their invasion of North Africa—called "Operation Torch"—they did not invite the Free French forces to participate.

This made de Gaulle mad, but he was even angrier when the Allies (the countries fighting against Germany, Italy, and Japan) made an agreement with a Vichy commander, Admiral Francois Darlan, allowing him to administer all of France's colonies in North Africa except Morocco and Algeria, which the Allies would occupy. After Darlan's assassination in December 1942, de Gaulle worked out a power-sharing arrangement with General Henri Giraud (who had strong links to the Vichy government) and established the French Committee of National Liberation. Soon, however, de Gaulle edged out Giraud, who faded into obscurity.

By 1944, de Gaulle had been recognized by nearly everyone as the leader of the Resistance Movement (now known as the France Combatante or Fighting French) both inside and outside of France. In Nazi-occupied France, the Gestapo (Hitler's secret state police) responded by rounding up and imprisoning members of de Gaulle's family who were still in the country.

A triumphant return to France

When the Allies were planning the massive troop landing on northern French beaches that came to be known as the Normandy Invasion or D-Day, de Gaulle and his forces were not included. But de Gaulle did land in France on June 14, 1944, eight days after the initial Allied invasion. On August 25 he made a triumphant return to Paris, whose citizens greeted him with joy and gratitude.

By September, de Gaulle had announced the formation of a temporary government with himself as president. He immediately started working on the economic reforms France needed so badly at this time of transition. In October, both the United States and Britain officially recognized de Gaulle's government as legitimate.

The Women of the French Resistance

When the German army marched into France and took control of the country, many French citizens vowed to do whatever they could to resist. While de Gaulle led the Free French movement outside France, many secret resistance movements formed inside the country. They carried on a variety of activities, from attacks on German officials by fighting groups called the Maquis, sabotage (destroying buildings and equipment used by the Germans), and spying, to printing propaganda (material intended to persuade the reader to adopt a certain viewpoint) against the Germans.

In the decades following World War II, the deeds performed by the French Resistance were well known, but it has only been in recent years that the important role played by French women in the movement has come to light. Like women in the United States, French women found their options expanded by the war: since so many men had been called away to fight, their contributions were crucial. And within the resistance movement, they found a measure of equality with men that had not existed in their prewar world.

The tasks performed by French Resistance women were many and varied. In the first few years of the German occupation, they resisted openly through protests and demonstrations against the shortages of food from which the French people suffered. They also called for the return of prisoners of war (POWs, French men who had been arrested and imprisoned by the Nazis) and for the right

Criticizing the Fourth Republic

Over the next few months, French leaders began planning their new, reorganized government, which they called the "Fourth Republic" and which would feature a strong legislative body and a weaker president. De Gaulle didn't like this plan. He believed the president should have more power. Claiming that he did not want to "preside, powerless, over the powerless state," de Gaulle resigned the presidency on January 10, 1946, and returned to his country home.

De Gaulle started writing his war memoirs, but he remained interested and active in politics and particularly in criticizing the Fourth Republic. In the late 1940s he formed an organization called the Rally of the French People, which to send packages to POWs. But as the occupation continued, they took on even more dangerous and secret responsibilities, all of which could lead to arrest, torture, imprisonment, or even death if they were discovered.

Some women assisted the resistance movement in traditional ways, by performing office work or nursing those injured in clashes with the Germans. They opened their homes to those who were being chased by the Gestapo, whether they were Jews, Allied pilots whose planes had crashed in France, or resistance fighters. Farm women hid weapons, and documents were stashed in the apartments of city women. Before the war, fathers had been in charge of families; now, with men away from home, mothers took that responsibility.

A number of French women worked for the resistance in untraditional ways, especially those who served as "liaison agents." They traveled around the country at great risk to their own safety, carrying messages and money and looking for good hiding spots for weapons and fighters and good sites for parachute drops. A few women also participated as Maquis fighters, though this was not common. Women proved to be flexible, adaptable members of the resistance who showed initiative and had good ideas about what could be done. After the war, they said that they had learned through their resistance work how much they could do, even though peacetime brought with it a return to traditional women's roles.

advocated a strong chief executive and which expressed its ideas through Nazi-style rallies. This group gained a fair degree of popularity for a short time but eventually collapsed, and de Gaulle officially dissolved it in the early 1950s.

Back into the political ring

Several circumstances brought de Gaulle back to the forefront of French government. A dull economy and political squabbling weakened the Fourth Republic in the mid-1950s. And in Algeria, which was still a French colony, tension was increasing between those who sought independence and those who wanted to maintain Algeria's colonial status, including army leaders.

Women Who Served in the French Resistance

Berty Albrecht: Before the war, she had been a pacifist (someone who does not believe in killing or violence for any reason) who fought for working women's rights. With a man named Henri Frenay, she helped found Combat, one of the most active resistance movements. Albrecht had the idea of publishing a secret newsletter, which was widely read. She was captured and tortured three times by the Germans, and it is thought that she finally committed suicide.

Celia Bertin: A literature student, she was recruited into the resistance because she spoke English and could help with the hiding of Allied pilots. While in hiding herself, she wrote a novel, and after the war she published many books.

Jeanne Bohec: She went to London after the Germans arrived in France, but she used her knowledge of chemistry and her experience working in an arms factory to help the Free French. Bohec parachuted into France's Brittany region and taught young men how to use weapons.

Sister Edwige Dumas: She helped care for the wounded of both sides after the Allies bombed the city of Calais, and she sheltered resistance fighters wanted by the Germans.

Genevieve de Gaulle-Anthonioz: General de Gaulle's niece, she followed the family tradition by becoming a member of the resistance, working with a movement of young people called Defense de la France. She was captured by the Germans and sent to the Ravensbruck concentration camp.

Marie-Louise Le Duc: Known as "Madame X" to the British, she helped those who wanted to escape from France (especially Allied airmen) by assisting with secret, nighttime pickups by British boats. She was arrested three times but always escaped.

Suzanne Vallon: She was an opthalmologist (doctor specializing in diseases of the eye) who fled to London but managed to be sent on active duty to North Africa. Later she accompanied Allied troops in their invasion of France.

Denise Vernay: She served as a liaison agent in Lyon, an unfamiliar city, which required her to memorize messages and addresses and to have few contacts with others. Vernay was caught by the Gestapo and deported (sent out of the country).

Members of the National Assembly were afraid there might be a coup (illegal government takeover, sometimes through physical force, by an unelected person or party), so in 1958 they called on de Gaulle to return to his leadership role.

He was considered the only figure strong enough to lead the nation at such a dangerous time.

Once again installed as France's president and the head of a new government called the "Fifth Republic," de Gaulle soon resolved the Algerian crisis by granting Algeria its independence. He spent the next decade improving France's position in the world, constantly asserting its independence from the United States, Britain, and the Soviet Union. He established ties with West Germany and diplomatic relations with the People's Republic of China, and he took steps to promote economic growth and modernization of industry.

Student and worker unrest

By the late 1960s France's economy had grown quite strong, but other problems were brewing. In 1968, French students revolted against their country's traditional political and educational systems and began demanding reforms as well as a voice in decision-making. Fighting broke out in the streets of Paris. Next a huge workers' strike threatened the survival of de Gaulle's government. Nevertheless, de Gaulle was reelected, partly because he had successfully convinced the voters that if he didn't win, the Communists (those who believe in a political system in which all property is owned by the community as a whole, rather than by individuals) might.

In 1969, de Gaulle proposed a number of reforms that would, he claimed, allow groups like students and workers to "share" power with government. When a referendum (public vote to express approval or rejection) on these reforms was defeated, De Gaulle resigned the presidency.

A quiet finale

De Gaulle again retired to Colombey and continued working on his memoirs, which he completed just before his death on November 9, 1970. At de Gaulle's request, no public ceremony was held to honor a man who had always been equally convinced of his country's greatness and his own fitness to lead it.

Where to Learn More

Books

Cook, Don. *Charles de Gaulle.* New York: Putnam, 1983.

Weinberg, Gerhard L. *A World at Arms.* Cambridge: Cambridge University Press, 1994.

Web sites

Colton, Joel. "Charles de Gaulle." [Online] Available http://www. grolier.com/wwii/wwii_degaulle.html (November 18, 1998).

Dwight D. Eisenhower

Born October 14, 1890
Denison, Texas
Died March 28, 1969
Washington, D.C.

U.S. Army general and 34th
president of the United States

U nlike two other famous American military leaders of World War II, General Douglas MacArthur and General George Patton (see entries), Dwight D. Eisenhower was an even-tempered, universally liked figure with a talent for getting people to work together. His management ability was really put to the test when, as commander of all Allied forces in Europe, he led an alliance of men from all the different branches of military service and from many different countries to victory over the German army. At the beginning of the war, Eisenhower was only a lieutenant colonel, but by the time it was over he had risen to the rank of five-star general. He overcame his lack of battle experience and with his brilliant strategies and his calm, likable personality won the trust and loyalty both of Allied political and military leaders as well as the men he led. After the war, the American people demonstrated their regard for Eisenhower by electing him president.

A poor but proud family

      Eisenhower was the third of six sons born to David Jacob and Ida Stover Eisenhower, who began their married life

Dwight D. Eisenhower commanded the three million soldiers, airmen, and sailors of the Allied Expeditionary Force during World War II— the largest such force ever led by one person.

Portrait: Dwight D. Eisenhower. *(Reproduced by permission of AP/Wide World Photos.)*

73

running a small grocery store in Hope, Kansas. When the store went bankrupt, David went to Denison, Texas, to find work, and his family eventually joined him there. Dwight was born in Denison, but less than a year later his father moved the family back to Kansas because he had been offered a job at a creamery in Abilene.

The Eisenhower family was quite poor—David never earned more than $100 a month—and the boys sometimes had to defend themselves against taunting and ridicule from other children. They were taught to work hard, to be independent and self-reliant. David and Ida were members of a fundamentalist Christian group called the River Brethren, and religious faith was also an important element in the Eisenhower household.

In grade school and high school Dwight was a fairly good student, but his real love was sports. It was at this time that his classmates gave him the nickname "Ike," which would stick with him throughout the rest of his life. After he graduated from high school, Dwight made an agreement with his older brother Edgar that he would work for a year while Edgar, who wanted to become a lawyer, attended college. The next year, Edgar would work while Dwight went to college. So Dwight took a job in the Abilene creamery.

Attending West Point

Then one of Dwight's friends encouraged him to take the entrance examinations for the U.S. Naval Academy and the army's Military Academy at West Point, New York. If he passed, Dwight would receive a free college education. The fact that his very religious parents were opposed to war made this a difficult decision, but he chose to take the exams.

Eisenhower passed both exams, but learned that he was already too old to apply to the Naval Academy. Even though the navy had been his first choice, Eisenhower entered West Point in 1911. Stern discipline had been part of his family life and this helped him adjust quickly to the school's rigorous routines.

At West Point, Eisenhower immediately began to pursue his main interest—sports. He played halfback on the school's football team, but an injury during his sophomore year ruined what had been a promising athletic career. Disappointed, Eisenhower lost interest in school and began to spend much of his time earning demerits (negative disciplinary marks) by smoking and playing cards. He graduated in 1915, ranking 61st in a class of 164 students.

A steadily advancing career

Eisenhower was assigned to the 19th Infantry Regiment at Fort Sam Houston in San Antonio, Texas. At a party, he met Mamie Geneva Doud, the daughter of a wealthy Denver businessman who had brought his family to Texas for the winter. The couple fell in love and were married in July 1916 in Denver. They had two sons, Doud Dwight (who died in infancy) and John Sheldon Doud, who would become a career army officer.

In 1917, as the United States was getting ready to enter World War I , Eisenhower was promoted to captain. He wanted to join the fighting in France, but instead he was assigned to command a tank training center in Camp Colt, Pennsylvania. Despite his frustration at being stateside during the war, Eisenhower earned a Distinguished Service Medal for his performance.

Eisenhower became a major in 1920, and in 1921 he graduated from the Army Tank School at Fort Mead, Maryland. In 1922 came a turning point in his career: he was transferred to the Panama Canal Zone (now the country of Panama) to serve as executive officer to the 20th Infantry Brigade. There he met General Fox Conner, who took a great interest in this bright, capable young officer. Conner instructed Eisenhower in military history and helped him sharpen his administrative and tactical skills.

Important advice from a general

Conner told Eisenhower that in the next war—which he felt was inevitable and which he predicted would be fought by a coalition (a temporary union for a common purpose) of nations rather than one nation against another—a colonel named George C. Marshall would lead the American forces. He encouraged Eisenhower to try for an assignment with Marshall. Conner also helped Eisenhower get into the Army Command and General Staff School in Leavenworth, Kansas. This time, Eisenhower was serious about his studies and career, and he graduated first in a class of 275.

Building a good reputation

From 1927 to 1933, Eisenhower built a reputation as a resourceful, energetic staff officer. In 1933, while he was working in the office of the assistant secretary of war, Eisenhower was assigned to serve under General Douglas MacArthur, a flamboyant, opinionated figure who appreciated Eisenhower's even temper and considerable administrative skills. When MacArthur was sent to the Philippines to serve as a military advisor to that country's army, Eisenhower accompanied him; MacArthur's flamboyant style led Eisenhower to say later that he spent those years studying "dramatics" under MacArthur.

Four years later, Eisenhower returned to the United States and, now a lieutenant colonel, was made chief of staff for General Walter Krueger, commander of the Third Army at Fort Sam Houston. Just before the Japanese bombed Pearl Harbor in late 1941, the Third Army took part in the biggest war games (a way of practicing warfare in order to prepare officers and troops for the real thing) the army had ever held. The brilliant strategies Eisenhower devised for this operation drew admiration from his superiors, and he was promoted to brigadier general.

A rapid rise to the top

The day after the Japanese bombed Pearl Harbor (December 7, 1941) the United States declared war on Japan. Within a week, Germany and Italy (who were aligned with Japan in a coalition called the Axis) declared war on the United States. General Marshall—now the army's chief of staff—called Eisenhower to his office and asked for his advice on what action the United States should take in Asia. Eisenhower's answer impressed Marshall, and he assigned Eisenhower to the War Plans Division.

During the first months of the war, Eisenhower's strategic talent, his skill in managing people, and his tendency to both share the credit for achievements and shoulder the blame for mistakes made him an valuable member of the team directing the U.S. military effort. His rapid rise through the ranks continued. In March 1942, he was promoted to major general, and in June he was sent to London to take command of the U.S. forces in Europe. Meanwhile, General Douglas MacArthur and Admiral Chester Nimitz were in charge of the Pacific theater (area of action).

Planning Allied strategy

Eisenhower's first task was to meet with the heads of all the British and American military services to determine a course of action. They decided that the United States would invade Axis-occupied North Africa, with Eisenhower in charge of all the ground, sea, and air forces. Called "Operation Torch," this successful campaign took place in November 1942. It was followed by the Allies' victorious invasions of Sicily and Italy in July and September of 1943.

Eisenhower was named the commander of the Supreme Headquarters Allied Expeditionary Forces in Europe (SHAEF), which meant that he was now in charge of all Allied forces in Europe. Eisenhower returned to London in December to plan for the Allied invasion of Normandy on the northern coast of France. Nicknamed Operation Overlord, and D-Day, this campaign would have a huge impact on the course of World War II. Describing Eisenhower's role in Operation Overlord, Stephen A. Ambrose wrote that it "bore his stamp. He was the central figure in the preparation, the planning, the training, the deception, the organization, and the execution of the greatest invasion in history."

The Normandy invasion or D-Day

The invasion was to be carried out by 156,000 troops who would cross the English Channel on boats and land on the beaches of Normandy. The troops would be supported by 6,000 ships, thousands of airplanes, and a staff of 16,312 officers and enlisted men (higher-ranking soldiers who are not officers). The Allies planned to push the Germans back to their own country while the Russians pushed from the other direction—through Eastern Europe and toward Germany. Just in case the mission didn't succeed, Eisenhower prepared a press release in which he took full blame for the failure.

General Dwight D. Eisenhower speaking with a group of paratroopers before the D-Day landing. *(Reproduced by permission of the National Archives and Records Administration.)*

Operation Overlord was originally scheduled to begin on June 4, 1944, but a storm held up the invasion until June 6, when Eisenhower, heeding the advice of his trusted weather forecaster, finally gave the order. On that day, the weather did clear, allowing the men to land. Eisenhower made regular visits to the battlefields; once, in fact, he even drove off at the wheel of a jeep and strayed behind enemy lines.

The Allies spent the next few months advancing through France, and they liberated Paris in August. In December, the Germans made one last stand in the Ardennes region on the border of France and Belgium. This was called the Battle of the Bulge because the Germans' success in pushing the Allies back in that region caused a "bulge" in the front line. Although the German attack took the Allies by surprise, they won the battle. Forced back into Germany and fatally weakened, the Germans surrendered on May 8, 1945.

Postwar activities

Eisenhower spent another six months in Europe as head of the occupation forces, which were Allied troops who kept order and provided assistance as the various European countries made their transitions to peacetime. Then he returned to Washington to replace General Marshall as army chief of staff. Eisenhower had become so popular with the American public that in the years immediately following the end of the war, both the Democratic and Republican parties urged him to run for president. He told them he wasn't interested.

In 1949, Eisenhower became the president of New York's Columbia University, but he left this job the next year to accept command of the North Atlantic Treaty Organization (NATO), which had just been formed to help protect Europe from the threat of Soviet aggression.

The 34th president of the United States

Meanwhile, as the 1952 election neared, the two major political parties continued their attempts to get Eisenhower to run for president. He decided he would run—as a Republican. Backed by moderate supporters, Eisenhower beat the much more conservative Senator Robert A. Taft for the Republican nomination. He also won the national race against Illinois Democratic governor, Adlai Stevenson; in fact, Eisenhower earned the largest number of popular votes to that time.

Eisenhower brought to his office a talent for administrative efficiency and a background in foreign relations, but not much experience with domestic issues. As president he was a consensus (agreement) seeker who tended to avoid controversy if he could.

One goal of Eisenhower's first term was to end the conflict in Korea which had started in 1950. The Korean War (1950–53) involved the Communists who occupied the northern part of the country and U.S.-backed South Korea. In July 1953, Eisenhower helped to negotiate a cease-fire and truce, stating that "There is no glory in battle worth the blood it costs."

Other major events of Eisenhower's first term included the 1954 Supreme Court decision to declare segregation (the separation and unequal treatment of black and white people) in public schools unconstitutional, and the campaign of Senator Joe McCarthy to expose and remove suspected Communists from the federal government, military, and other realms of American life. Eisenhower remained quiet on both these issues.

A second term as president

In September 1955, Eisenhower had a heart attack while vacationing, and his supporters feared he would be unable to run for president again. However, he had recovered by election time, and his continuing popularity led to a victory over Adlai Stevenson. His political party was not as successful, though, and the Democrats gained control of Congress.

Eisenhower's second term as president was not quite as smooth as his first. Despite his good relationship with both Republican and Democratic congressional leaders, he faced opposition on some of his legislative measures from both parties. And he was forced to take action on the Supreme Court's segregation decision when a mob of angry white southerners blocked the integration of a high school in Little Rock, Arkansas. Eisenhower sent military units to enforce the court-ordered integration.

In addition, the progress Eisenhower had made in easing the tension between the United States and the Soviet Union was shattered when Russian premier Nikita Khrushchev refused to take part in a planned summit meeting with Eisenhower. Khrushchev was angered after an American U-2 spy plane that had been taking photographs of military sites in Russia was shot down. Critics faulted Eisenhower for allowing such an espionage (spy) operation to jeopardize peace between the two countries.

A relaxing retirement

In 1960, after Eisenhower's two terms as president were complete, John F. Kennedy, a Democrat who had been a senator from Massachusetts, was elected to the office. Eisenhower retired and divided his time between his farm at Gettysburg, Pennsylvania, and a home in Palm Springs, California. He continued to speak occasionally on public issues, and he worked on his memoirs. His favorite retirement activities, though, were playing golf and bridge.

Healthy and active for the first few years of his retirement, Eisenhower suffered serious heart attacks in 1965 and 1968. In December 1968 a Gallup poll showed that he still led the list of the ten most-admired Americans. He died at Walter Reed Army Hospital in Washington, D.C., on March 28, 1969, and was buried in Abilene, Kansas, on the grounds of the presidential library he had established there a few years earlier.

Where to Learn More

Books

Ambrose, Stephen. *The Supreme Commander: The War Years of General Dwight D. Eisenhower* New York: Doubleday, 1970.

Burk, Robert. *Dwight D. Eisenhower, Hero and Politician.* Boston: Twayne Publishers, 1986.

Darby, Jean. *A Man Called Ike.* Minneapolis, MN: Lerner Publications, 1989.

Jacobs, William Jay. *Dwight David Eisenhower: Soldier and Statesman.* New York: Franklin Watts, 1995.

Sandberg, Peter Lars. *Dwight D. Eisenhower.* New York: Chelsea House, 1986.

Van Steenwyk, Elizabeth. *Dwight David Eisenhower, President.* New York: Walker, 1987.

Periodicals

"The Father Figure: Dwight Eisenhower." Special Report: The Strategists of War. *U.S. News and World Report* (March 16, 1998): 59.

Web sites

Ambrose, Stephen and George H. Mayer. "Dwight D. Eisenhower." [Online] Available http://www.grolier.com/wwii/wwii_eisenhower.html (April 21, 1999).

Hermann Göring

Born January 12, 1893
Rosenheim, Germany
Died October 15, 1946
Nuremberg, Germany

Nazi political leader and commander of the Luftwaffe, the German air force; second in command to Adolf Hitler

"I pledge my destiny to you [Adolf Hitler] for better or for worse. . . ."

In the years leading up to World War II, Hermann Göring achieved a position of great power in Germany because of his relationship with Adolf Hitler (1889–1945; see entry), Germany's dictator from 1933 through 1945. Hitler put Göring in charge of such important matters as the organization of the police force and rebuilding Germany's air power. Although he had held fairly liberal beliefs as a young man, Göring adopted Hitler's views on the superiority of the German people and the need to eliminate their enemies. He played an active role in carrying out the horrors of the Holocaust (the period between 1933 and 1945 when Nazi Germany systematically murdered millions of Jews, Roma, homosexuals, and other innocent people).

Dreams of greatness

Born in Rosenheim, Bavaria (a state in the southeastern part of Germany), a little town located south of Munich, Göring was the son of a German government official. He was the youngest of four children born to his father's second wife (he had five siblings from his father's first marriage). When

Portrait: Hermann Göring.
(Reproduced by permission of USHMM Photo Archives.)

Göring was three months old, his parents went to live in Haiti, where his father was to serve as consul general. They left their new baby in the care of family friends for three years, a period that was very difficult and unhappy for him.

As a young boy Göring was sent to live with his godfather, an Austrian physician named Hermann von Epstein, who had been born Jewish but had converted to Christianity. When Göring wrote a school essay praising his godfather, his teacher scolded him because it was not considered proper to think well of Jewish people. This disturbed Göring so much that he left the school.

Next Göring attended two military academies where he proved an excellent student and a self-confident, athletic boy who enjoyed mountain climbing and horseback riding. One day he hoped to become a great German hero. He graduated at the top of his class in 1912.

A World War I hero

Göring joined the military after graduation. During World War I (1914–18; a war that started as a conflict between Austria-Hungary and Serbia and escalated into a global war involving thirty-two nations) he proved to be an exceptionally brave pilot who won his country's highest military honor, the Pour le Merite or "Blue Max." In July 1918 he was made commander of the Richthofen Squadron, a famous and daring group of aviators that was also known as the "Flying Circus."

Discouraged after the war

When World War I ended, many Germans resented the outcome of the war and its aftermath. They had been led to believe that their country would win, but they had lost. Now the German people were being punished by the victorious Allies (including Great Britain, the United States, France, and Russia), who insisted Germany pay reparations (huge sums of money) for the damages incurred during the war.

Germany also faced a terrible depression (an economic downturn that causes many businesses to close and people to lose their jobs) that started around 1930. Although this depression began in the United States, it soon spread to all of the industrial countries in Europe. Germany was hit harder than any other major European country. Germany relied heavily on exports and the countries that had been buying its goods could no longer buy them. There were few jobs available—one out of every three Germans was out of work—which led to widespread poverty and dissatisfaction with the government.

Like many former soldiers, Göring felt that he had no future in Germany. He went to Sweden and became a pilot and salesman for a Swedish airline. There he met a Swedish baroness, Carin von Lock-Kantzoa, a delicate beauty with an interest in mysticism. Even though she was already married, Carin and Göring fell in love. Carin soon divorced her husband. She married Göring in 1923, and the couple returned to Germany.

Becoming Hitler's follower

Meanwhile, an ambitious politician named Adolf Hitler took advantage of the widespread dissatisfaction in Germany. He formed the National Socialist German Workers' Party, better known as the Nazis. Hitler's party was based on the belief that the Germans were a superior race whose purity was threatened by the harmful presence of Jews and other people they considered undesirable. In particular, the Nazis blamed Jews for their country's defeat in World War I.

Even though Göring had not previously been anti-Semitic (anti-Jewish), he was so impressed by Hitler that he became a devoted follower, gradually dropping all of his more liberal views and adopting the Nazi philosophy. Recognizing his potential, Hitler put Göring in charge of the SA or *Sturmabteilung*—also called Storm Troopers and Brown Shirts—an organized group of men who terrorized anyone who opposed the Nazis. And it was in Göring's hometown—Munich—where the Nazis planned to take over the German government. Their attempt, called the Munich Beer Hall Putsch (1923), failed and led to the arrest and imprisonment of Hitler and other Nazi leaders.

Göring was badly wounded but managed to escape to Austria, finally making his way to Switzerland. In severe pain, he was given morphine (a strong pain medication related to opium) and quickly became addicted, a condition that led to stints in several psychiatric institutions. He was off drugs by 1926, but his addiction would continue to plague him throughout the rest of his life. Göring had also become obese, and over the next two decades his enemies would often make fun of him, nicknaming him "der Dicke" (the fat one).

Returning to success in Germany

In 1927, Germany's president pardoned all political prisoners, including Hitler and the other Nazi leaders arrested after the Munich Beer Hall Putsch. Göring no longer had to fear being arrested and punished for his involvement in the Putsch and returned to his country. He and his wife settled in Berlin, where Göring became successful selling BMW cars. He again got involved with Hitler, who realized that Göring's many social, business, and military connections could be helpful to the Nazi party.

Running on the Nazi ticket, Göring was elected to the Reichstag (Germany's legislative or law-making body) in 1928 and became its president in 1932 (the top office in the Reichstag, but not the same as president of a country). Hitler was also gaining power during this period, and in January 1933 he was made chancellor (chief executive or top leader) of Germany. In only a few months, Hitler took control of the government and outlawed all political parties except the Nazis. He made himself not only Germany's head of state but also its military commander. In other words, Hitler had become a dictator (a ruler with absolute authority).

A prominent role in Hitler's government

Hitler gave Göring the job of interior minister to Prussia (a large state within Germany that ceased to exist after July 1945). Later that year, acting as commandant of police, Göring replaced the regular police force with the Secret State Police. This ruthless group became known as the Gestapo and quickly gained a reputation for brutality. They carried on a reign of terror against Jews and Catholics and members of other minority groups as well as anyone who disagreed with Hitler. So many arrests were made that the jails overflowed, so Göring constructed concentration camps where large num-

The Chief of the SS

Members of the SS—which stood for Schutzstaffel or security squad—served as Hitler's bodyguards and also worked as guards in the various concentration camps. They were involved in many cruel acts against those in the camps, and they murdered millions of innocent victims. The man who commanded the SS was Heinrich Himmler, a weak, dull person who had once dreamed of becoming a soldier.

Born in Munich, Germany, in 1900, Himmler was the son of a poor soldier who taught his children to develop ties to the upper classes; he also advised his son to keep a daily diary, in which Himmler would later record all of his murderous activities.

Himmler wanted very much to serve in Germany's army during World War I but he had only just completed officer training when the war ended. He spent a brief period as a farmer, then entered the University of Munich. Giving up his dream of military glory, Himmler studied agriculture. It was during his years at college that he became an anti-semite (person who hates Jews) and was drawn toward politics.

Graduating from college in 1922, Himmler got a job with a fertilizer company. The next year, he joined Adolf Hitler's (1889–1945; see entry) National Socialist German Workers' Party (the Nazis). Later he moved with his new wife Marga to a chicken farm. He continued to work for the Nazis and proved himself efficient and alert to details, even if he did have a very dull personality. In 1929, Himmler was promoted to the rank of Reichsfuhrer (equivalent to a general in the U.S. Army) of the SS.

Himmler remained in charge of the SS for the next 16 years. Although the organization had originally been intended to provide protection for Hitler and other high-ranking Nazis, Himmler expanded it to include 50,000 soldiers who could carry out anything Hitler ordered, including the punishment and murder of those the Nazis considered "enemies of the state."

bers of these so-called "enemies of the state" could be confined. Ironically, Göring did not have the stomach for violence and soon turned his Gestapo and concentration camp duties over to others.

In 1931, Göring's beloved wife Carin died. Now very wealthy (due to income from his various political offices,

Heinrich Himmler *(Reproduced by permission of The Library of Congress.)*

The Nazi idea of "racial purity" made Germans the highest form of humanity, and the ideal German was tall, blonde, and blue-eyed. Those considered racially impure included Roma (commonly known as Gypsies), handicapped people, homosexuals, and others but especially Jews, who were blamed for all of Germany's troubles. Since the SS was to provide the leaders of a new German race,

Himmler ruled that SS soldiers who wanted to marry had to prove that their fiancees were of pure blood and not "contaminated" by that of other, lesser races. At the SS Bride School, women were taught how to be good Nazi wives.

Much more alarmingly, though, Himmler began to set up concentration camps where those arrested by the Nazis were sent to be imprisoned, interrogated, tortured, and often murdered. Himmler himself stayed in the background while gangs of crisply uniformed SS soldiers in shiny black boots terrorized the Jewish population, rounding up and killing thousands of people.

In May 1945, several weeks after Germany had surrendered to the Allies, Himmler was caught by British soldiers while—disguised as a low-ranking soldier— he was trying to flee the country. Several days later, Himmler realized that he was not going to receive any special treatment from the Allies, and he bit into a cyanide capsule he had managed to conceal in his mouth. He died almost immediately.

investments, and business interests), he built a grand estate that he named Carin Hall in his dead wife's memory. He furnished this home with fine art and spent much of his time there. In 1935 Göring married a German actress, Emmy Sonnemann, and the couple's daughter Edda was born three years later. Over the next few years the Görings entertained many famous visitors from all over the world at their lavish estate.

The Luftwaffe leads the war effort

The terms of the treaty signed at the end of World War I prohibited Germany from having an air force, but Göring—who had been named reichminster of aviation in 1933—built one anyway, in secret. By 1936, his Luftwaffe (the name by which the German air force was known) was ready, just as Hitler's plans to wage war began to take shape. Hitler's stated goal at this time was to make sure that all of the German-speaking people in the world were under Nazi rule; later it would become clear that he also wanted to acquire more territory for Germany. At the same time, he was restricting the freedom of ordinary Germans while totally eliminating that of the Jews who lived in Germany.

Germany launched World War II in September 1939 by invading Poland. Much of the credit for this successful attack was given to the air force, and as head of the Luftwaffe Göring became a hero. When Holland, Belgium, and France also surrendered to the Germans he received even more attention and praise. In these first few years of the war, the German air force was considered the best in the world. Pleased with his second-in-command and with the progress of the war, Hitler made Göring a field marshal—the highest rank in the German army—and even spoke of him as his successor (the person who would take over his position when he left office).

Out of favor with "der Führer"

As the war continued, though, Göring fell out of favor with Hitler even though he never stopped idolizing "der Führer" (the leader). The main cause for Hitler's displeasure was the failure of the air force on three occasions. The first was the Battle of Britain, at which the Germans were defeated. On the second occasion, the Luftwaffe was unable to defend Germany against air raids by the Allies. The third was when the air force could not rescue the German Sixth Army when they were stranded in Stalingrad in the Soviet Union. Hitler blamed Göring for these disasters and began treating him with scorn, and leaving him out of important military decisions.

Disillusioned with the way things were going, Göring began taking drugs again. He retreated into the fantasy world he had created for himself, neglecting his official

duties while traveling around Europe in his private train. He was notorious for stealing priceless works of art from the countries Germany had conquered and decorating his various homes with them.

As the war drew to a close, Soviet troops invaded Germany and made their way toward Berlin, where Hitler had gone into hiding in an underground bunker. Having fled (and

Hermann Göring receiving reports from pilots of the Luftwaffe.
(Reproduced by permission of AP/Wide World Photos.)

destroyed) Carin Hall, Göring was convinced—quite logically—that Hitler might soon be captured. He sent his leader a message that he was prepared to take over: "If I should receive no reply by 10 P.M., I shall assume that you have been deprived of your freedom of action and shall act in the best interests of our country and people."

Hitler was enraged by Göring's assumption, and on April 23 he ordered him charged with treason and arrested. By April 30, Hitler knew that the war was lost, and he committed suicide in his bunker.

On May 9, having been freed by his Nazi captors, Göring surrendered to the American troops who had occupied Germany. He was pleased with the special treatment he received at first, when he was given good food and wine. But this had just been a trick to make him offer up information about the Nazis, and he soon became an ordinary prisoner of war.

Tried and convicted at Nuremberg

The Allies (the countries that had joined together to fight Germany) tried the surviving Nazi leaders for their war crimes in a series of famous trials held in Nuremberg, Germany, in 1946. This well-publicized event exposed the full horror of Nazi Germany, in particular the Holocaust. After months in prison, Göring was drug-free and much slimmer. Observers agreed that he gave a brilliant performance at the trial, speaking with intelligence and confidence as he tried to justify what he and others had done. He argued that government officials could not be judged by the same standards as ordinary citizens.

Nevertheless, Göring was found guilty of conspiracy to wage war, crimes against peace, war crimes, and crimes against humanity. He was sentenced to death by hanging, and his request to be executed by firing squad, in the military tradition, was denied. Just two hours before he was to be executed, Göring took poison (it is still not known how he got it) and died. The next day, his body was cremated and the ashes thrown away, along with those of others who had been executed that night.

Where to Learn More

Books

Butler, Ewan, and Gordon Young. *The Life and Death of Hermann Göring.* San Bernardino, CA: Borgo Press, 1990.

Hoyt, Edwin P. *Angels of Death: Göring's Luftwaffe.* New York: Forge, 1994.

Irving, David. *Göring: A Biography.* New York: William Morrow, 1989.

Mosley, Leonard. *The Reich Marshal: A Biography of Hermann Göring.* Garden City, NY: Doubleday, 1974.

Skipper, G.C. *Göring and the Luftwaffe.* Chicago: Children's Press, 1980.

Web Sites

Sauer, Wolfgang. "Hermann W. Goering." [Online] Available http:/www.grolier.com/wwii/wwii_goering.html (January 21, 1999).

Hirohito

Born April 29, 1901
Tokyo, Japan
Died January 7, 1989
Tokyo, Japan

124th emperor of Japan

Powerless to prevent his country from entering World War II, Hirohito played an important role in Japan's surrender to the Allies in 1945.

Portrait: Hirohito.
(Reproduced by permission of Archive Photos.)

Hirohito's reign as emperor of Japan—the longest of any monarch in modern times—was a period of great turmoil and change. Although he chose as the name for his reign the word "Showa," which means "Enlightened Peace," he ruled during one of the least peaceful periods in history. Hirohito's enemies considered him the head of a brutal, militaristic country and felt that he should be punished as a war criminal for atrocities (extreme cruelty and violence) committed by the Japanese military against Chinese citizens during World War II. But others now argue that Hirohito was powerless to prevent the war with the Allies, that he was not in charge of the military campaigns, and that he personally opposed the war. He was a shy, self-conscious person whose life had been devoted not to governing a country but to playing the mainly symbolic role of emperor.

A privileged but lonely childhood

Born at Aoynama Palace in Tokyo, Hirohito was the son of Crown Prince Yoshihito and grandson of Mutsuhito, known as the Meiji ("Enlightened Ruler") Emperor. His mother was Princess Sadako, a member of a family that had provided royal brides for many centuries. When he was less than three months old, Hirohito was sent to live with foster parents, the Count and Countess Kawamura Sumyoshi. In accordance with a long-standing custom, he was to be raised in a normal family away from the ceremonial trappings of palace life, and he was to be treated (and disciplined) like any other child of that family.

Count Kawamura Sumyoshi died when Hirohito was five years old, and the boy was returned to his parents' official residence, Akasaka Palace, which had been modeled after France's famous Versailles palace. But Hirohito and his two brothers rarely saw their parents. Growing up in the palace, he had little contact with children outside the family. Hirohito was a small, weak, very shy little boy with a shuffling walk and an extremely solemn manner.

Two schools for royalty

At the age of eight, Hirohito was sent to the Peers' School and became a member of a class of twelve boys whose parents were also members of the Japanese royalty. There he studied modern languages, military and technical sciences, politics, and history. He developed a special (and, as it turned out, lifelong) interest in marine biology, and when he complained that he could not conduct field work with so many servants and other people hanging around him, he was allowed to go out alone in a little boat to collect specimens. Hirohito's beloved headmaster, Count Maresuki Nogi, taught him to practice the values of discipline, hard work, loyalty, and bravery.

With the death of the Meiji Emperor, Hirohito's father took the throne and Hirohito became the crown prince. Hirohito graduated from the Peers' School in 1914 and went on to the Crown Prince's Institute, located right on the palace grounds. His class was made up of five other royal students. It was during these seven years of study that Hirohito expressed some doubt that his family really was descended from gods, a belief that was rooted in Shinto (the dominant religion) tradition.

The Shinto Religion

Shinto is the traditional religion of Japan. It has existed since ancient times, even before the arrival of Buddhism (another major religion practiced in Japan), and is still practiced today. After World War II, however, when a new constitution called for the separation of church and state and freedom of religion, the role of the Shinto religion in Japanese life changed.

Shinto involves the worship of a variety of gods and forces called kami, which are honored with ceremonies performed in shrines as well as festivals and other activities. The most important deity is Amaterasu, the "great heavenly illuminating goddess." Although there are no specific doctrines (official beliefs) or scriptures (written documents), followers of Shinto believe that their religion creates unity and harmony among the people of Japan.

From ancient times until the reign of Hirohito, Japanese emperors were considered direct descendants of Amaterasu, and their duties included not only political activities but religious service. In the nineteenth century, the Meiji government took steps to make Shinto a national religion (even though the Japanese constitution guaranteed freedom of religion) by building shrines, teaching about Shinto in public schools, and making Shinto festivals national holidays. By 1945, there were 218 national shrines in Japan.

At the end of World War II, an occupation government arrived in Japan to help the country rebuild itself as a democracy, which meant that church and state would have to exist separately. Hirohito had to announce to his people that he was not, in fact, a descendant of a Shinto goddess. The Japanese government had to break its ties (including giving public funds) with the shrines.

Some Japanese felt that this change went too much against Japan's cultural traditions, while others tried to find ways to keep the important role of Shinto in Japanese life strong without threatening religious freedom. By the 1980s, there were about 80,000 Shinto shrines in Japan, and about 75 million believers.

Engagement and overseas travel

In 1918 Hirohito became engaged to Princess Nagako. This was a somewhat controversial match, because she was not a member of the famous bride-supplying family, like his mother. Nevertheless, after a six-year engagement (during which they met only nine times, and never without a chaperone) the two were married. Over the years they had seven children (one of whom died at age two).

After graduating from the Crown Prince's Institute in 1921, Hirohito broke with tradition by becoming the first crown prince to go on a six-month tour of Europe. Following stops in Hong Kong, Singapore, and Cairo, he visited Belgium, France, and Italy. But his favorite place was England, where the family of King George V warmly welcomed the shy, bespectacled prince. Hirohito was especially impressed with Great Britain's constitutional monarchy, in which the role of royalty was mostly to put the stamp of approval on policies determined by other government leaders. This model strongly influenced Hirohito's ideas about his own role in Japan.

A reign of "enlightened peace"?

Returning from his journey in November 1921, Hirohito found his father in poor health, and he was appointed regent (acting emperor). Yoshihito died in late 1926, and Hirohito took the throne as the latest in a line of divinely descended emperors that stretched back more than two thousand years. He chose Showa, "Enlightened Peace," as the name of his reign. No longer was he to be treated as an ordinary mortal—now doctors used silk gloves when they treated him, tailors were not allowed to touch his body, and food tasters tested his food before he ate.

Soon after Hirohito became emperor, Japan's economy went into a slump. At the same time, the military was growing in strength and hoping to extend Japan's reach into other parts of Asia, especially China. Meanwhile, although Hirohito was emperor, his role in governing the country was limited to his silent attendance at "Imperial Conferences," where his presence meant that the "Imperial Will" approved of whatever policy was being discussed. Government matters were decided by the prime minister and other government and military leaders, without Hirohito's involvement. Hirohito did take a more active role on a few occasions. For instance, in 1936 he recommended quick and harsh punishment for some military officers and soldiers who had tried to take over the government.

Moving toward war

With Hirohito's approval, Japan went to war against China in July 1937; in fact, he took a great interest in the military conflict. In September 1939 Germany started World War II by invading Poland, and Japan's military leaders and aggressive prime minister, Hideki Tojo (1884–1948; see entry) began to make their own plans for war against the West. Their main target was the United States, which had been trying to stop Japan from expanding its empire. The Japanese military believed that through aggressive actions they could force the United States into allowing Japan to control East Asia.

During an Imperial Conference on December 1, 1941, Hirohito's advisors recommended going to war against the United States. He approved the plan, but he later said that this did not reflect his own wishes. Ever since his visit to Great Britain as a young man, Hirohito had believed in cooperation with Western powers, including the United States. But according to his own ideal of constitutional monarchy, he did not think it was his right to intervene; in later years, he wrote that he was also sure he would have been assassinated if he protested.

President Franklin D. Roosevelt (1882–1945; see entry) sent Hirohito a personal note on December 6, urging Japan to keep the peace. Tojo rejected the note, and Hirohito did not have a chance to reply. The next day, Japan attacked the U.S. naval base at Pearl Harbor, Hawaii, destroying many ships and airplanes and killing thousands of people. Hirohito's request that the United States be given notice of the attack had been ignored, so it came as a complete surprise.

The war goes downhill

During the war, Hirohito remained on the palace grounds in Tokyo, despite frequent bombings by Allied planes. He was often confined to a stuffy, thick-walled air raid shelter that was adjacent to the royal library. By June 1942, Japan had suffered several major defeats in battle, and it appeared they might lose the war. Tojo wanted the Japanese people to try harder to win, so he began to mention the emperor often in his public announcements, calling on citizens to make sacrifices in Hirohito's name.

By the summer of 1945 it was obvious that Japan could not win the war, but many Japanese leaders wanted to continue the fight. On August 6, the United States dropped an atomic bomb on the city of Hiroshima, with immediate and devastating effects. Another bomb fell on Nagasaki on August 9, and on the same day Soviet forces (the Soviets were fighting with the Allies) invaded Japanese-held Manchuria in northern China.

In Tokyo, leaders debated about Japan's next step: surrender or keep fighting. Finally, in a meeting that took place in the emperor's air raid shelter, Tojo asked Hirohito to make the most important decision of his life. Convinced that Japan would be completely destroyed if the war continued, Hirohito chose surrender. His own fate, he knew, would be in the hands of whatever Allied commander led the forces that would occupy Japan.

Japan surrenders and rebuilds

At 7:21 A.M. on August 15, the Japanese people were informed that, for the first time in history, they were about to hear the voice of their emperor. In a poor but audible radio transmission, Hirohito told his people that they must "endure the unendurable" and surrender to the Allies.

The officer chosen to head the occupation government in Tokyo and to put Japan on the path toward a democratic society was U.S. general Douglas MacArthur (1880–1964; see entry). There had been much talk around the world about whether Hirohito would be tried as a war criminal, but MacArthur had already decided that Hirohito should not be punished—that his respected position with the Japanese people could be used to enforce the reforms that would have to be introduced.

Hirohito, however, did not know that MacArthur had already made a decision on this issue. He asked MacArthur to meet with him, and at their meeting made the following statement: "I come to you, General MacArthur, to offer myself to the powers you represent as the one to bear sole responsibility for every political and military decision made and action taken by my people in the conduct of the war."

MacArthur later wrote that he was "moved ... to the very marrow of my bones" by "this courageous assumption of a responsibility" that could lead to Hirohito's death, since many war criminals were executed. The general informed Hirohito that he would not be held responsible for the war, but that he would play an important role in Japan's recovery. Over the next few years, the two men met often, and MacArthur gave Hirohito credit for helping his people adjust to a new kind of government and way of life.

Japan's new constitution abolished Shintoism as the official state religion, and on January 1, 1946, Hirohito made a public statement declaring that he was *not* a descendant of gods. (This was actually a relief to Hirohito, who considered himself a scientist and had never believed the myth anyway.) Instead, the emperor was now "a symbol of the state and of the unity of the people."

A peaceful twilight

During the rest of Hirohito's life, the Japanese government tried to bring the emperor into much closer contact with his people. Still shy, awkward, and self-conscious, Hirohito made many public appearances. He also found time for his study of marine biology; he published the first of his several books on the subject in 1962. In 1959, another long-standing Japanese tradition was broken when Hirohito's son, Crown Prince Akihito, married a woman who was a commoner (not royalty).

When Hirohito traveled to Europe in late 1971 and early 1972 (the first Japanese emperor to go abroad) he found that there were some people around the world who still considered him a war criminal. But he had a friendly reception from U. S. president Richard M. Nixon, whom he met during a stopover in Anchorage, Alaska. In 1975, Hirohito made an official state visit to the United States. He was given a Mickey Mouse watch as a gift, and this watch—along with his beloved microscope—was buried along with him when he died of stomach cancer in 1989.

Where to Learn More

Books

Behr, Edward. *Hirohito: Beyond the Myth.* New York: Villard Books, 1989.

Crump, Thomas. *Death of an Emperor: Japan at the Crossroads.* Oxford: Oxford University Press, 1991.

Hoobler, Dorothy and Thomas Hoobler. *Showa: The Age of Hirohito.* New York: Walker, 1990.

Hoyt, Edwin P. *Hirohito: The Emperor and the Man.* New York: Praeger, 1992.

Mosley, Leonard. *Hirohito, Emperor of Japan.* Englewood Cliffs, NJ: Prentice Hall, 1966.

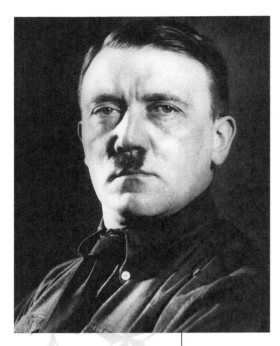

Adolf Hitler

Born April 20, 1889
Braunau, Austria
Died April 30, 1945
Berlin, Germany

Dictator of Nazi Germany from 1934 to 1945

Adolf Hitler created a political party based on racial hatred and violence, and waged an unsuccessful war against the Allied nations.

A dolf Hitler was the dictator or absolute ruler of Germany from 1934 to 1945 and leader of the National Socialist German Workers' Party, known as the Nazi Party. He took advantage of Germany's economic hardships and the bitterness of its citizens after World War I to attract followers, eventually taking complete control of the country. Hitler had a deep hatred of Jews and he used the idea of "racial purity" to justify harsh measures—and eventually mass murder—against them as well as other groups he called "enemies of the state." Hitler's skills as a persuasive speaker and his willingness to use violence to get what he wanted led to a twelve-year reign and sparked a war that led to the deaths of some fifty million people.

Dreams of becoming an artist

Born in Braunau, a small Austrian town close to the German border, Hitler was the son of Alois Hitler, a customs inspector. His mother, Klara, was her husband's second cousin and much younger than he; she had served as his maid before marrying him. Hitler's father was a harsh, demanding man disliked by his son, but Klara was a doting mother whom Hitler adored. He and his sister Paula were the only two of Klara's six children to survive infancy, and they were raised with two stepbrothers from their father's earlier marriage.

In 1899 the Hitler family moved to a small village near the town of Linz. As a child, Hitler did well in school and enjoyed art, poetry, and music. When he became a teenager, he expressed a wish to become an artist but his father did not approve of the idea. Hitler began to rebel against his father and teachers, and he worked hard only on subjects he liked.

In 1903, when Hitler was fourteen, his father died. Hitler convinced his mother to let him quit school, and he spent the next three years wandering through the streets of Linz, visiting the library, opera, and theater. He developed a special passion for the music of German composer Richard Wagner, whose operas were full of gods and goddesses from old German legends.

An aimless life in Vienna

When he was eighteen, Hitler traveled to Vienna, Austria. After taking the entrance exam for the Academy of Fine Arts, he was shocked and disappointed when the drawings he had submitted were not considered good enough to gain him admittance. The school's director suggested that Hitler apply instead to the School of Architecture, but since this meant that he would first have to finish his high school studies, he refused.

Hitler's mother died in 1907, which was a heartbreaking loss for him. He applied to the academy again in 1908 but was rejected. For the next five years, Hitler lived the life of a drifter in Vienna, making money here and there by painting portraits, postcard scenes, and store posters.

Learning to hate

During this period, Austria (which then included Hungary) was a socialist society (one in which the government controls the production and distribution of goods and cooperation, rather than competition, is stressed) struggling with the problems of modernization and rapid industrialization. Many people were out of work, which caused conflicts between the country's different ethnic groups (including Germans, eastern Europeans, Slavs, Italians, and others) as they competed for jobs.

It was in this climate that Hitler's anti-Semitism (opposition to Jews) began to grow, as he blamed the Jews for his own lack of success. He paid attention to how public events were handled and learned about the use of propaganda (material such as pamphlets and speeches designed to persuade people to adopt a certain view) and, as he later wrote in his autobiography, *Mein Kampf* (*My Struggle*), of the use of "physical terror" to control large numbers of people.

A German soldier in World War I

By the start of World War I in 1914, Hitler had moved to Munich, Germany. World War I was a world-wide conflict that involved twenty-eight countries fighting against Germany, Austria-Hungary, Turkey, and Bulgaria. Hitler did not wish to serve in the Austrian army and instead volunteered for the German army. Accepted into the 16th Bavarian Reserve, Hitler left for France in October 1914. He spent the next four years—which he was to call the "greatest and most unforgettable" of his life—near the front lines as a message runner. He was a good soldier who enjoyed the orderliness and excitement of army life. Wounded twice, he was awarded the Iron Cross medal.

In *Mein Kampf* (*My Struggle*), Hitler wrote about a World War I experience that changed the course of his life. When he was temporarily blinded by poison gas (a common weapon at that time), Hitler had what he called a vision. He saw himself as an Aryan (white) hero like those in Wagner's works, called upon by the gods to lead his country into a glorious "1000-Year Reich" (reich means empire).

World War I ended in 1918 with Germany's surrender, and the country was forced to sign the Treaty of Versailles, which severely limited its power and forced it to pay other countries for damages from the war. Like many Germans, Hitler was very bitter about the outcome of the war, and he was convinced that Germany had been defeated because of socialists, liberals, and Jews.

The German Workers' Party

While still in the army, Hitler was chosen in 1919 to become a special agent. His main task was to speak to German troops about loyalty. He also took this opportunity to discourage liberal attitudes that were gaining some popularity at the time. He was very good at this job; in particular, he had an obvious skill for public speaking. But in 1920, Hitler retired from the army to devote all his energies to the German Workers' Party, a tiny group based on opposition to Jews and Communists (communism is a political system that involves group, instead of individual, ownership of property).

Hitler began to recruit new members to the party, which was soon renamed the National Socialist German Workers' Party, or Nazi Party for short. The Nazis' main position was that Jews should lose all civil rights and be banished from the country. Hitler did so much to build the party that he was able to take over its leadership by threatening to leave. The members agreed to put him in charge, and he soon demanded that they refer to him as "mein führer" (my leader).

The Munich Beer Hall "Putsch"

In November 1923 Hitler led a group of Nazi soldiers called "storm troopers" into a Munich beer hall where high-level government officials were meeting and staged a "putsch" (an attempt to seize power). Hitler and his followers planned to take over the German government and start a new Germany based on Nazi principles, but they were defeated. Brought to trial, Hitler used the occasion to publicize his views. He said that his accusers were the traitors, stating, "I feel myself the best of Germans, who wanted the best for the German people."

Sentenced to five years in jail, Hitler's fame and popularity actually increased during his imprisonment, which only lasted nine months due to a special amnesty (granting of freedom) for political prisoners. In his cell at the Landsberg prison (where prisoners were allowed to drink beer and wine and have visitors whenever they wanted), Hitler began working on *Mein Kampf*. Assisted by his devoted follower Rudolf Hess (1894–1987), he explained his theory of racial superior-

"The Father of Lies": Joseph Goebbels

Adolf Hitler built his power partly through the use of propaganda, official government communications to the public that are designed to influence public opinion. Nazi propaganda made the Jews appear as subhuman creatures who had caused all of Germany's problems, and it portrayed Hitler himself as Germany's savior. Hitler chose as his master of propaganda a well-educated man who was a devoted follower of Hitler. Joseph Goebbels had a Ph.D. in literature and was a published novelist, but he used his talents in the service of hatred and violence.

When Germany entered World War I in 1914, Goebbels volunteered to serve in the army but was rejected because of his limp and his small size (for all of his adult life, he was only five feet tall and weighed less than one hundred pounds). In 1917, Goebbels entered the University of Bonn to study literature. His studies were interrupted when he was called by the military—now in desperate need of men—to perform an office job.

After the war, Goebbels returned college, and earned his Ph.D. in 1922. In 1924, he became an editor of political journals, and the next year he joined the National Socialist German Workers' Party (Nazi for short), which was led by Hitler. Goebbels became a great admirer of Hitler, who put him in charge of one of the party's chapters.

By 1928, Goebbels had become one of twelve Nazi deputies, and Hitler made him head of party propaganda and public information in 1930. During the elections between 1930 and 1933, when the Nazis were gaining ground and winning more and more seats in the national legislature, Goebbels managed the party's campaigns. When Hitler became the dictator of Germany in 1933, Goebbels was made reichminister of propaganda. In this position he took control of the media so that it could only publish information approved by the Nazis. He arranged for the burning of books disliked by the Nazis, and made sure that all artistic and cultural expressions conformed to the Nazi viewpoint.

Perhaps most important, Goebbels worked to create in the public mind an image of Hitler as a superior human being

ity, claiming that Aryans were "creators of culture" and the "Master Race," while others—especially Jews, the "alien race"—were "destroyers of culture" and should be eliminated. This book was to become the most important document of Nazism.

Joseph Goebbels salutes a German soldier.
(Reproduced by permission of AP/Wide World Photos.)

Goebbels planned one of the most dramatic anti-Jewish events, which came to be known as Kristallnacht (Crystal Night, also called "the night of broken glass"). On November 9, 1938, many thousands of Jews were forced from their homes and taken to concentration camps, while their businesses, schools, and nearly 300 synagogues (Jewish places of worship) were destroyed.

Goebbels continued his crusade against the Jews in every way he could, including portraying them—in movies and propaganda—as ugly and evil. Called "the father of lies," Goebbels lied to the German people about other things as well, telling them, for instance, that the war was going well when in fact Germany was losing. After Hitler committed suicide in his underground bunker, Goebbels told his last lie, informing the public that the Führer had died while leading his troops into battle.

The day after Hitler's death, Goebbels and his wife injected their six children with lethal poison, then also killed themselves.

who never made mistakes and who lived simply, denying himself luxuries.

Although he had not been raised to hate Jews, Goebbels became an anti-Semite (anti-Jewish) during the 1920s, when Germany was suffering great economic hardship. Like Hitler and others, Goebbels blamed the Jews for Germany's problems, and he believed that it would be necessary to exterminate the Jews completely in order to "cleanse" Germany of their presence.

Rebuilding the Nazi Party

When he was released from prison in 1925, Hitler began rebuilding the Nazi Party. His success was partly due to the desperation of the German people, who were suffering from the devastating effects of a worldwide economic depression, including unemployment and inflation, and partly to Hitler's own talents. He spoke to Germany's frustrations and fears, and encouraged citizens to blame Jews for the poor condition of their country. His very effective speaking style, which could become almost hypnotic, produced strong emotion in his listeners. At the same time, he used his disciplined but brutal storm troopers both to maintain order at Nazi rallies and to terrorize his opponents.

The failure of the Munich Beer Hall Putsch had convinced Hitler that he must use legal means to achieve his goals, which meant election to public office. In the 1928 elections, the Nazi Party won 2 percent of the votes, but by 1930 they had earned 18.3 percent. Surrounded by such supporters as Hess, Hermann Göring (1893–1946; see entry), Joseph Goebbels, and Heinrich Himmler (see sidebars on pages 104 and 86), Hitler attracted more followers and the party's popularity increased.

Chancellor of Germany

In the 1932 election, Hitler ran against German president Paul von Hindenberg. He won 37 percent of the votes and lost, but the Nazi Party now formed the largest political group in the Reichstag (the parliament, Germany's legislative body). Meanwhile, the population was increasingly angry and it seemed that violence would soon erupt. To prevent this from happening, Hindenberg made Hitler chancellor (the person who runs the day-to-day business of government) of Germany. Government leaders who disagreed with the Nazis' violent tactics thought they would still be able to control the Nazis, but they were wrong.

The Nazi Party continued building public support through propaganda and violence. In February 1933 a fire destroyed part of the Reichstag building, and Hitler used this event as an excuse to begin a series of terrorist acts against politicians he considered his enemies. Although there was never any proof as to who started the fire, Hitler told the people that the fire was part of a Communist plan to start a revolution in Germany. The next day Hitler issued an emergency decree, approved by the nervous Reichstag and Hindenburg, that gave him special powers, supposedly to protect the nation against possible Communist acts of violence. The decree gave

Adolf Hitler in Munich, 1931.
(Reproduced by permission of AP/Wide World Photos.)

the government the power to ignore almost all German citizens' rights as granted by their constitution. This was the beginning of the "Third Reich," the name by which Hitler's regime and this period in Germany history became known.

The Nazis in control of Germany

The Nazis began by eliminating civil rights and the legal system and giving the state police force, the Gestapo , the right to arrest and imprison anyone for any reason. Laws no longer protected citizens, and soon the Gestapo arrested all the members of the Reichstag. In fact, the Nazis were the only legal political party, and many of Hitler's opponents—including some from within his own party that he considered threatening—were assassinated.

At the same time, the Nazis enacted a series of harsh measures against the Jewish population in Germany. Starting around 1933 they were not allowed to hold public jobs and their businesses were boycotted. Propaganda was used to stir up hatred against the Jews, and they were made to wear yellow Stars of David (a symbol of the Jewish religion) on their clothing to identify them and meant to humiliate them. They were prevented from using many public facilities, and forced to attend only all-Jewish schools.

The rest of the world looked on with disapproval as Hitler reshaped Germany. Then he angered the international community by pulling Germany out of the League of Nations (an organization that promoted cooperation between countries, and the forerunner of the United Nations). He built up the German army, navy, and air force, which was in direct violation of the Treaty of Versailles. Hitler also eliminated from the armed forces any officers who did not cooperate with the Nazis, and he started Hitler Youth movements to train young people to become Nazi soldiers. He also introduced a draft (requiring able young men to serve in the armed forces).

At the peak of popularity

When Hindenberg died in August 1934, Hitler became head of state, and he also made himself commander of all military forces. He was now in complete control of Germany, and he demanded that all of its citizens refer to him as "Führer." He made many appearances before huge crowds in large halls, using military music, elaborate ceremonies, and dramatic speeches to demonstrate the glory of Germany and of his own leadership.

A popular vote showed that 90 percent of the population agreed with Hitler's policies, due in part to the fact that under his reign unemployment had almost ceased and the national income had doubled. But Hitler's popularity was also enforced by the Gestapo—along with Hitler's private bodyguard unit, the "blackshirts" or SS—who were free to torture or kill anyone who didn't agree with the Nazis. Most of the people who openly disagreed with Hitler's policies were either dead or in prison camps.

Germany invades nearby countries

By the end of the 1930s, Hitler was ready to expand Germany's empire by taking over nearby countries. He began by conquering Austria and some German-speaking sections of

Czechoslovakia. Anxious to avoid war with Germany, the region's other powerful countries, Great Britain and France, agreed to these actions, providing that Hitler did not take over any more territory in Europe. Hitler soon broke this agreement and took over the rest of Czechoslovakia. In less than a year, he had added ten million people to the population of Germany, as the citizens of the countries he invaded became German citizens.

In 1939, Hitler signed a "Pact of Steel" with Italy's dictator, Benito Mussolini (1883–1945; see entry), and the two countries became known as the Axis nations; Japan joined the Axis in 1940. Finally, Great Britain and France decided that if Hitler carried out his threatened invasion of Poland, they would go to war with Germany. On September 3, 1939, the German military attacked Poland, and Britain and France soon declared war.

Hitler's "Final Solution"

Meanwhile, Hitler had been acting on his "racial purity" policies against Jews. Many had already left Germany, but there were still about 500,000 Jews remaining in the country in addition to those who lived in the areas Germany had conquered. Hitler began sending Jews—along with other people he deemed undesirable, such as Catholics, Roma (commonly known as Gypsies), homosexuals, and political opponents—to labor or concentration camps in Poland.

In 1941 Hitler ordered the "Final Solution" to what he and his followers called the "Jewish problem": the mass killing of European Jews. In the camps, prisoners were often separated from their families, forced to work for no wages, given little food, and in many other ways treated cruelly. Eventually, most would be killed in gas chambers (sealed rooms into which lethal gas was piped) and their bodies cremated. This horrible event in history is now called the Holocaust. Before World War II was over, an estimated six million Jews and about one million others had been murdered by the Nazis.

The war goes downhill

The first few years of the war went well for Germany. They quickly conquered Denmark, Norway, Belgium, Luxembourg, and finally France, and they terrorized Great Britain with bombing raids. The bombing of Berlin by the British air force was a slight setback (Hitler had vowed no bombs would fall in his country), but Germany went on to invade Bulgaria, Hungary, and Romania.

But Hitler made a fatal mistake. In 1939 he had signed an agreement with Joseph Stalin (1879–1953; see entry), the leader of the Soviet Union; the agreement stated that the two countries would not invade each other. In June 1940, Hitler broke the agreement by attacking the Soviet Union. At first Hitler's army moved quickly, making its way east toward the Soviet capital of Moscow. But Hitler had underestimated the strength of this new enemy, which fought back valiantly over two bitterly cold winters. German troops were not prepared for the harsh weather, and they were not able to progress according to plan.

The Soviets kept the Germans from taking Moscow, then retook the city of Stalingrad. With the Soviet victory at Kursk in mid-1943, the Germans were forced to retreat.

The entry of the United States into the war in December 1941 also greatly decreased the chances of a German victory, as did the defeat of General Erwin Rommel's (1891–1944; see entry) seemingly unbeatable troops in North Africa. The Americans provided the additional men and supplies the Allied forces needed to finally start pushing the German army back into Germany.

Trapped in the bunker

After the successful Allied landing on the beaches of Normandy in northern France (known as D-Day) in June 1944 it became clear that the German war effort was doomed, but Hitler refused to admit it. Although many of his opponents had made attempts over the years to assassinate him, one attempt almost succeeded. In the summer of 1944, some military officers tried to bomb a meeting at which Hitler and other leaders were present. The plot failed, and Hitler ordered about 5,000 people he suspected of being involved in the plot to be killed. Hitler claimed that the failure of the attempt was just "more proof that fate has selected me for my mission."

In January 1945, as the Allies pressed toward Germany, Hitler was forced to move into an underground bunker or shelter beneath his Berlin headquarters. By now his physical and mental health had declined sharply: he walked with a stoop, often spoke irrationally, and was suspicious of everyone. For Germany's defeat Hitler blamed not himself but the military leaders and the German people themselves, claiming that they were all too weak to realize Germany's great destiny. He now ordered a "scorched earth" policy, which meant that German land and property was to be destroyed to keep it out of Allied hands.

About fifteen years earlier, Hitler had met a teenage shop clerk named Eva Braun. She became his mistress and in 1936, she had moved into his Bavarian villa, Berchtesgaden. Now Eva joined Hitler in the bunker, and on April 29, 1945, they were married. Hitler was urged to flee the bunker, but he refused, and he began preparing for his own death. He wrote a will in which he restated his hatred for the Jews, calling on Germany's future leaders to continue their "merciless opposition" to the Jewish people.

The next day, as the Soviet Union bombed the area above the bunker, Hitler shot his beloved German shepherd, Blondi, then put the gun to his own head. Eva also committed suicide by taking poison. The two bodies were burned in the garden above, even as shells were exploding around them.

Some people refused to believe the news of Hitler's death. For years, rumors persisted that he was still alive and in hiding. In 1972, a dental forensic expert (a person who examines teeth and dental records for evidence to be used for legal purposes) compared pictures of the dentures taken from a body found near Hitler's bunker with X-ray head plates of Hitler that were taken in 1943. The two were a perfect match. The dental expert told the Sixth International Meeting of Forensic Sciences that this was conclusive proof that Hitler had died in Germany as reported.

With Hitler's death Nazism was finished, for, according to Hitler biographer John Toland, "without its true leader, it burst like a bubble." Germany surrendered to the Allies on May 7, 1945.

Where to Learn More
Books

Fuchs, Thomas. *The Hitler Fact Book*. Los Angeles: Fountain Books, 1990.

Harris, Nathaniel. *Hitler.* London: B.T. Batsford Ltd., 1989.

Marrin, Albert. *Hitler.* New York: Viking Kestrel, 1987.

Shirer, William L. *The Rise and Fall of Adolf Hitler.* New York: Random House, 1961.

Speer, Albert. *Inside the Third Reich.* New York: Macmillan, 1970.

Toland, John. *Adolf Hitler.* Garden City, NY: Doubleday, 1976.

Wepman, Dennis. *Adolf Hitler.* New York: Chelsea House Publishers, 1985.

Oveta Culp Hobby

Born January 5, 1905
Killeen, Texas
Died August 1995

Director of the Women's Army Corps (WAC) and first secretary of the Department of Health, Education, and Welfare

W omen have played a role in every war in American history, usually as nurses or in other supportive positions. World War II marked the first time, however, that women other than nurses served within the ranks of the U.S. Army. The original purpose of the Women's Army Auxiliary Corps (WAAC), which later became the Women's Army Corps, was to "free men for combat" by having women perform many of the military's noncombat duties. But it also allowed women to demonstrate their loyalty to their country while showing that they could perform as well as men did in the same positions. Oveta Culp Hobby had already achieved much in her life by the time she became the WAC's first director, and she went on to manage the agency with dedication and energy.

A busy and talented young woman

Born in Killeen, Texas, Hobby was an excellent student who attended the Mary Hardin Baylor College for Women. She decided to become a lawyer like her father, and she attended the University of Texas Law School. By the time she was only twenty years old, Hobby had become Houston's assistant city

Oveta Culp Hobby led more than 100,000 WACs serving in approximately 200 noncombatant positions in 400 U.S. military installations and every overseas theater of World War II.

Portrait: Oveta Culp Hobby.
(Reproduced by permission of the U.S. Army.)

attorney as well as the parliamentarian of the Texas legislature (an expert in the formal procedures used by legislative bodies).

In 1931, when she was twenty-six, Oveta married William Hobby, a former governor of Texas and the publisher of the *Houston Post* newspaper. She went to work at the *Post*, starting as a book editor and working her way up to the position of executive vice president.

Between 1933 and 1941, Hobby was remarkably busy and productive: she worked as the parliamentarian for the Texas legislature, helped her husband manage the *Post,* served as president of the Texas League of Women Voters, had two children to raise, and even wrote a book on parliamentary practice (*Mr. Chairman,* 1936).

A way for women to serve

Meanwhile, the United States was about to get involved in World War II. In Washington in early 1941, Congresswoman Edith Nourse Rogers of Massachusetts had introduced a bill to establish a separate women's corps of the army. Rogers knew that women would serve in and help the army in the coming war, just as they had in World War I (1914–1918) and other conflicts. She wanted to make sure they received the same benefits and protection as men did (such as food, living quarters, legal protection, and medical care).

Although many people felt that women should not be involved in the work of war—especially if they would be serving alongside men—the army's chief of staff, General George Marshall (1880–1959; see entry), agreed that women would be well suited to perform not only office work but some communication jobs that required manual dexterity and patience. He and other army leaders believed that if women could fill many noncombatant jobs, more men would be available to fight the enemy.

Finally, Congress passed the bill authorizing the Women's Auxiliary Army Corps (WAAC), even though the final version featured some compromises Rogers did not want to make. For example, women serving as WAACs would be paid less than men of the same rank and position, and they would not get the same protection when they served overseas (including overseas pay, life insurance, veterans' medical coverage, and death benefits).

Taking command of the WAAC

Hobby was already in Washington when the bill was signed; she had earlier been assigned to head the new Women's Division of the War Department's Bureau of Public Relations. In fact, Hobby had helped push the bill through Congress and had testified in its favor. On the day the bill was signed—May 15, 1941—Hobby was named director of the WAAC. Her record of personal achievement and experience in local and national politics qualified her for the job. It was also thought that her attractive and "ladylike" demeanor would persuade conservative critics that the WAAC was a respectable organization.

Public response to the WAAC bill was enthusiastic. By November, the goal of 25,000 recruits to the WAAC had already been met, so a new limit of 150,000 was authorized. When the first WAAC training center was set up at Fort Des Moines, Iowa, over 35,000 women signed up for fewer than 1,000 positions.

Soon after accepting her new position, Hobby appeared at a press conference to answer questions about the WAAC and its role in the military. Some of the questions were rather silly (such as what color underwear the women would wear under their uniforms, and whether they would be able to wear makeup) but Hobby answered all of them calmly and seriously. In other speaking engagements, she explained that "the gaps our women will fill are in those noncombatant jobs where women's hands and women's hearts fit naturally. WAACs will do the same type of work which women do in civilian life. They will bear the same relation to men of the Army that they bear to the men of the civilian organizations in which they work."

The WAACs are trained and assigned

In July 1941 the first WAAC officer candidate training class (which included 440 recruits) started its six-week course at Fort Des Moines. The average officer candidate was twenty-five years old and a college graduate with experience in office work

"Rosie the Riveter": American Women at Work on the

As World War II heated up in Europe in 1939 and 1940, it seemed likely that the United States would eventually be drawn into the conflict. Yet it was clear that the U.S. military was not prepared, that it lacked not only the large number of soldiers but the equipment (such as guns, ammunition, tanks, and airplanes) that would be needed. In May 1940 President Franklin D. Roosevelt (1882–1945; see entry) announced that the United States must become the "great arsenal of democracy" for the rest of the world. This meant that the country must produce the materials that would allow democracy's defenders to win the war over dictators like Adolf Hitler and Benito Mussolini (see entries).

To accomplish this goal, Roosevelt authorized a huge buildup in the industrial production of war materials, while other products (such as automobiles, household appliances, and bicycles) were put on hold. Meanwhile, many men were joining the armed forces, especially after Japan's attack on the U.S. naval base at Pearl Harbor, Hawaii, and the entry of the United States into the war. So who would take up the millions of factory jobs that had been created by the buildup? Who would make up this huge new workforce?

The answer was women. Even though the majority of American women of this period had been taught that their place was in the home, taking care of their families while their husbands earned money to support them, they were now called upon to help the war effort by working in industry and other areas. The U.S. government joined with industry to encourage women to take factory jobs, putting up posters that showed strong, determined female workers who did their parts to help their country win the war, and whose husbands were proud of them.

In February 1943 a song called "Rosie the Riveter" began to be heard over radios all over the country. Written by Redd Evans and John Jacob Loeb and sung by a group called the Four Vagabonds, the song

or teaching. Many of them had friends and relatives already serving in the military. A separate platoon of forty African American officer recruits was also established; these women attended class and ate meals with the white women, but all of the post's service clubs, theaters, and beauty shops were segregated.

In August, the first class of auxiliary or enlisted women reported. These recruits were slightly younger than the officer celebrated the historic role that women were playing in the war. Soon the term Rosie the Riveter (which the songwriters had chosen for its sound, not to honor any specific worker) came to be used as a fond nickname for the more than six million women who had joined the workforce.

Women were working in factories, shipyards, and steel mills, employed as welders, electricians, mechanics, engineers, and chemists, operating everything from cranes to streetcars and even driving taxi cabs. Dressed in coveralls and heavy shoes, they were performing jobs that had previously been the domain of men only, and they were proving to themselves and the world just what women could do.

In addition to the industrial work performed by women, about two million of them took clerical jobs, about half of these were hired by the federal government. Women also took charge of farms, and many worked as Red Cross volunteers—serving as air raid wardens, messengers, and drivers and checking the skies for enemy airplanes.

The figures for total wartime production in the United States are amazing: the country produced 296,429 airplanes, 102,351 tanks and self-propelled guns, 372,431 artillery pieces, 47 million tons of ammunition, and 84,620 warships, as well as other kinds of equipment. This massive output—which played a major role in the Allied victory—could never have been accomplished without the help of Rosie the Riveter and her friends, who came by the millions to answer their country's call for help.

After the war, most of these women were laid off from their jobs—many unwillingly—both because production decreased and because space was being made for men returning from war. Nevertheless, the war years changed forever Americans' ideas about what women could or should do in the workplace, and led to the great changes in women's roles that happened over the next five decades.

candidates, and most had only a high school education and less work experience.

The first qualified WAACs were sent to the Aircraft Warning Service units of the U.S. Army Air Corps. About half of the women filled office positions such as file clerk, typist, or stenographer. Others worked in such diverse jobs as weather observer and forecaster, cryptographer (working with codes and secret messages), radio operator, parachute rigger, photograph analyst, and control tower operator. Women working for the Army Transportation Corps helped process men for overseas assignments; members of the Quartermaster Corps maintained supply depots; and women assigned to the Signal Corps operated telephone switchboards and served as photographers and map analysts.

Reactions to the work of the WAACs

In general, the response to the work done by the WAACS was positive. For example, General Dwight D. Eisenhower (1890–1969; see entry), commander of all the Allied forces in Europe (and future president of the United States), commented in 1945: "During the time I have had the [WAACs] under my command they have met every test and task assigned to them...their contributions in efficiency, skill, spirit, and determination are unmeasurable."

In 1943, however, there was a backlash of public opinion against the WAACs when rumors spread that most of the women were functioning as prostitutes and that a large number of them had become pregnant. This uproar—which showed how uncomfortable many people were when women took on nontraditional roles—died down after Hobby testified before Congress and provided evidence that the rumors were untrue. In fact, Hobby had always insisted that the WAACs maintain a high standard of performance, discipline, and morality in order to avoid such controversies.

The Army's high regard for the WAAC was confirmed in July 1943, when the organization became a part of the army itself and its name changed to the Women's Army Corps (WAC). This meant that the women would receive the same pay, privileges, and protection as men.

The war draws to a close

By the end of the war, WACs had served in a wide variety of positions in locations all over the world. For example, 300 WACs assisted in the planning of the D-Day invasion of France. An African American battalion worked in England and France redirecting the tons of mail sent to all of the U.S. personnel fighting in Europe. More than 600 WACs received

medals and citations for their work during the war, including Hobby, who received the Distinguished Service Medal. With the war over, Hobby, still just forty-years-old, resigned her command and returned to Houston.

Returning to public service

A little less than ten years later, in 1953, President Eisenhower appointed Hobby the first secretary of the new Depart-

Oveta Culp Hobby being sworn in as secretary of the Department of Health, Education, and Welfare by President Eisenhower. *(Reproduced by permission of AP/Wide World Photos, Inc.)*

ment of Health, Education and Welfare (HEW). This made her the only female member of the president's cabinet, and only the second female cabinet member in American history.

In this position Hobby had responsibility for the Public Health Service, the Food and Drug Administration, the Office of Education, and the Bureau of Old Age and Survivors Insurance. In 1955, Hobby oversaw the distribution of the polio vaccine, the discovery by Jonas Salk that virtually eradicated what had been a major public health menace. That same year, she returned to Houston to care for her sick husband. When Hobby resigned, Treasury Secretary George Humphrey reportedly exclaimed, "What? The best man in the Cabinet?"

Running a successful newspaper

Hobby's husband died in 1964, and the following year she became Chairman of the Board of the Houston *Post*. Over the next few decades she resided over the buildup of the *Post* into a $100-million business. In 1983 Hobby was listed in *Texas Business* magazine as one of the twenty most powerful Texans (and the only woman on the list). She died in 1995.

Where to Learn More

Books

American Decades, 1940–1949. Detroit: Gale Research, 1995, 276-77.

Periodicals

Bellafaire, Judith A. "The Women's Army Corps: A Commemoration of World War II Service." U.S. Army Center of Military History. [Online] Available http://www.army.mil/cmh-pg/WAC.HTM (November 30, 1998).

Time (August 28, 1995): 27.

Web sites

"Oveta Culp Hobby" [Online] Avialable http://199.173.224.3/history/hobby.html (November 30, 1998).

Franz Jaggerstatter

Born May 20, 1907
St. Radegund, Austria
Died August 9, 1943
Berlin, Germany

Austrian farmer and conscientious
objector during World War II

During Adolf Hitler's reign as leader of Germany, those who lived in countries ruled by the Nazi Party (the National Socialist German Workers' Party) were subjected to an iron rule. Refusing to follow Nazi orders brought swift, brutal punishment and often death. Few people had the courage to resist. Yet Franz Jaggerstatter, an Austrian farmer with a wife and three young daughters, did show such courage—even when everyone around him said he should go along with the Nazis. He refused to enter military service because he believed it would violate his religious beliefs, knowing very well that his refusal would lead to his execution. Since his death, Jaggerstatter has become a strong role model for other conscientious objectors (those who refuse to fight and kill others on religious or moral grounds).

"We must love God even more than family, and we must lose everything dear and worthwhile on earth rather than commit even the slightest offense against God." Franz Jaggerstatter was executed by the Nazis for refusing to serve in the military.

A lively young man

Jaggerstatter was born in the rural town of St. Radegund, located along the banks of the Salzach River in northern Austria (and only about an hour's drive from Braunau, Hitler's birthplace). His mother, Rosalia, worked as a maid when she became pregnant with Franz; her baby's father, Franz Bachmeier, was also a servant and the two never married. Bachmeier was killed in 1915 while fighting in World War I (1914–18). In 1917, Rosalia married a farmer named Jaggerstatter, who adopted young Franz and began to instill in him a love of books and reading.

Franz attended the local school in St. Radegund, and as he grew up he gained a reputation as a lively—or even wild—young man who enjoyed games, dancing, and driving his motorcycle (the first one seen in St. Radegund) loudly around the village streets. When he was twenty years old, Franz went away for three years to work in the iron ore industry in Steiermark, Austria. Then he returned to St. Radegund and began farming.

Experiences religious awakening

In 1936 Franz married a local girl named Franziska. The couple traveled to Rome for their honeymoon, and during that time in Italy Franz experienced a renewal of his Roman Catholic faith. After the couple's return to St. Radegund, Franz continued his farm work. He attended daily mass and served as sacristan (a church officer in charge of the room in which priests' garments and other items used in the Mass are kept) in St. Radegund's small church. During the next few years, three daughters were born to the Jaggerstatters. Franz was known as an especially devoted father, and even took one of his babies out in a carriage—something the men of that time and place usually didn't do.

"A beautiful train ... to hell"

While Franz and Franziska were running their farm and raising their family, Adolf Hitler was busy taking power in Germany. It was during this period that Jaggerstatter had a frightening dream about "a beautiful train" that was "going to hell." It seemed that the train stood for National Socialism (the National Socialist German Workers' Party or Nazi Party; a political system devised by Hitler and his subordinates), which promised order and prosperity but actually involved hatred, cruelty, and murder. Jaggerstatter was alarmed at the way everybody around him seemed eager to jump on this train and join the Nazis, and he shared his views and his distrust of Hitler with his friends and neighbors at local gatherings.

In 1938, Austrians voted on whether their country should join Hitler's empire, which was called the Third Reich. Jaggerstatter was the only person in St. Radegund to vote against the *Anschloss,* or the joining together of the two countries.

A difficult decision

Jaggerstatter received his first call to military duty in June 1940. Despite his doubts about Hitler and National Socialism, he reported for duty, but was released in 1941 because his farm work was deemed more important than military service at that time. Meanwhile, he thought more about the conflict between his religious beliefs and fighting for a system he did not support. Jaggerstatter was not a pacifist (a person who does not believe in fighting or killing others for *any* reason); in fact, he stated that he would have become a soldier in an instant if Austrians had chosen to oppose, rather than join, the Nazis. But it was becoming more and more clear to him that he could not kill in the name of Hitler and his followers.

In February 1943 Jaggerstatter received his second call to military duty. Still struggling with his conscience, he consulted the Catholic bishop in the nearby town of Linz. He asked the bishop, "Who can be a soldier for Christ and a soldier for National Socialism at the same time?" The bishop's response was that Jaggerstatter's duty to his country and to his family must take priority over all other concerns. Jaggerstatter's friends and relatives agreed with the bishop and urged him to join the military.

Nevertheless, Jaggerstatter went to the local induction center (where military recruits signed up for service) and told the commanding officer that he had decided to refuse to serve in the military. Jaggerstatter was arrested and taken to the prison in Linz, then transferred to the Brandenburg Prison in Berlin.

Explains his position in letters from prison

While waiting for his trial, Jaggerstatter wrote several letters to his friends and loved ones, as well as a statement

What Is a Conscientious Objector?

A conscientious objector is a person who refuses to participate in a war because his or her own conscience tells him or her that it would be wrong to take part. This stand may be based on religion (some religions believe that violence and war are never justified), politics (a person may disagree with the reason a country has gone to war), or philosophy (someone may object to the idea of war without being a follower of a religion).

There are several types of objectors. Some refuse to serve in combat but will agree to perform noncombatant duties, while others also refuse noncombatant service but will work in civilian jobs rather than fight. A third type of objector, often called an absolutist, not only refuses to fight but also to accept any alternative to fighting.

Conscientious objectors have existed throughout history. The ancient religions of Buddhism and Jainism (which date back to the sixth century before Christ) were based on nonviolence, and the early Christians refused to serve in the Roman army. During the Middle Ages, Christians began to see a difference between just and unjust wars.

After the Protestant religions broke off from the Roman Catholic Church, some of them began to include conscientious objection in their beliefs. These included the Mennonites, the Society of Friends or Quakers, and the Brethren, all of which still exist and still promote nonviolence. In the 19th and 20th centuries, they were joined by such churches as the Jehovah's Witnesses and the Seventh-Day Adventists.

Indian leader Mohandas K. Gandhi, who took a nonviolent stand as he led his country to independence, had a major influence on the way people viewed the conscientious objector. Now groups like the Fellowship of Reconciliation and

explaining why he had taken such an unusual and dangerous stance. In a letter to his three daughters (the oldest of whom was not yet six), he wrote: "I would have liked to spare you the pain and sorrow you must bear because of me. But you know we must love God even more than family, and we must lose everything dear and worthwhile on earth rather than commit even the slightest offense against God." To his wife, Jaggerstatter asserted that he did not want to live like a "halfway Christian, that is more like vegetating than living."

War Resisters International try to provide support for those who refused to fight.

The United States did not have a draft (by which qualified young men are required to serve in the armed forces) before World War I, except during the Civil War, when an objector was allowed to send someone to war in his own place. During World War I, U.S. law recognized objectors if they were members of churches that had nonviolence as part of their official beliefs. These objectors still had to report to duty, but they were assigned to noncombatant units. Some of those who refused noncombatant service were sent to work on farms, while many absolutists were imprisoned. Conscientious objectors in Austria-Hungary and Germany were sent to insane asylums, while those in France were often shot as deserters.

During World War II, about 100,000 Americans were classified as conscientious objectors. United States law recognized those who refused to fight "by reason of religious training and belief," but those who objected on political or philosophical grounds were excluded. Objectors performed alternative service in such areas as reforestation, flood control, soil conservation, dairy testing, and caring for mental patients. About 6,000 absolutists were imprisoned.

Great Britain had the same three categories of objectors as the United States (no combat, no noncombatant service, no service whatsoever) but conscientious objector status could be claimed on religious, political, or philosophical grounds. In Germany, as Jaggerstatter's case shows, conscientious objectors were shot or sent to concentration camps, while in Japan some objectors entered the army but then refused to aim their guns at the enemy.

Jaggerstatter's statement from prison begins with this declaration: "These few words are being set down here as they come from my mind and my heart. And if I must write them with my hands in chains, I find that much better than if my will were in chains. Neither prison nor chains nor sentence of death can rob a man of the Faith and his free will." Jaggerstatter asserted that he did not owe worldly leaders "blind obedience," and that God had granted him the grace and strength to die for his beliefs.

Trial and execution

Jaggerstatter's trial, held on July 6, 1943, was presided over by military judges who were from the regular army, not Hitler's Schutzstaffel, the Security Squad (known as the "SS"). Even the judges attempted to talk Jaggerstatter out of his position, but he continued to assert that he would not fight for National Socialism. According to the official court proceedings, Jaggerstatter was convicted of the charge of "undermining our military forces" by his "stubborn refusal to fulfill his patriotic duty as a soldier in Germany's perilous war for survival." He received the death sentence.

On August 9, 1943, Jaggerstatter was beheaded at Brandenburg Prison. His remains were cremated and buried on the prison grounds. Back home in St. Radegund, he was regarded as a religious fanatic, and his wife was criticized for not forcing him to change his mind. For almost twenty years, Jaggerstatter was remembered only by his closest survivors.

Jaggerstatter's story comes to light

Jaggerstatter might still be unknown today if not for the efforts of American sociologist Gordon Zahn, who uncovered his story while he was in Europe conducting research on German Catholic support for World War II. Zahn had learned of Father Franz Reinisch, a Catholic priest executed in 1942 for refusing to pledge unconditional obedience to Hitler, from another priest, Father Kreuzberg. In a book written by Father Kreuzberg, Zahn discovered the story of "Franz II," as Kreuzberg called Jaggerstatter.

Intrigued by Jaggerstatter, Zahn (who had also been a conscientious objector during World War II) traveled to St. Radegund and interviewed his widow and others who had known him. He learned that after the war, Jaggerstatter's ashes had been returned to his home village and buried near the door of the St. Radegund church. A sympathetic priest had also insisted—despite protests that Jaggerstatter was a coward who refused to fight while other men sacrificed their lives for their country—that Jaggerstatter's name be added to a list of St. Radegund's war dead.

In 1964, Zahn's book *In Solitary Witness: The Life and Death of Franz Jaggerstatter* was published. In Austria, public opinion about Jaggerstatter remained mixed, but much of the rest of the world embraced him as a religious martyr (a person who makes a great sacrifice for the sake of a belief or principle) and role model. His example helped to persuade the Catholic Church to officially support the individual's right to object to military service based on religious and moral grounds. His name was also cited when, in 1970, the United Nations expanded the Universal Declaration of Human Rights to include a provision for conscientious objection.

Jaggerstatter's legacy

Although some individuals still question Jaggerstatter's position, his homeland has come to celebrate him as a hero of conscience. Streets in Vienna, Linz, and other Austrian cities have been named for him, celebrations in his honor have been held, and a petition has been submitted to the Vatican to have him named a saint. The Jaggerstatters' old family farmhouse has been turned into a center for study and meditation. In a gesture of reconciliation and goodwill, a cycle of twelve etchings on Jaggerstatter by Austrian artist Ernst Degaspari has been displayed at Yad Vashem, the center for Israel's Holocaust Memorial.

In addition to these public tributes, Jaggerstatter's words and courage inspire those individuals struggling to follow their own consciences. In an article in the *New Statesman and Society,* Bruce Kent writes that "Jaggerstatter's life continues to give courage to conscientious objectors around the world from many different religious and non-religious backgrounds."

Where to learn more

Books

Balfour, Michael. "A Portrait Gallery: Franz Jagerstatter." In *Withstanding Hitler in Germany 1933–45,* pp. 231–33. London: Routledge, 1988.

Zahn, Gordon. *In Solitary Witness: The Life and Death of Franz Jaggerstatter.* New York: Holt, Rinehart, and Winston, 1964.

Periodicals

Jabusch, Willard F. "A Tale of Two Towns." *America* (July 16, 1994): 4.

Kent, Bruce. "The Man Who Said No to Hitler." *New Statesman and Society* (May 6, 1994): 20.

Moore, Donald J. "Franz Jagerstatter: Conscience vs. Duty." *America* (February 19, 1994): 12.

Zahn, Gordon. "In Celebration of Martyrdom." *America* (February 19, 1994): 8.

Web sites

Putz, Erna. "Against the Stream: Franz Jaggerstatter" (translated by Michael Duggan). [Online] Available http://c3.hu/ bocs/jager-a.htm (October 23, 1998).

Fred T. Korematsu

Born 1919
Oakland, California

Japanese American working as a welder
at the beginning of World War II

Between 1941 and 1944, approximately 120,000 Japanese Americans were forced to leave their homes and move into internment camps. At the time, the U.S. government said that it feared these people might spy for Japan or otherwise threaten the safety of Americans. Yet many people believe the real reason was racism. After all, the United States was also at war with Italy and Germany, but Italian Americans and German Americans were left alone.

Of the 120,000 people forced to move, Fred Korematsu is one of a few Japanese Americans who challenged the evacuation order in court, charging that it went against the U.S. Constitution. Although he did not set out to become a hero, he played an important role in an episode that proved how the freedoms Americans often take for granted must always be protected.

Born and raised in the USA

Korematsu was a "nisei," a member of the first generation of Japanese Americans to be born in America. His parents

Fred T. Korematsu defied the U.S. government's call for the "evacuation" of all Americans of Japanese descent to internment camps, and challenged the order in court.

Portrait: Fred T. Korematsu.
(Copyright 1998 Shirley Nakao. Reproduced by permission of the Asian Law Caucus.)

were immigrants who settled in Oakland, California, where they ran a flower nursery. Although the family spoke only Japanese at home and observed some Japanese holidays, Korematsu and his three brothers also enjoyed such American pastimes as playing tennis, basketball, and football. He was first called "Fred" by a teacher who found his real name, Toyosaburo, difficult to pronounce; he liked his new name and kept it for the rest of his life.

By June 1941 it seemed inevitable that the United States would get involved in World War II. Korematsu went with his friends to his local post office to volunteer to serve in the armed forces, but the officer in charge refused to give him an application. He said that he had been ordered not to allow any Japanese Americans to sign up.

"Potential enemies"

On December 7, 1941, the Japanese bombed Pearl Harbor, killing thousands of American servicemen. A wave of anti-Japanese hysteria swept over the country—especially on the West Coast, where curfews restricting the activities of Japanese Americans were implemented, as well as limits on how far they could travel. Some military and political leaders were pressuring President Franklin D. Roosevelt (1882–1945; see entry) to do something about the "threat" posed by Japanese Americans. One of the most vocal was General John DeWitt, who issued a report stating that the United States could probably expect another attack from Japan, that Japanese Americans living on the West Coast were "potential enemies," and that there was a "military necessity" to evacuate them and place them into camps.

On February 19, 1942, Roosevelt issued an executive order directing that all Japanese Americans and resident aliens (immigrants who have not yet achieved citizenship) be sent to inland internment camps. The first (and possibly most famous) camp was established at Manzanar in southern California; in all nine more camps were set up in California, Arizona, Wyoming, Colorado, Utah, and Arkansas. On March 31, those affected were ordered to report to control stations to register the names of people in their families, then told where and when to report for relocation to temporary "assembly areas." Finally, from there they would be sent to internment camps.

Uprooted lives and businesses

Japanese Americans were given between four days and two weeks to move. They were allowed to bring only what they could carry with them, so they had to decide what to do with property and possessions. Many were forced to sell their businesses, homes, cars, and other belongings at very low prices, and in some cases these things were illegally confiscated. It is estimated that total losses were between $810 million and $2 billion.

Korematsu defies the order

When the United States entered World War II, the twenty-two-year-old Korematsu had been working in the defense industry as a welder. His family was ordered to go to the Tanforan assembly area (a former racetrack where internees had to camp in empty horses' stalls), but he did not want to go with them. He had been dating an Italian American woman whose parents disapproved of their mixed-race relationship, and now he urged her to go with him to Nevada, where they could get married and avoid the internment order. His girlfriend decided she didn't want to leave her family, so Korematsu stayed in Oakland while planning to go to Nevada later.

Taking the case to court

He moved into a boarding house and changed his name to Clyde Sarah, presenting himself as a person of Spanish and Hawaiian heritage. He even had surgery on his eyelids so that he would look more like a Caucasian person. But on May 30, 1942, someone who knew Korematsu recognized and reported him, and he was arrested in San Leandro, California, and imprisoned in the San Francisco County Jail.

He stands up for his rights

Ernest Besig, a lawyer who worked for the American Civil Liberties Union (ACLU), read about Korematsu's situation in the newspaper and went to visit him in jail. He asked Korematsu if he would be willing to test the legality of the internment order in court, and Korematsu agreed. Freed on bail, Korematsu joined his family at Tanforan; they were later sent to the Topaz camp in the Utah desert. Other internees, fearful of more trouble, tried to talk Korematsu out of going to court.

⬛ The Nisei Prove Their Loyalty

After the December 7, 1941, bombing of the U.S. naval base at Pearl Harbor, Hawaii, anti-Japanese hysteria swept the country, and thousands of Japanese Americans living on the West Coast were forced to move into internment camps. At the same time, many young Japanese Americans were eager to prove their loyalty to the United States by joining the fight against the Axis nations (Germany, Italy, and Japan).

In response to their pleas, Congress authorized the formation of the U.S. Army's 442nd Regimental Combat Team, made up entirely of niseis (the first generation of Japanese to be born in the United States to immigrant parents) who had volunteered to serve. This 3,000-member team, made of mostly of young men from Hawaii—as well as some who had come out of internment camps on the mainland—was to become the most decorated army unit in U.S. history.

After training at Camp McCoy in Wisconsin and Camp Shelby in Mississippi, the Japanese American soldiers were sent in September 1943 to North Africa and then to Italy, where Allied troops were preparing for an invasion. They took part in bloody fighting throughout the following spring, losing one-fourth of the regiment but performing valiantly and living up to their motto, "Go for Broke." Then the 442nd Regiment moved on to France, where they achieved a daring, unexpected rescue of the "Lost Battalion," a unit of 211 Texas soldiers who had been surrounded by Germans in a mountainous region.

By the end of the war, the 442nd Regiment had earned 18,143 individual decorations, including more than 3,600 Purple Hearts, and had been responsible for 9,486 enemy casualties.

One distinguished member of the 442nd Regiment was Daniel Ken Inouye, the son of a Honolulu file clerk, who had

At Korematsu's trial, the judge agreed that the executive order was racially biased (no other ethnic group was affected) but he still found Korematsu guilty of defying it. He was sentenced to five years probation and returned to Topaz with his family. Meanwhile, Korematsu's attorneys had filed a suit in the Ninth Circuit Court of Appeals. But their argument that the executive order was unconstitutional was again rejected. Now Korematsu's legal team took

Daniel K. Inouye *(Courtesy of Daniel K. Inouye. Reproduced by permission.)*

Distinguished Service Cross, the Bronze Star, and the Purple Heart.

Soon after the war ended, Inouye learned that the war against racial prejudice was not yet over. Needing a haircut, he walked into a San Francisco barbershop wearing his army uniform, heavily decorated with the ribbons and medals he had earned, with its empty right sleeve pinned up. Inouye was told, "We don't serve Japs here."

Inouye returned to Hawaii and became a lawyer, then entered politics. In 1959 he was elected to the new state's first seat in the U.S. House of Representatives, becoming the first Japanese American to serve in Congress. Inouye became a strong supporter of civil rights and a spokesperson for the Asian American community. He spoke out against racism in an important speech at the 1968 Democratic convention, and he played a key role in the 1974 Watergate hearings, which led to the resignation of President Richard M. Nixon.

dropped out of the premedical program at the University of Hawaii to join the unit. While fighting on Mount Nebbione in Italy, Inouye lost his arm in an assault on a German infantry position, but destroyed three enemy machine-gun nests even after being wounded. For his bravery during this and other combat, Inouye won the

the case to the highest legal authority in the United States, the Supreme Court.

Justifying the internment order

By the time the Supreme Court reached its decision (in December 1944), the government had already closed down the internment camps. The Court came to a "split decision": even though three of the nine judges ruled in Korematsu's

President Clinton presents Fred Korematsu with a Presidential Medal of Freedom in 1998.
(Photograph by Dennis Cook. Reproduced by permission of AP/Wide World Photos.)

favor, six ruled against him, and he lost the case.

Justice Hugo L. Black wrote the majority opinion, stating that the government had not acted "because of hostility to [Korematsu] or his race" but "because we are at war with the Japanese Empire, because the ... military authorities feared an invasion of the West Coast." Disagreeing with this analysis, Justice J. Frank Murphy stated that the executive order "goes over the very brink of constitutional power and falls into the ugly abyss of racism."

New evidence spurs Korematsu to action

After the war, Korematsu moved to Detroit, Michigan, in search of a new start. Over the next forty years he married, raised two children, and worked as a draftsman. But in 1982, Korematsu was contacted by Peter Irons, a lawyer and historian who had uncovered new evidence. Irons learned that the government attorneys had intentionally disregarded reports from the FBI and Naval Intelligence that concluded that Japanese Americans were not security risks.

Korematsu and others who had fought the internment order during the war agreed to retry the case, aided by a group of two dozen attorneys from California, Washington, and Oregon who worked pro bono (for free). The attorneys filed suit in San Francisco's federal court on January 19, 1983, arguing that *Korematsu vs. United States* should be overturned because the government had falsified, suppressed, and withheld evidence that showed that there was no "military necessity" to banish Japanese Americans to the camps.

At an October 4 hearing attended by a large number of Japanese Americans, Korematsu stated: "I still remember forty years ago when I was handcuffed and arrested as a criminal here in San Francisco....I would like to see the government admit that they were wrong and do something about it so this will never happen again to any American citizen of any race, creed, or color."

The old case is overturned

Judge Marilyn Hall Patel overturned Korematsu's conviction, arguing that it had been "based on unsubstantiated facts, distortions and representations of at least one military commander, whose views were seriously infected by racism."

After the trial, Korematsu moved back to San Francisco and became an active, respected member of the Japanese American community. In 1983, he received the prestigious Earl Warren Human Rights Award from the ACLU. Further acknowledgment of the wrong done by the U.S. government came in 1988, when Congress passed a bill formally apologizing to Japanese Americans for the internment, and providing for a one-time payment of $20,000 to any living person who had spent time in the camps. In 1998 Korematsu was honored with the nation's highest civilian award, the Presidential Medal of Freedom.

Where to Learn More

Books

Chin, Steven A. *When Justice Failed: The Fred Korematsu Story.* Austin, Texas: Raintree Steck-Vaughn, 1993.

Fremon, David K. *Japanese-American Internment in American History.* Springfield, NJ: Enslow Publishers, 1996.

Irons, Peter. *Justice at War: The Story of the Japanese American Internment Cases.* Oxford: Oxford University Press, 1983.

Levine, Ellen. *A Fence Away from Freedom.* New York: Putnam's, 1995.

Web sites

Ehrlich, Dorothy. "Honoring Fred Korematsu and the Day of Remembrance." [Online] Available http://www.aclunc.org/opinion/9802223 -internment.html (January 25, 1999).

Douglas MacArthur

**Born January 26, 1880
Little Rock, Arkansas
Died April 5, 1964
Washington, D.C.**

**American general; commanded the Allied forces in
the Southwest Pacific and served as civilian
administrator of occupied Japan**

"Preparedness is the key
to success and victory."

Portrait: Douglas
MacArthur. *(Reproduced by
permission of Archive Photos.)*

One of the most memorable figures of the World War II period, Douglas MacArthur was a colorful character and an excellent self-promoter whose image frequently appeared in newspapers and newsreels (news films, often shown before movies). He was always seen wearing sunglasses and smoking an oversized corncob pipe, looking fearless as he commanded the Allied forces in the Pacific. He was known as a complicated person who could be charming and modest or vain and arrogant, and he often clashed with his superiors. In fact, President Franklin D. Roosevelt (1882–1945; see entry) once called MacArthur one of the "two most dangerous men in America" (the other was Louisiana senator Huey Long, another colorful character). However, his theatrics should not cloud MacArthur's real accomplishments, especially his campaign to liberate the Philippines from Japanese control and his term as civilian administrator of Japan after the war.

A boy bound for glory

Almost from birth, MacArthur seemed destined for greatness. He was the third child and second son of General

Arthur MacArthur, who earned a Congressional Medal of Honor for his courage during the Civil War and who was the U.S. Army's top-ranking officer by 1906. Coincidentally, the elder MacArthur also once served as military governor to the Philippines, which had been under American control since the Spanish American War (April to August 1898). Douglas MacArthur's mother, Mary Pinkney Hardy, was devoted to her son and would eventually use her many social connections to help him advance in his career. She encouraged all of her children to remember their duty to others and to be honest, but she paid special attention to Douglas, telling him that he was certain to achieve glory.

MacArthur spent his childhood living on a variety of army posts and was attracted to the military life at an early age; he claimed to have learned to ride horses and shoot before he learned to read and write. He was close to his older brother, Arthur, who died of appendicitis in 1926 in the midst of a promising career in the navy. In 1897 the family moved to St. Paul, Minnesota, and for the rest of his life MacArthur considered that city home. His father decided that MacArthur should attend the U.S. Military Academy at West Point, New York. Before he was accepted he had to take a competitive examination, and he later remembered how rigorously he had prepared for it: "I never worked harder in my life. It was a lesson I never forgot. Preparedness is the key to success and victory."

MacArthur passed the exam and entered West Point in 1899, when he was nineteen. During his years at the academy he had an excellent academic record; he also played baseball, managed the football team, and served as president of the student body during his senior year. At graduation in 1903 he won the rank of first captain, the school's highest military honor, and also was first in his class in academics.

The "Fighting Dude"

After graduation he was made second lieutenant of engineers, and he served briefly in the Philippines, then in San Francisco. In 1905 he was assigned to serve as an aide to his father, who had been appointed the U.S. Army's official observer of the war between Russia and Japan. The next year MacArthur returned to Washington to work as an aide to President Theodore Roosevelt, a friend of his father's. Over the next ten years, MacArthur served a number of different assignments. When the United States joined World War I (1914–18) in 1917, he was working in the office of the Army General Staff in Washington, D.C.

It was during World War I that MacArthur made his reputation—both for exceptional courage and for exceptional arrogance. In response to the military's need to recruit more men into the armed forces and to unite the country behind the war effort, MacArthur suggested the formation of a "Rainbow Division," which would be made up of National Guard volunteers from each state. MacArthur was assigned to lead this division and given the temporary rank of colonel.

In June 1918, when he was only thirty-eight years old, MacArthur was appointed brigadier general, and two months later he was given command of the Rainbow Division's 84th Infantry Brigade. He led his troops in several major battles in France, including those at St. Mihiel, Meuse-Argonne, and Sedan. MacArthur became famous both for his bravery (he earned seven Silver Stars as well as four other U.S. medals and nineteen honors from the other Allied countries) and for his "uniform," which went completely against army regulations. It consisted of riding breeches, a turtleneck sweater, a four-foot-long scarf, and a soft cap instead of a helmet. He also smoked his cigarettes in a long holder. Called the "Fighting Dude" by the troops, MacArthur was once taken prisoner by an American soldier who thought he must be a German because of his unusual uniform.

Between two wars

Returning to the United States in 1919, MacArthur was named superintendent of West Point— the youngest officer ever to hold that post. During his three years at the academy, he modernized the curriculum, reorganized the athletic program, and made other changes that allowed the school to double in size. In February 1922, he married a wealthy, divorced socialite named Henrietta Louise Cromwell Brooks, and in August of the same year he was assigned to serve in the Philippines.

After three years in the Philippines, MacArthur returned to the United States to command the army's 3rd Corps Area, stationed in Baltimore. In 1928, he was named president of the U.S. Olympic Committee and spent a summer in Amsterdam overseeing the games. Then he returned to the Philippines, but this time his wife did not accompany him; the following June, the two were divorced by mutual consent.

In the fall of 1930, MacArthur returned to Washington, D.C., and was named the army's chief of staff—the highest post in the U.S. military—by President Herbert Hoover. Only fifty years old, MacArthur attained the rank of four-star general. Only eight other generals in U.S. history had reached that rank. The country was in the midst of the Great Depression (1929–39; a period of sharp economic decline during which many businesses went bankrupt and many people were jobless) and there was not much extra money for military use; nevertheless, MacArthur managed to modernize and strengthen the army during his five years as chief of staff. The only controversy of his term occurred when he was accused of taking too personal a role in a troop action that ended the "Bonus March," a demonstration by impoverished World War I veterans demanding assistance from the government. MacArthur was accused of trying to make himself look good by personally appearing on the scene; in addition, it was said that the troops had used too much force against the veterans.

Advisor to the Philippines

MacArthur's next job was as a military advisor to the newly-formed Philippine Commonwealth, which was scheduled to become fully independent, but the United States would still be in charge of the country's defense. MacArthur's job was to create and train military forces for the Philippine government. One young officer who accompanied him on this assignment was Major Dwight D. Eisenhower (1890–1969; see entry), who would later achieve his own measure of greatness as commander of Allied forces in Europe during World War II.

In April 1937, MacArthur wed Jean Faircloth, a Tennessean he had met on the boat to the Philippines; he later described the marriage (which turned out to be long and happy) as "perhaps the smartest thing I have ever done." Later that year, MacArthur retired from the U.S. Army, remaining in the Philippines, and the couple's son, Arthur MacArthur III, was born in early 1938.

Trying to defend the Philippines

By the middle of 1941, Japan's aggressive actions in the Pacific region alarmed the American government. President Franklin D. Roosevelt recalled MacArthur from retirement and made him the head of all the U.S. Army forces in the Pacific area, including the entire army of the Philippines, which was immediately inducted into the U.S. Army. MacArthur quickly began preparing the forces in the Philippines, raising the number of soldiers from 22,000 to 180,000. These men, however, were mostly untrained troops.

On December 7, 1941, Japan bombed Pearl Harbor, taking everyone by surprise and destroying much of the U.S. Navy's fleet. The United States declared war on Japan and three days later Japan's allies, Germany and Italy, declared war on the United States. The United States joined the Allied powers that were working together to defeat Germany, Italy, and Japan.

Instead of making sure that the U.S. planes and other equipment at Clark Air Field in the Philippines were out of harm's way, MacArthur did nothing—apparently he believed that Japan would leave the Philippines alone. But nine days after Pearl Harbor, Japan struck the airfield, following their attack with a full-fledged invasion of the Philippines.

By Christmas, MacArthur and his friend Manuel Quezon, the president of the Philippines, were forced to abandon the country's capital, Manila. They took refuge at Corregidor, the island fortress at the entrance to Manila Bay. Meanwhile the combined U.S. and Filipino troops fought it out in the jungles of the Bataan peninsula. Soon it was clear that the Philippines could not be saved, and President Roosevelt ordered MacArthur to leave. With his family and a few staff members and officers, MacArthur escaped to Australia, traveling 560 miles by PT boat (a coastal patrol vessel), followed by a flight in a B-17 Flying Fortress airplane with the Japanese in pursuit. Before leaving the Philippines, MacArthur proclaimed "I shall return" (even though the U.S. government had recommended that he say "We shall return").

Determined to return

MacArthur felt that the United States broke its promise to protect the Philippines, and he was determined to rescue

Admiral Nimitz Leads in the Pacific

While General Douglas MacArthur led his troops to a "leapfrogging" victory in the South Pacific, the top officer in the U.S. Navy commanded Allied forces in the northern and eastern parts of the region. Admiral Chester Nimitz was a quiet, easygoing man with a big job.

Born in 1885 in Fredericksburg, Texas, Nimitz graduated from the U.S. Naval Academy at Annapolis, Maryland, in 1905. He served in the Philippines, and later became an expert on submarines. During World War I Nimitz was chief of staff of the Atlantic Submarine Force.

By the time World War II began, Nimitz had been promoted to rear admiral and was serving as chief of the navy's Bureau of Navigation. About ten days after the Japanese attack on Pearl Harbor, Nimitz took over command of the Pacific Fleet. He flew out to Hawaii and began rebuilding the fleet, which had been devastated by the attack. Nimitz was soon overseeing raids on the Marshall Islands, then on the Gilbert Islands. It seemed that despite the blow it had taken, the U.S. Navy was on the attack.

In an operation designed to protect Australia from possible Japanese invasion, Nimitz gathered together Allied forces for the Battle of the Coral Sea, which took place in early May 1942. This victory was followed by another one at Midway Island in June. During the next year, Nimitz's forces worked their way across the central Pacific, rooting out the Japanese from their island strongholds and pounding the Japanese navy. Finally the Allies achieved a decisive victory at Kwajalein Atoll in the Marshall Islands in February 1944.

In July, 1944 Nimitz met with President Franklin D. Roosevelt (1882–1945; see entry) and other military commanders to discuss MacArthur's wish to liberate the Philippines. Nimitz finally agreed with MacArthur that it was the right thing to do, and in October the Battle for Leyte Gulf took place. The Allies came out on top, and MacArthur was able to wade ashore as the returning victor.

Nimitz was promoted to five-star admiral in December 1944. The war ended with the Japanese surrender, which took place on September 2, 1945, aboard the USS *Missouri*. Nimitz was among the Allied officers who signed the treaty agreement. He left his Pearl Harbor command in November and the next month became the commander in chief for the U.S. Fleet. Two years later Nimitz retired from the military. He died in 1966.

the country from the Japanese. But first he had to convince the other Allied military commanders—who were inclined to focus first on the defeat of Germany—that conquering the Japanese should be a high priority. That done, he would have to convince those who thought American forces should bypass the Philippines on the way to attacking Japan.

Meanwhile, Australia was vulnerable to Japanese attack. Named Supreme Commander of the Southwest Pacific Area in April 1942, MacArthur prepared Australian and American troops for battle, and from October to December 1942 he led a campaign in New Guinea that kept the Japanese at bay. By 1943, the United States was sending more troops and airplanes to the Pacific. The War Department had divided the region into two theaters or areas of attack: Admiral Chester Nimitz (1885–1966; see sidebar on page 141) would lead the navy west across the central Pacific and toward Japan, while MacArthur and the army would move north from Australia.

"Leapfrogging" to victory

MacArthur used a unique "leapfrogging" strategy that proved highly successful. The strategy involved "hopping" from island to island, bypassing the places where enemy troops were waiting in large numbers, and attacking where they were least expected. In this way, MacArthur worked his way toward the Philippines—with Japan as the final goal—making eighty-seven amphibious landings (a joint action of land, sea, and air forces that invade from the seas) and minimizing casualties (deaths or wounding of his own soldiers).

Finally the Allies were ready to retake the Philippines, and MacArthur waded ashore with his troops at Leyte island in October 1944 and on the mainland at Luzon three months later. With his first landing he made a radio broadcast proclaiming, "People of the Philippines, I have returned," and he became an instant hero to his listeners. He was not such a hero, however, with some of his officers and soldiers. They felt that he wanted to keep all of the glory for himself.

To Japan for a new role

After the Allied forces cleared the Philippines of all remaining Japanese soldiers, they prepared to invade Japan.

MacArthur was named commander of all U.S. ground troops in the Pacific, while Nimitz commanded the naval forces. The plans were made unnecessary, however, when the United States dropped atomic bombs on the Japanese cities of Hiroshima and Nagasaki. On August 15, Japan surrendered to the Allies. MacArthur was promoted to Supreme Commander of the Allied Powers on August 15. He flew to Tokyo, where he received the Japanese surrender aboard the USS *Missouri* on September 2, 1945.

Immediately after the end of the war, MacArthur was made civilian administrator of occupied Japan. This important position involved helping the country recover from the devastating effects of war as well as encouraging a democratic form of government—instead of the type of government they had in place during the war, one headed by an emperor and dominated by the military. MacArthur arrived in Tokyo with no weapons but plenty of self-confidence. He set up his headquarters in the Dai Ichi Building in Tokyo. From there he issued various rules and regulations to disarm the country, restore the economy, begin land reform, and create and strengthen labor unions. Emperor Hirohito (1901–1989; see entry) was allowed to remain as a symbol of unity and tradition, but he was stripped of almost all of his power.

Although some viewed MacArthur as an almost dictatorial ruler who did not listen to criticism, most observers praised his evenhanded approach as well as the way he won the trust of the Japanese people. MacArthur himself felt that this was his most successful role and greatest accomplishment.

Back in the United States, MacArthur was mentioned as a possible presidential candidate for the 1948 election. He did not discourage his supporters, and was said to be quite disappointed when Thomas Dewey beat him for the Republican nomination.

A showdown with President Truman

After World War II, the country of Korea was divided into two countries, Communist North Korea and South Korea, which had an authoritarian (where power is concentrated in an authority that is not responsible to the people) government. The North Koreans wanted to reunite Korea under Communist rule, and on June 25, 1950, North Korean forces attacked South Korea. The United States was concerned about the spread of communism throughout Asia. President Harry S. Truman (1884–1975; see entry) placed MacArthur in charge of the U.S. troops in the region, directing him to protect South Korea. Soon he was made commander of the United Nations forces sent to help South Korea.

MacArthur's personal determination to fight communism led him to go against the advice of other military leaders and launch a bold strike against North Korea with an amphibious landing at Inchon in September 1950. His troops succeeded in pushing the enemy back across the 38th parallel (the line dividing North and South Korea), and they continued driving the North Koreans toward the Yalu River, which formed the boundary between North Korea and China. MacArthur ignored warnings that the Chinese might join the North Koreans in their struggle. The Chinese did join the fight, and the American and United Nations troops had to withdraw.

MacArthur asserted that instead of retreating, the United States should bomb strategic sites in China; he thought that to crush communism in Asia, they would have to crush China, the largest Communist country. But Truman and other western leaders disagreed. They were not ready to start another big war. MacArthur was unwilling to accept this judgment, and he made public his conflict with Truman over U.S. policy in Korea. Truman firmly believed that a military officer must not question the civilian leader of the United States, and therefore he relieved MacArthur of his command on April 11, 1950.

A hero goes home

A week later, MacArthur returned to the United States for the first time in fifteen years. He received a hero's welcome, with about 20,000 admirers waiting to greet him when his airplane landed. He made a speech before Congress, quoting a line from an old ballad, "Old soldiers never die, they just fade away": "And like the old soldier of that ballad, I now close my military career and just fade away—an old soldier who tried to do his duty as God gave him the light to see that duty."

MacArthur spent his remaining years living at the Waldorf Astoria Hotel in New York City with his wife. With the death of General George C. Marshall (1880–1959; see entry).in 1959, MacArthur became the army's top-ranking officer (just as his father had been earlier in the century), with the rank of General of the Army. He remained on active duty—though without assignment—until his death. MacArthur was buried in one of the old uniforms he'd worn during his days in the Pacific, adorned only (from among all the many decorations he had earned) with the U.S. and five-star insignias.

Where to Learn More

Books

Darby, Jean. *Douglas MacArthur*. Minneapolis, MN: Lerner, 1989.

Devaney, John. *Douglas MacArthur: Something of a Hero*. New York: Putnam's, 1979.

Finkelstein, Norman H. *The Emperor General: A Biography of Douglas MacArthur*. Minneapolis, MN: Dillon Press, 1989.

Perret, Geoffrey. *Old Soldiers Never Die: The Life of Douglas MacArthur*. New York: Random House, 1996.

Scott, Robert A. *Douglas MacArthur and the Century of War.* New York: Facts on File, 1997.

Wittner, Lawrence S., ed. *MacArthur.* Englewood Cliffs, NJ: Prentice-Hall, 1971.

Periodicals

"The Emperor: Douglas MacArthur." *U.S. News & World Report* (March 16, 1998): 54.

George C. Marshall

Born December 31, 1880
Uniontown, Pennsylvania
Died October 16, 1959
Washington, D.C.

American general and army chief
of staff from 1939 to 1945

I n describing the role that General George Marshall played in World War II, British prime minister Winston Churchill (1874–1975; see entry) called him "the true organizer of victory." Although he was neither as flashy nor as famous as military leaders like George Patton (1885–1945; see entry) and Douglas MacArthur (1880–1964; see entry), some historians compare Marshall favorably to the first U.S. president, George Washington. Like Washington, Marshall was a rare combination of soldier and statesman who believed strongly that in a democracy the military must be under civilian control. He also resembled Washington in his intelligence, integrity, quiet self-confidence, and moral authority. Marshall was a great organizer and a perceptive judge of people, qualities that served him well in his job as army chief of staff. He led the buildup of a very small, underequipped U.S. Army into a mighty fighting force. As secretary of state, Marshall led the effort to help Europe recover from the devastation of World War II.

George C. Marshall oversaw the buildup of U.S. military forces and helped plan war strategies and later served as secretary of state.

Following family traditions

Marshall came from an old Virginia family. He was a descendant of John Marshall, the third chief justice of the

Portrait: George C. Marshall. *(Reproduced by permission of The Library of Congress.)*

147

Supreme Court. Marshall noted in later years (as reported by Lance Morrow in *Smithsonian*, that he didn't approve of his father's frequent references to this fact, because he thought it was "about time for somebody else to swim for the family." A tall, skinny boy, Marshall developed an interest in outdoor activities. He decided to become a soldier after seeing how enthusiastically troops returning to his town from duty in the Philippines during the Spanish-American war (April to August 1898) were greeted and how well they were treated.

Several male members of Marshall's family, including his older brother Stuart, had attended the Virginia Military Institute (VMI). When Marshall heard Stuart—with whom he did not get along very well—telling their mother that he hoped George would not attend VMI, he made up his mind that was exactly what he would do. In a letter to the school's superintendent, Marshall's father wrote, "I send you my youngest son. He is bright, full of life and I believe he will get along well."

A young officer begins his career

Marshall earned good (though not excellent) grades at VMI and demonstrated that he could be a leader. He graduated in 1901 with the rank of first captain of his class (a high honor at the school). Just after he was commissioned as a second lieutenant in the army, Marshall married Elizabeth "Lily" Coles, a young woman several years older who had previously been courted by his brother. Lily stayed in the United States when Marshall went to serve his first assignment in the Philippines (which at that time was under the control of the United States), but she joined him at his second post in Oklahoma.

In 1907, Marshall graduated at the top of his class from the army's Infantry and Cavalry School at Fort Leavenworth, Kansas. Then he attended Staff College for a year, staying on as an instructor until 1911. After serving assignments in Massachusetts, Arkansas, and Texas, Marshall was assigned to the 13th Infantry in the Philippines, where he served as an aide to General Hunter Liggett. Returning to the United States, he became General J. Franklin Bell's aide. At this time Marshall was performing exceptionally well (one commanding officer even wrote in an evaluation that he would like to serve *under* this young junior officer) but was not progressing the way he thought he should be; as a result, he considered leaving the army.

Taking part in a world war

In 1917, however, the United States entered World War I (1914–1918; a war that started as a conflict between Austria-Hungary and Serbia and escalated into a global war involving thirty-two countries) and Marshall was called into action. Made a captain with the First Division, Marshall left on the first boatload of troops headed for France. There he worked in operations (the collecting and moving around of soldiers and equipment), quickly gaining a reputation as a brilliant organizer of men and supplies. He served as chief planner of the St. Mihiel battle and supervised the transfer of 600,000 soldiers and 900,000 tons of supplies (including 2,700 guns) into the Meuse-Argonne area, where another battle took place.

During the war, Marshall had earned the temporary rank of colonel, but when the war ended he went back to his former rank of captain. From 1919 to 1924 he served as an aide to General John J. Pershing, the army's chief of staff (highest ranking officer). Marshall had met and impressed the general during the war when he had angrily defended his superior officer, whom Pershing had criticized. Marshall's friends predicted that his career was doomed after this incident, but in fact Pershing liked Marshall's honesty and loyalty and wanted him to join his staff.

Between two wars

Marshall helped Pershing with such tasks as drawing up legislation and preparing reports on World War I, and he took part in many high-level meetings with government leaders. These years gave him experience in dealing with politicians and other officials—lessons that would serve him well in later years.

Marshall was sent to Tianjin, China, in 1924, where he served as the executive officer of the 15th Infantry for three years. In 1927, after Marshall had returned to the United States and was teaching at the Army War College, his wife died suddenly. In an effort to overcome his grief Marshall threw himself with even more vigor into his new assignment. He was soon made assistant commandant of the Infantry School at Fort Benning, Georgia, where he was in charge of training.

The "Benning Revolution"

This was an important period in Marshall's career, because he was able to play a major role in shaping the army of the future. He oversaw what came to be known as the "Benning Revolution." Faculty members were reassigned, manuals rewritten, and curriculum redesigned to emphasize the new *mobile* warfare (conducted with tanks, airplanes, and movable weapons and covering a wide area of ground) that modern soldiers would have to wage. Marshall taught his students not to rely on the "school solution" or standard response to problems, but to be bold and innovative.

During Marshall's reign, about 150 future generals came through the school as students, and fifty more served as instructors, including such famous World War II figures as generals Omar Bradley, Joseph W. Stilwell, Matthew Ridgway, and Walter Bedell Smith. Marshall entered the names of the most promising officers in a "little black book" which was to become famous a decade later when it influenced the leadership of the wartime army.

In 1930 Marshall married Katherine Tupper Brown, a widow with three children (one of whom died in 1944 while fighting in World War II) and a former Shakespearean actress. General Pershing served as best man at the wedding. During the 1930s Marshall served a number of assignments, including several as director of Civilian Conservation Corps (a program President Franklin D. Roosevelt created to improve the environment while giving unemployed people jobs) camps in Georgia, Florida, South Carolina, and Washington. By now he had been promoted to colonel.

Called to an important job

As the 1930s ended, war was looming in Europe and Asia as Germany and Japan moved aggressively to expand their empires. In the summer of 1938, President Roosevelt called Marshall to Washington to head the War Department's War Plans Division, and promoted him to major general. Only three months later, he was made deputy chief of staff of the army. Marshall made a strong impression on Roosevelt when, during a White House conference, he respectfully but decisively disagreed with the president on a policy issue. Those present told Marshall he'd committed political suicide, but in fact Roosevelt—like Pershing many years earlier—decided that Marshall's honesty made him even more valuable.

In the spring of 1939, Marshall was nominated for the chief of staff position, and after serving for four months as acting chief of staff, he was sworn in on September 1—the same day Germany launched World War II by invading Poland. Marshall had now to begin the awesome task of getting the army and Army Air Corps ready for combat, in case the United States should enter the war in the next few years. As it was, the army's size (a little less than 200,000 soldiers) was pitiful, putting it in the same rank as the much smaller countries of Portugal and Bulgaria. Its weapons were outmoded and its bases were neglected.

Marshall lobbied Congress to send more money the army's way, even as others—such as the navy and the Lend-Lease Program (a program that allowed the United States to send troops and supplies to help the countries fighting Germany)—were competing for the same funds. He convinced Congress to approve a draft (requiring all qualified young men to serve terms of military service) and funding that boosted the army's ability to train and equip recruits as well as possible. One of Marshall's most important moves was to change the laws regarding retirement so that older officers could be removed and younger, more capable ones could be rapidly promoted. This practice offended some of Marshall's old colleagues, but he believed that the modern army needed new blood.

Playing a crucial role in the war

With America's entry into World War II (on December 7, 1941) Marshall put his skills into high gear, becoming one of the leading planners of Allied strategy. The Allies were the countries who fought against the Axis countries—Germany, Italy, and Japan—during World War II. Great Britain, the United States, and the Soviet Union were the primary Allied powers. Marshall was present at all the important conferences at which the Allies decided their next moves, including those at Casablanca (Morocco) and Tehran (Iran) in 1943, Quebec in 1944, and Malta, Yalta, and Potsdam in 1945. Marshall often demonstrated his intelligence and analytical ability by inviting forty or fifty reporters to ask him questions one after

Facts About the Normandy Invasion: D-Day, June 6, 1944

History's Largest Amphibious Landing

- The invasion involved ground, air, and naval forces that had been gathering in England for months. More than 4,400 ships and landing craft were used to carry 154,000 troops (50,000 would make the initial assault on the beaches) and 1,500 tanks to the area. In the air were 11,000 fighter planes, bombers, transports, and gliders to provide protection for the ground troops.

Where It Took Place

- Troops crossed the English Channel (the body of water that lies between England and France) to land on a 50-mile stretch of beaches on the Normandy region of northern France. The U.S. First Army landed on Utah and Omaha beaches to the west, while the British Second Army landed on Gold, Juno, and Sword beaches to the east.

Who Took Part

- Forty-seven Allied division took part in the invasion. Of these, twenty-one were American and the rest were British, Canadian, and Polish. French, Italian, Belgian, Czech, and Dutch troops also fought. All of them were under the supreme command of General Dwight D. Eisenhower (1890–1969; see entry). General Bernard Montgomery (1887–1976; see entry) headed up the overall ground forces, with General Omar Bradley in charge of the American First Army and General Sir Miles Dempsey in charge of the British Second Army.

What About the Germans?

- Altogether there were about sixty Germany divisions in France and the Low Countries (the Netherlands, Belgium, and Luxembourg). In the area in which Allied troops would invade, there were nine Germany infantry divisions and one tank division.

A Deception Plan

- The Germans knew the Allies were planning an invasion, but they thought they would land on the Calais coast, not on the beaches of Normandy. In order to fool the Germans, the Allies had stationed

another, then giving a long response in which each question was answered and all issues were tied together in a logical way.

Along with the secretary of war, Henry Stimson, Marshall was in favor of a "Germany First" approach to winning the war in Europe. He thought the Allies should regain France (which the Germans had invaded in May 1940) and then press

Soldiers help another wounded soldier ashore during the Normandy invasion. *(Reproduced by permission of AP/Wide World Photos.)*

sion. Originally it was scheduled for June 4, but stormy weather forced Eisenhower to postpone the invasion until June 6. But even before the troops landed, British and American paratroopers dropped into France behind German lines to capture bridges, roads, railroads, and airfields the Allies would need for their advance.

The Invasion Begins

- At 6:30 A.M. on June 6, the Allied troops began their landing. The well-entrenched Germans fought back hard, and casualties (wounded or killed) were high. The Americans who landed at Omaha Beach were the worst hit, suffering 2,000 casualties, whereas those at Utah Beach lost only 210. Allied D-Day casualties totaled about 15,000, which was about the same for the German side. The Allies moved inland and by the end of the month German field marshal Erwin Rommel (1891–1944; see entry) would report that the Germans had lost 28 generals, 354 field commanders, and about 250,000 men.

some landing craft off Calais, and they had made up a fake unit called the First United States Army Group, which was supposedly commanded by General George S. Patton (1885–1945; see entry).

The Weather Interferes

- Planners used weather and tide forecasts to plan the exact date of the inva-

on to attack Germany. But the British plan—starting in North Africa, then driving through Italy and finally to Germany—won out. Meanwhile, Marshall continued to push for a cross-channel (the English Channel, which separates England and France) attack on the Germans, and at the end of 1943 the rest of the Allied leadership finally agreed with him.

Roosevelt makes a decision

"Operation Overlord" called for the Allies to land troops and equipment on the beaches of the Normandy area in northern France. The attack was scheduled for June 4, 1944 (it didn't actually take place until June 6, 1944), and nicknamed D-Day. Roosevelt had to decide who would direct the campaign. Marshall seemed a good choice, and he had certainly earned the honor. Roosevelt asked Marshall whom he should choose, but Marshall refused to promote himself, even though such an assignment would surely be the crowning achievement in his military career. He left the decision to Roosevelt, who finally chose General Dwight D. Eisenhower (1890–1969; see entry), telling Marshall, "I did not feel I could sleep at ease if you were not in Washington."

D-Day was successful, and by May 1945 the Germans had surrendered; the war continued until August, when the Japanese surrendered as well. Marshall retired in November, but only a few days later, President Truman (who had succeeded Roosevelt upon the latter's death in April 1945) called him to serve as a special envoy to China. The ruling Nationalist Party (also called the Kuomintang), under Chiang Kai-Shek (1887–1975; see entry), and the Communists led by Mao Tsetung were vying for control of the country, although a full-scale civil war had not yet erupted. Marshall was able to halt the hostilities only temporarily, and finally had to return to the United States in defeat.

The Marshall Plan

Once again President Truman recognized Marshall's abilities and experience by appointing him secretary of state in 1947. In June of that year, Marshall made a momentous speech at Harvard University's commencement (graduation) ceremony, proposing that the United States provide aid (in the form of both money and supplies) to help the European nations recover from the war. Pointing out that economic and political chaos in those countries could bring about yet another war or wars, Marshall stated the new plan would be "directed not against any country or doctrine, but against hunger, poverty, despotism and chaos. Its purpose shall be the revival of a working economy in the world so as to permit the emergence of political and social conditions in which free institutions can exist."

Through the European Recovery Act—the formal name for what was commonly known as the "Marshall Plan"—sixteen countries received $13 billion in assistance. Before leaving his position in 1949, Marshall also helped to lay the foundation for the North Atlantic Treaty Organization (NATO), an alliance set up to shield Europe from the threat of the Soviet Union's expansion plans.

One more job to do

After a brief stint as head of the American Red Cross, President Truman again summoned Marshall. The Korean War had started and there was a need for strong leadership. Truman appointed Marshall secretary of defense, and his accomplishments included enlarging the army, increasing weapons production, and helping to put into action the NATO agreements that had been drawn up when he was secretary of state.

Marshall's fifty-year career in public service came to an end on September 1, 1951, when he retired for the last time. A five-star general, he remained on active status, the highest-ranking officer in the U.S. military. In 1953, Marshall was awarded the Nobel Peace Prize for his efforts to assist in Europe's recovery, becoming the first member of the military to receive the prize. In his acceptance speech, he referred to the military's role in bringing about and maintaining peace: "There had been considerable comment over the awarding of the Nobel Peace Prize to a soldier. I'm afraid this does not seem quite so remarkable to me as it quite evidently does to others."

Marshall refused to write any memoirs, which he considered a self-centered activity, but he did agree to be interviewed by historians from the Marshall Foundation. After suffering a stroke in early 1959, he died in October of that year and was buried in Arlington National Cemetery.

Where to Learn More

Books

Cray, Ed. *General of the Army.* New York: Norton, 1990.

Pogue, Forrest C. *George C. Marshall,* 4 vols. New York: Viking Press, 1963-1987.

Stoler, Mark. *George C. Marshall.* New York: Macmillan, 1989.

Periodicals

Morrow, Lance. "George C. Marshall: The Last Great American?" *Smithsonian* (August 1997): 104.

Mulvoy, Thomas F., Jr. "George Marshall's Influence Was Felt Through World War II and on Into the Cold War." *Knight-Ridder News Service* (August 25, 1994): 0825K2928.

"The Straight Shooter: George Marshall." *U.S. News & World Report* (Special Report: The Strategists of War) 124, No. 10: 64.

Bernard Montgomery

Born November 17, 1887
London, England
Died March 24, 1976
Alton, England

British field marshal

Considered by some historians the greatest British general of all time, Bernard Montgomery was the best known and most successful officer to lead British troops during World War II. He transformed the demoralized 8th Army into a skilled fighting machine that defeated German field marshal Erwin Rommel's (1891–1944; see entry) fierce Afrika Korps in the North African desert. Although he was a hero to many people, he was also a controversial figure; it is said that he possessed a difficult personality—his bluntness, egotism, and stubborn streak often got him into trouble with his military colleagues. Whatever Montgomery's reputation with fellow officers, his careful planning and desire to minimize casualties (dead and wounded) made him popular with the soldiers who served under him.

Bernard Montgomery led his troops to decisive victories in North Africa and contributed to Allied successes in Sicily, Italy, and France.

Launching a military career

Montgomery was the fourth of nine children born to a clergyman and his wife. His mother was stern and too busy with her church work to devote much time to her children. Montgomery later recalled that "If I could not be seen any-

Portrait: Bernard Montgomery. *(Reproduced by permission of AP/Wide World Photos.)*

157

where, she would say, 'Go and find out what Bernard is doing and tell him to stop it.'" When Montgomery was two years old the family moved to Tasmania, an Australian island in the south Pacific Ocean, where his father had been appointed bishop. After their return to London in 1901, Montgomery attended St. Paul's School.

In 1906, already planning a military career, Montgomery entered the Royal Military Academy at Sandhurst, where he was better at sports and making mischief than at academics. During his last years at school, however, he improved his grades and in 1908 he graduated thirty-sixth in a class of 150. Commissioned a lieutenant, Montgomery wanted to serve in India (which was then a colony of England) where he could support himself well on little pay, but his grades had not been high enough to earn him a spot in the Indian army. Instead, he signed up with the Royal Warwickeshire Regiment, which had a battalion in India.

The influence of World War I

After several years in India, Montgomery returned to England in 1912. When World War I (1914–18) began in 1914, he was immediately called into battle in France. Only two months later, he was shot in the chest. His life was saved by another soldier who had come to help him and was himself shot; the dead man's body fell over Montgomery and shielded him from taking further bullets. Montgomery was assumed dead for several hours, but finally he was able to indicate that he was alive. He was rescued and taken to a hospital in England.

Promoted to captain and awarded the Distinguished Service Order, Montgomery returned to the fighting in France in 1916. He was a staff officer for the remaining two years of the war, serving as a lieutenant colonel in command of the 17th Battalion Royal Fusiliers (fusiliers are muskets—the guns this battalion once carried).

Montgomery's experiences during World War I strongly affected his attitude toward the military—especially how officers should treat the troops serving under them. He had witnessed suffering and death that he considered unnecessary, and he had seen officers sacrifice soldiers needlessly in hopeless battles. Thus he believed in careful, detailed planning before sending troops to fight, and in making sure that the soldiers were extremely well trained and equipped.

He also believed that explaining to soldiers the importance of certain decisions and battles helped make them feel good about what they were doing. To this end he encouraged personal contact between officers and their men. Montgomery believed that commanders who remained distant from their troops could not command as much loyalty and dedication as those who saw and talked to as many soldiers as possible. In later years, Montgomery would be criticized for refusing to begin battles before his plans, troops, and equipment were ready, but those fighting under his command appreciated his concern for their lives.

Between wars

In the years between World War I and World War II, Montgomery served in a number of locations around the world, rising steadily through the ranks of the army. After serving with the occupation forces in Germany, Montgomery attended the army's Staff College at Camberley, then spent some years in Ireland. In 1926 he became an instructor at the Staff College, and in 1929 he was assigned to head the committee to rewrite the army's manual on infantry training. Montgomery ruffled some feathers when he ignored the other committee members' opinions and wrote the manual himself.

When he was thirty-nine years old, Montgomery shed his bachelor status and married Betty Carver, the widow of an officer who had died in World War I. The marriage was happy and produced a son, David, born in 1928. After ten years, however, Betty died from an insect bite. Montgomery was devastated by her death, but reacted by throwing himself even more deeply into his work.

Another world war begins

During the 1930s, Montgomery served in India, Egypt, and Palestine (where he helped in the effort to keep peace between Arabs and Jews). By 1939—as war loomed on the horizon—he was in command of the army's Third Division, one of the few units ready for combat. The war began in September 1939 after Germany invaded Poland. In the sum-

Admiral Mountbatten: Allied Commander in Southeast Asia

While Montgomery dominated the scene in North Africa and Europe, another British officer was making a name for himself in another part of the world. As supreme commander of Allied Forces in Southeast Asia, Admiral Louis Mountbatten led his troops into several successful offensives against Japan.

A member of the British royal family, Mountbatten was the great-grandson of Queen Victoria and Prince Albert. Born in 1900, he joined the British navy and served as a midshipman during World War I, specializing in the use of signals. Just before the outbreak of World War II he was assigned to command the Fifth Destroyer Fleet.

Mountbatten took the helm of the battleship HMS *Kelly* in August 1939 and was soon involved in many clashes with German submarines. In the spring of 1940, the *Kelly* was almost sunk several times by torpedoes from German airplanes. Eventually, in fighting off the Greek island of Crete, the ship was sunk and Mountbatten almost drowned.

After a short period as commander of the aircraft carrier *Illustrious,* Mountbatten was named by Prime Minister Winston Churchill (1874–1965; see entry) to become an advisor on combined operations, which put him in charge of the Commandos (British units that staged raids against German positions in Norway and France). After the United States entered the war at the end of 1941, military leaders began to talk about an eventual invasion of France, and Mountbatten's experience in conducting amphibious landings (made by combined land, air, and naval forces who attack from the sea) became valuable.

In March 1942, Mountbatten was made chief of combined operations and promoted to the rank of vice admiral. In August, Mountbatten oversaw the raid on the German position at Dieppe, France. This mission was a great failure—3,336 of the 5,000 men who took part were killed—but it did provide crucial information that helped in the planning of the Normandy invasion, which would take place in June 1944.

mer of 1940 Germany invaded France. Montgomery was sent as part of the British Expeditionary Force sent to help fight off a German invasion. The campaign was not successful, and the British troops had to be evacuated from Dunkirk, on the northern shore of France. France surrendered to the Germans on June 22.

In 1943 Mountbatten was transferred to another part of the world, becoming Supreme Commander of Allied Forces in Southeast Asia, where, said Churchill, "a young and vigorous mind" was needed. The Japanese had overtaken the country of Burma (now Myanmar), and the Allied troops stationed in India were suffering both from low spirits and from a number of tropical diseases. They felt ignored and called themselves the "Forgotten Army."

Like Montgomery, Mountbatten knew that personal attention from high-level commanders could lift the men's spirits, so he began to visit as many units as possible, trying to convince the troops that their role was important and appreciated. Meanwhile, U.S. leaders were pushing for an invasion of Burma, which was a key strategic location because of its nearness to China. Mountbatten took charge of the invasion, and by July 1945 the Allies had recaptured Burma.

The next month, two atomic bombs were dropped on Japan, and the war ended with the official Japanese surrender in September. Mountbatten soon received the surrender of all Japanese forces in southeast Asia.

After the war, Mountbatten (who was named Earl Mountbatten of Burma in 1947) became viceroy of India, which was still a British colony. He was involved in the negotiations that led to India's independence in 1947 (as well as the establishment of Pakistan, which broke off from India to become a separate country). Mountbatten served as governor-general of India until 1948, when he returned to England to rejoin the navy.

Over the next several decades, Mountbatten served in various command positions in the British navy. From 1959 to 1965 he was chief of the United Kingdom Defense Staff and chairman of the Chiefs of Staff Committee. When he retired in 1965, Mountbatten had reached the rank of admiral of the fleet. While on holiday in Ireland in 1979, he was killed by members of the Irish Republican Army (a group that often uses terrorism to protest Great Britain's presence in northern Ireland) who had nothing against Mountbatten personally but wanted to show that no one was immune.

England was now in grave danger of invasion by the German forces, so Montgomery was assigned to lead the 5th Corps in protecting the coastal Dorset and Hampshire regions. Instead of following the conventional military tactic of concentrating only on the beach areas, Montgomery spread his troops out to a variety of locations, using the double-decker buses favored by tourists to transport them. Meanwhile, he focused on training and rigorous physical fitness to keep his men ready for possible attack.

Even though his abrasive personality and arrogance had made him unpopular with some people, Montgomery's skills and experience were noted by his superior officers. By December 1941, he had been made a lieutenant general and put in command of the whole South East Command.

Fighting Rommel in the desert

One of the places in which the Germans had established a stronghold was North Africa, where the Afrika Korps under Field Marshal Erwin Rommel (1891–1944; see entry) threatened to take the strategically important Suez area of Egypt. The British 8th Army had been fighting Rommel's troops in the desert and were exhausted and demoralized. Looking for a new commander for the 8th Army, Prime Minister Winston Churchill (1874–1965; see entry) considered Montgomery but ultimately chose General "Strafer" Gott. But when Gott was killed in a plane crash on his way to his new job, Montgomery was assigned to head the 8th Army.

Arriving in northern Egypt, Montgomery quickly set out to improve the spirits of his troops. One of his first steps was to adopt a distinctive hat, first an Australian bush or slouch hat, and finally the black beret he wore for the rest of the war. Montgomery claimed the beret was "worth two divisions" because it made him immediately recognizable to his troops during his daily visits to their units.

Montgomery left much of the detailed battle planning to his staff—especially his trusted chief of staff, Francis de Guingand—and concentrated instead on building up his men's fighting spirit. He told them: "Here we will stand and fight; there can be no further withdrawal....we will stand and fight *here*. If we can't stay here alive, then let us stay here dead."

Montgomery's troops adopted his determination. They won a decisive victory against Rommel's troops at Alam Halfa in late August and early September. In October his forces fought the battle of El Alamein where Montgomery cemented his reputation as a great commander. After twelve days of fierce fighting, the 8th Army emerged victorious and chased the

Afrika Korps across the desert as far as Tunisia, a distance of 2,000 miles. Montgomery had proved his skills in organizing, training, and motivating troops, and his efforts were formally recognized when England's King George VI knighted him.

Military victories and personality conflicts

The battles in Sicily and Italy that followed the successful North African campaign were somewhat less glorious for Montgomery, for they exposed more of his weaknesses. In Sicily, he was annoyed to be given a lesser role in the fighting. In addition, he did not want to work alongside General George S. Patton (1885–1945; see entry) of the United States, who also had a reputation as being difficult and overbearing. In Italy, Montgomery came into conflict with U.S. general Mark Clark when Montgomery's forces were supposed to meet up with Clark's forces to launch a combined attack. Clark accused Montgomery of moving slowly so that Clark's forces would have to bear the brunt of the fighting.

In December 1943, even before the Italian campaign was over, Montgomery was called away to take part in planning for the Normandy invasion, code-named Operation Overlord (also called D-Day). In this invasion the Allies hoped to get a foothold on the northern shores of France and then drive the Germans out of France and back into Germany. The D-Day landing took place on June 6, 1944, with Montgomery in charge of all land forces and American general Dwight D. Eisenhower (1890–1969; see entry) in overall command.

An important role in the Normandy invasion

During the Normandy battle, Montgomery demonstrated his usual energy, organizational skills, and ability to cut to the core of problems. Once again, he worked hard on bolstering his troops' morale; one of the ways he did this was to travel around Normandy during and after the initial invasion to meet with the soldiers. It is said that he was personally seen by as many as a million men, whose lives he promised not to waste and whom he encouraged to have faith in an eventual victory.

When the initial phase of the successful Normandy invasion was over and the Allies prepared to move across France toward Germany, the command structure changed.

Bernard Montgomery (r.) headed the land forces for the D-Day invasion. Here he is en route to Normandy with Bertram Ramsey (l.), head of the naval forces for D-Day, and Dwight D. Eisenhower (c.), commander in chief of the operation.
(Reproduced by permission of AP/Wide World Photos)

Eisenhower stepped in to command the land forces directly, while Montgomery was assigned to head the 21st Army Group (part of the Normandy invasion forces), which included one British and one Canadian army. Meanwhile, Montgomery had been made a field marshal, the highest rank in the British army.

Clashing with the high command

Montgomery continued to have difficulty cooperating with his Allied colleagues, including—and most dangerously—Eisenhower. While Eisenhower favored a "broad front" approach to moving the troops forward, Montgomery pushed him to adopt a "single thrust" approach.

In September, Montgomery's plan, nicknamed Operation Market Garden, was to land Allied troops behind the northernmost section of Germany's front line, and create a gap through which more troops could pour in and surround the

German army from behind. The troops landed behind Germany's line and faced stronger-than-expected resistance. The operation was a failure. More than 5,000 men were killed or taken prisoner.

Then came the Battle of the Bulge, which took place in the Ardennes region of Belgium in December. In a last desperate attempt to gain some ground, the Germans had managed to push the Allies back along one portion of the front, creating a "bulge" in the line. Eisenhower was forced to put two American units that had been caught above the northern "bulge" under Montgomery's command. In a press conference held after the Allied victory, Montgomery implied that he had rescued the Americans and had been solely responsible for cleaning up a real mess. Montgomery would have been in even worse trouble with Eisenhower over this if not for the efforts of his chief of staff de Guingand to soothe the American general's temper.

The end of the war and beyond

Montgomery's troops took part in the Allied advance across northern Europe, liberating the Netherlands and finally driving into Germany. On May 4, 1945, Montgomery accepted the surrender of 500,000 Germans. The remaining German forces surrendered to the Allies on May 7. The war in Europe was over, and Montgomery took command of Great Britain's Army of Occupation in Germany. (An occupation army takes control of the conquered country and oversees its transition into peacetime.)

In early 1946, Montgomery was made viscount of El Alamein. He was appointed chief of the Imperial General Staff, and stayed in that position until 1948. Then he became chairman of the Western European Union's (with representatives from Great Britain, the Netherlands, France, Belgium, and Luxembourg) Commanders in Chief Committee. From 1951 to 1958, Montgomery served as deputy supreme allied commander in Europe for the North Atlantic Treaty Organization (NATO)—set up to protect Europe from Communist aggression—in charge of training, equipping, and integrating NATO forces.

Montgomery retired in 1958 and went to live with his son David at Isington Mill in Alton, Hampshire, where he worked on his memoirs. He died in 1976 and was buried in a country churchyard near his home.

Where to Learn More

Books

Hamilton, Nigel. *Monty*, 3 vols. 1981–1986. New York: Random House, 1996.

Howarth, T.E.B., ed. *Monty at Close Quarters*. New York: Hippocrene Books, 1985.

Lewin, Ronald. *Montgomery as Military Commander*. New York: Stein and Day, 1971.

Thompson, R. W. *The Montgomery Legend*. New York: Ballantine Books, 1967.

Benito Mussolini

Born July 29, 1883
Predappio, Italy
Died April 28, 1945
Milan, Italy

Fascist dictator of Italy from 1922 to 1943

During his two decades as dictator of Italy, Benito Mussolini created a regime still remembered for stripping its citizens of most rights and freedom and for violently punishing those who resisted his government. Although Mussolini's power (as well as his life) came to an end in the middle of World War II, he played a major role in the conflict through his alliance with Adolf Hitler (1889–1945; the leader of Germany from 1934–1945; see entry). Hitler modeled parts of his own dictatorship after Mussolini's, and the two leaders formed what they termed an "Axis" to oppose the Allied forces (the major Allied powers were Great Britain, the United States, and the Soviet Union).

A rebellious young man

At the time of Mussolini's birth, most people in Italy were poor. The country had only recently been joined together from many different independent states into one country ruled by a king. A few rich people owned most of the land, and the poor people worked the fields for meager wages and food. But this work didn't last all year, and people were suffering and unhappy with the way their country was governed.

After taking control of the government and naming himself dictator, Benito Mussolini sought to return Italy to the glory it had known during the Roman Empire. He formed a close friendship with and was a military ally of Germany's dictator, Adolf Hitler.

Portrait: Benito Mussolini. *(Reproduced by permission of AP/Wide World Photos.)*

Mussolini's father, Alessandro, was a blacksmith and an atheist (someone who does not believe in God) with strong ideas about social injustice. He believed that poor people should rebel against those in charge in order to improve their lives. Mussolini's mother, a schoolteacher, was a devout Catholic who wanted her children to succeed in life and thought that education was the best path to success.

Mussolini's parents named him after Benito Juarez, a Mexican revolutionary leader, and as he grew he seemed to follow the example of his rebellious namesake. He was aggressive and stubborn; he didn't want to do what the teachers told him to do, and because he bullied other children he had few friends. When he attended a Catholic boarding school, Mussolini noticed that the poor students were treated differently than the richer ones, and this angered him. He started thinking about revolution, and he also started working on his public speaking skills.

Becoming a Socialist leader

Despite his unhappiness in school, Mussolini got good grades and, at his mother's insistence, he qualified as a teacher. He didn't like teaching, though, and in 1902 he left home to work in Switzerland (the lack of jobs in Italy made this a common choice for young Italian men). While in Switzerland Mussolini was arrested for vagrancy (homelessness), and he spent some time in jail. After that traumatic experience, he joined a group of socialists. Socialism is a political system in which land and factories are owned collectively by society or by the government. Socialists believe government should control the distribution of goods and services. Mussolini began working for the rights of Italian workers by writing articles about the problems they faced. He attempted to organize the workers to rise up against the authorities.

Mussolini returned to Italy in 1904 to perform the two years of military duty that all young Italian men were required to serve. When that term was finished, he spent a few years in Austria, where he worked on the staff of a newspaper. He returned to Italy to become the editor of a newspaper called *La Lotta di Classe* (*The Class Struggle*) and the secretary of his local Socialist Party.

In 1910, Mussolini married Rachele Guidi, who also came from a poor family. The couple had four children, and Rachele remained a devoted wife throughout Mussolini's life despite his affairs with other women. He even fathered a child with one of his mistresses.

Italy went to war against Turkey in 1911. Mussolini was very much opposed to this war, and he was imprisoned for spreading propaganda (pamphlets and other material intended to persuade people to adopt a certain viewpoint) in favor of peace. Now the editor of a publication called *Avanti!* (*Forward!*), Mussolini built a reputation as a strong Socialist leader. He talked about the need for workers to unite into one powerful "fasci" or bundle—and this is where the idea that would grow into fascism had its start.

A whole new philosophy

When World War I (1914–1918; a war that began as a conflict between Austria-Hungary and Serbia and escalated into a global war involving thirty-two nations) started, Mussolini surprised and shocked his Socialist friends by reversing his usual stance on war. He said that Italy should join the fight on the side of the Allies (the United States, Great Britain, France, and the Soviet Union). Perhaps he thought that if Italy went to war its government would collapse, so that the workers could bring about their revolution. In any case, the Socialists believed in neutrality (not taking sides) and they expelled Mussolini from the party.

Mussolini now started his own newspaper, *Il Papolo d'Italia* (*The People of Italy*) with the help of some new supporters, who were capitalists (those who believe that property and means of production such as land, factories, and labor should be privately owned, and that competition should determine the price of goods and services) and who agreed with his prowar opinions. The Italian government did join the Allies during World War I and Mussolini served in the Italian army for seventeen months, until he was wounded during grenade training.

The end of World War I brought more unrest to Italy. The Allies had won the war, and many Italians had given their lives to help bring about that victory. The people of Italy were disappointed, though, with how little their country had gained from their sacrifice; they were especially unhappy about their weak economy.

The Fascist Party takes root

Meanwhile, Mussolini's views were almost the reverse of those he'd held as a younger man. He and his followers wanted to take advantage of the mood of dissatisfaction that dominated their country and take over the Italian government. In 1919, they joined with some other conservative groups to form the *Fasci di Combattimento* (Union for Struggle or Fighting Leagues), which eventually became the Fascist Party. Mussolini organized squads of black-shirted young men, most of them war veterans, who used violent force against people with differing opinions. They became an even more powerful force when they put an end to a large workers' strike.

Mussolini was becoming more and more captivated by the idea of personal power and less concerned about the rights of workers. He began to envision himself as a supreme ruler or dictator. In 1921, Mussolini won a seat in the Italian parliament (the branch of the government that makes laws). His supporters continued to use violence to terrorize their opponents, particularly Socialists and Communists, and the government did little to stop them.

By 1922, all of the social unrest and public fears that the Communists or Socialists might actually take over the country created a mood of anarchy (a state of lawlessness brought about by a lack of governmental control) in Italy. Then, claiming that someone had to bring order to the country, Mussolini and his Fascists threatened to "March on Rome." Attempting to avoid a complete takeover by the Fascists, Italy's King Victor Emmanuel III invited Mussolini to become the country's prime minister. The March on Rome turned into a celebration for all those who supported the Fascists.

"Il Duce"

When Mussolini became prime minister (and at thirty-nine, he was the youngest leader in Italian history) he had widespread support, even from those who held more liberal views than he did but who feared complete political breakdown. He was given the nickname "Il Duce" (pronounced ill doo-chay which means the leader). Mussolini used his knowledge of journalism and the power of propaganda to create a public image of himself as a strong leader who could solve all of Italy's problems. The armed gangs of "black shirts" who served as his personal army were always ready to punish those who opposed him, but there were few who did.

Within a few years, Mussolini had used his very effective propaganda and the threat of physical terror to build up his power so much that he could declare himself independent of parliament and responsible only to the king (who was a popular figure but had no real power). By 1926, Mussolini had become a dictator. He dissolved the parliamentary system and all political parties, took control of the press, and put himself in charge of the military and most of the government ministries. "Il Duce" demanded absolute obedience from everyone, and anyone who resisted would soon be crushed.

Mussolini's goal was to make Italy as great as it had been during the days of the ancient Roman Empire, when its reach had extended far beyond its national borders. He set about improving roads and buildings, building up Italy's army and navy, and trying to increase its industrial strength. Mussolini's experience as a journalist served him well as he used all available media to publicize his goals.

Just as the early Roman rulers had expanded their empire, Mussolini wanted to conquer other nations. To do this, he started a war with Ethiopia in 1935. His successful invasion of this East African country cost Italy a lot of money and many lives. It also made Mussolini unpopular with other nations; in particular, the League of Nations (an international organization made up of nations working for world peace) opposed Italy's actions.

An alliance with Hitler

Meanwhile, Mussolini had an admirer in Germany. Adolf Hitler's political ideas (especially the use of violence to reach his goals) were close to Mussolini's. Even before he came to power, Hitler had admired Mussolini's Fascist dictatorship and had borrowed some of his phrases and symbols for his own speeches and propaganda. Hitler invited Mussolini to visit Germany, and the Italian leader was impressed by the military discipline and splendor of Hitler's regime.

The two leaders became allies not only because they thought alike but also because they had isolated themselves from the rest of the world. In 1936, Germany and Italy formed an alliance that was known as the "Axis"; this term came from Mussolini's reference in a speech to the need for the European powers to work together around a common axis. Soon Mussolini put into place some of the same anti-Jewish laws (even though he had never opposed Jews before and had many Jewish friends and supporters) that Hitler had imposed in Germany. Hitler and Mussolini became even closer partners in 1939, when they signed the "Pact of Steel" in which each nation agreed to protect the other from aggression.

Getting involved in World War II

As Hitler's forces moved across their own borders and conquered other countries (such as Austria and Czechoslovakia), it was clear that another world war was looming on the horizon. Even though Mussolini had proclaimed that "the prestige of nations is determined absolutely by their military glories and armed power," he knew that Italy's military power was not great and that his country was unprepared for war. When Germany finally invaded France in 1940, Mussolini officially entered the war as Hitler's ally. He made plans to ride out on a white horse after all of Italy's victories.

Meanwhile, Mussolini's countrymen had grown dissatisfied with his rigid policies and harsh tactics. Moreover, Mussolini's health was declining (he suffered from ulcers and possibly syphilis, a sexually transmitted disease). It soon became clear that Mussolini was the "junior partner" in the alliance with Germany and that Hitler was really in charge.

These problems were worsened by Italy's poor performance on the battlefield. Mussolini never got a chance to ride out on his white horse, because the Italian troops were defeated on all fronts, including North Africa, Greece, and Egypt. Many lives were lost, and the Italian economy became even weaker. In 1943, the United States invaded Sicily, an island off the southern coast of Italy. That military action signaled the inevitable invasion of the Italian mainland.

Removed from office

Mussolini's years as dictator of Italy ended on July 25, 1943, when the Fascist Grand Council voted to remove him from office. The next day he was dismissed by the king and taken into custody. The Italian authorities moved Mussolini from place to place to hide him from the Germans, but nevertheless he was rescued in a daring maneuver by German paratroopers.

Mussolini was flown to Munich, Germany. He met with Hitler, who set him up as the head of a new country—called the Italian Socialist Republic or the Republic of Salo—in northern Italy. Although Mussolini was not really in charge (Hitler was), he used what little power he had to capture and execute some of the former Fascist colleagues. One was his son-in-law, Galeazzo Ciano.

On September 3, 1943, the Allies invaded southern Italy. The Italian government immediately surrendered and joined the Allies in their fight against Germany. The combined armies began their drive north. Mussolini tried to flee to Switzerland, but he was captured by Italian partisans (an armed group that operates behind enemy lines, or in occupied territory during a war) near Milan on April 27, 1945. Along with his loyal lover, Clara Petacci, and twelve other Fascist leaders, Mussolini was shot the next day. His body and those of his companions were hung by the feet in a Milan gas station and subjected to public ridicule.

When they reached this scene, the Allies ordered the bodies taken down and buried. Mussolini's body eventually came to rest in Predappio, the little village in which he'd been born.

Where to Learn More

Books

Collier, Richard. *Duce!* New York: Viking Press, 1971.

Fermi, Laura. *Mussolini.* Chicago: University of Chicago Press, 1961.

Hartenian, Lawrence Raymond. *Benito Mussolini.* New York: Chelsea House, 1988.

Kirkpatrick, Ivone. *Mussolini, A Study in Power.* New York: Hawthorn Books, 1964.

Mulvihill, Margaret. *Mussolini and Italian Fascism.* London/New York: Franklin Watts, 1990.

Web sites

Smith, Denis Mack. "Benito Mussolini." [Online] Available http://www.grolier.com/wwii/wwii_mussolini.html (December 3, 1998).

The Navajo Code Talkers

Approximately 400 young Navajo men were recruited from their reservation (which includes parts of Arizona, New Mexico, and Utah) to join the U.S. Marine Corps and become "Code Talkers." The Navajo Code Talkers developed a code based on the Navajo language that was never deciphered and that played an important role in military communication

Some of World War II's most important and toughest battles took place in the islands of the western Pacific Ocean. Fighting the Japanese for control of the region, the Allies had to contend not only with a strong, determined enemy but also with dense jungle terrain. Secure communications by radio and telephone were crucial to the success of both planning and fighting battles. But the Japanese were good at cracking codes—they seemed to quickly decipher every one the Allies came up with. It wasn't until a World War I veteran suggested that members of the Navajo nation (a Native American people who live in the American Southwest) become "Code Talkers" that the U.S. Marines found a truly unbreakable code. Although the Navajo Code Talkers have never received much recognition from the public, they took part in every battle the marines fought in the Pacific from 1942 to 1945. They contributed greatly to the Allied victory over Japan (the Allies were all the countries fighting against Germany, Japan, and Italy, which were called the Axis. Britain, the United States, and the Soviet Union were the major Allied powers).

Two American code-breaking specialists who were called in to test the Navajo code could not even transcribe the sounds of the words, much less decipher their meaning.

Two Navajo Code Talkers in Bougainville.
(Reproduced by permission of Archive Photos.)

A boy grows up in Navajo country

The Allied strategy in the Pacific was to "leapfrog" from island to island, bypassing areas with high concentrations of Japanese troops. They would attack where they were least expected, in less protected areas. The Allies needed secret communications to succeed. The Japanese were so good at breaking codes that there was something called the "twenty-four-hour rule": a code could only be used for twenty-four hours, because after that period the Japanese were sure to have figured it out.

The answer to this dilemma finally came from a World War I (1914–1918; a war that began as a conflict between Austria-Hungary and Serbia and escalated into a global conflict involving thirty-two countries) veteran who was too old to fight in World War II but still wanted to help his country's war effort. Back in 1896, young Philip Johnston had traveled with his family into Navajo country where his father served as a Christian missionary. Philip spent all of his time with Navajo children and soon spoke their language fluently. He played Navajo games, ate Navajo food, and joined his friends in hunting with a bow and arrow and riding horses bareback.

When he was only nine years old, Johnston traveled with his father and some representatives of the Navajo and Hopi nations to Washington, D.C., to request that a certain piece of land be set aside as a reservation. Young Philip served as a translator when the group met with President Theodore Roosevelt.

Johnston loved his childhood, and even after his family moved to Los Angeles, California, he kept up his ties with the Navajo community. He went to the University of California and earned a degree in civil engineering, and he was working for the city of Los Angeles when World War II started. Aware of the military's problem with finding a safe code, Johnston wondered if some of the smart, capable Navajo men he knew could be used as communicators, talking to each other by radio in the Navajo language.

A successful demonstration

The Navajo language seemed an ideal choice for such a task, because it was spoken almost exclusively by Navajos (a population of about 50,000 in 1942) living in an isolated area, and it was estimated that only about thirty non-Navajos spoke the language at that time. Navajo is mostly an oral language and has no written alphabet. It is very complex and its tonal qualities and dialects make it very difficult to learn.

Early in 1942, Johnston brought his idea to Major J. E. Jones, a communications officer at Camp Elliot in San Diego, California. Although doubtful that the plan would work, Jones told Johnston to bring some Navajos to San Diego for a demonstration. Johnston rounded up four Navajos from the reservation and found another who was already serving in the Marine Corps. The men were to demonstrate their skills to General Clayton B. Vogel, commander of the Amphibious Corps, Pacific Fleet.

First the Navajos were given forty-five minutes to translate six military messages into their native language. There were many terms with no equivalents in Navajo, so they had to make up simple translations. Then they showed that they could translate a written or verbal message into Navajo and transmit it by radio to another Navajo in a different room, who would then translate the message back into English. The men proved that they could encode, transmit, and decode a three-line message in English in only twenty seconds, whereas it took thirty minutes for a coding machine to do the same thing.

Recruiting and training the "Code Talkers"

The marines were convinced. The next step was to recruit Navajo men to serve as what came to be known as "Code Talkers." The first recruiters who went to the reservation were met with suspicion, so Chee Dodge, the chairman of the Navajo nation, got involved in spreading the word that the marines needed men to serve as special communications agents. Notices went up around the reservation, and men started to volunteer.

In February 1942 twenty-nine Navajos (known thereafter as "The First 29") were inducted into the marines. They boarded trains in Flagstaff, Arizona, and Gallup, New Mexico, to go to boot camp (general training) in California. Four of the men began to devise a code and to teach it to the others. The Navajo marines were required to memorize the entire code

The Code Talker Alphabet

Letter	Navajo Word	Meaning
A	Woh-la-chee	Ant
B	Na-hash-chid	Badger
C	Moasi	Cat
D	Be	Deer
E	Dzeh	Elk
F	Ma-e	Fox
G	Klizzie	Goat
H	Lin	Horse
I	Tkin	Ice
J	Tkele-cho-gi	Jackass
K	Klizzie-yazzie	Kid
L	Dibeh-yazzie	Lamb
M	Na-as-tsosi	Mouse
N	Nesh-chee	Nut
O	Ne-ahs-jah	Owl
P	Bi-sodih	Pig
Q	Ca-yeilt	Quiver
R	Gah	Rabbit
S	Dibeh	Sheep
T	Than-zie	Turkey
U	No-da-ih	Ute
V	A-keh-di-glini	Victor
W	Gloe-ih	Weasel
X	Al-a-as-dzoh	Cross
Y	Tsah-as-zih	Yucca
Z	Besh-do-gliz	Zinc

McClain, S. *Navajo Weapon. Books Beyond Borders, 1994.*

during their training period; there would be nothing written down for them to use in battle.

The code was soon tested in combat, and when it worked well, authorization was given for another 300 Navajos to be recruited. Despite his age, Johnston was allowed into the marines so that he could help train and recruit the Code Talkers. Recruits fresh from boot camp were now sent to Staff Sergeant Johnston for training in how to use the code. In early 1943, Johnston worked with professional code makers to develop an even more sophisticated code.

How the code worked

The Navajo Code Talkers used from one to three Navajo words to stand for each letter of the English alphabet. For instance, the Navajo word for ant, "woh-la-chee," stood for a; "na-hash-chid" or badger was b; and "moasi" or cat was c. Words would then be spelled out letter by letter. For nearly 400 military words and expressions, the Code Talkers came up with symbolic Navajo names: the Navajo word for "chicken hawk" meant dive-bomber, "iron fish" meant submarine, "fast shooter" was machine gun, and "hummingbird" was fighter plane.

The code was so ingenious that Navajos who hadn't been trained in its use could not decipher it. Some of them were known to say "That's crazy Navajo!" when they heard it. One Navajo soldier who was captured while fighting in the Philippines was ordered by his Japanese captors to decipher the code, but of course he couldn't. He later said,

"I never figured out what you guys who got me into all that trouble were saying." Two American code-breaking specialists who were called in to test the code could not even transcribe the sounds of the words, much less decipher their meaning.

By 1943, 191 Code Talkers were serving in the marines; by the end of the war around 400 had served. Their job was to talk back and forth to each other, transmitting information on tactics, troop movements, and orders. As long as there was a Navajo Code Talker at each end of the telephone or radio connection, the code could be used. Intelligence officers in the field were skeptical at first about how secure it would be to have soldiers talking back and forth to each other in battle, but they soon saw that the code was effective.

An Example of a Translated Order

The order in English...

Request for artillery and tank fire at 123 B, Company E move 50 yards left flank of Company D.

Would be translated into Navajo words that meant...

Ask for many big guns and tortoise fire at 123 Bear tail drop Mexican ear mouse victor elk 50 yards left flank ocean fish Mexican deer.

McClain, S. Navajo Weapon. *Books Beyond Borders, 1994.*

Some Code Talkers' experiences

The experiences of King Mike are an example of the work done by the Code Talkers. Mike traveled from the remote Monument Valley in Arizona, where he was living on his wife's family's sheep farm, to take part in some of the bloodiest battles in the Pacific. After his entire brigade was wiped out in an attack on the island of Guam, Mike was reassigned to the 6th Division of the 22nd Regiment just before the U.S. invasion of Okinawa (a large island in the Pacific Ocean).

Mike was assigned to a five-person regimental intelligence team made up of a demolition (explosives) specialist, a soldier fluent in Japanese, a communications expert, a technician, and a Navajo Code Talker. After the U.S. Navy had bombed a particular shore area, the team would land on the beach and make their way behind enemy lines, then radio back information on how much damage the enemy had taken and how and when U.S. forces could invade. Much of this work was done at night, and there was constant danger of capture and

Some Terms Used By The Code Talkers		
Term	**Navajo word**	**Meaning**
Major General	So-na-kih	Two Stars
Colonel	Astah-besh-legai	Silver Eagle
Fighter Plane	Da-he-tih-hi	Hummingbird
Transport Plane	Astah	Eagle
Aircraft Carrier	Tsidi-ney-ye-hi	Bird carrier
Destroyer	Ca-lo	Shark

McClain, S. Navajo Weapon. Books Beyond Borders, 1994.

death. But the information Mike's team gathered was crucial to the Allies' success on Okinawa and in other battles.

Another Code Talker, Teddy Draper, Sr., took part in the battle of Iwo Jima—later made famous by the memorial in Washington, D.C., that shows a group of marines valiantly raising the U.S. flag. This was a hellish, thirty-six-day battle that involved hand-to-hand combat. The Navajo code was the only code used at Iwo Jima, and during the first two days of the battle, six Code Talkers worked around the clock to send and receive 800 messages, which they completed with no mistakes. Major Howard Connor, signal (communications) officer of the 5th Marine Division, is quoted on the Navy and Marine Corps World War II Commemorative Committee's web site saying: "Without the Navajo Code Talkers the Marines would never have taken Iwo Jima."

During one battle on the island of Saipan, Code Talkers successfully redirected some American troops who were accidentally firing on their own troops—those shooting could not be convinced they were firing at Americans until they heard the Code Talkers confirm it.

A secret until 1968

When he heard the story of the Navajo Code Talkers after the war, Japanese intelligence chief General Setzo Avisue said, "Thank you, that is a puzzle I thought would never be solved" (quoted on web site *Passages West: The Navajo Code Talkers* by Gerald Knowles). Some believe that the code devised and carried out by the Navajos may have been the only unbreakable code in military history.

The Code Talkers returned to their reservation and underwent the traditional Navajo "Enemy Way" ceremony to cast away their painful memories and chase away any lingering ghosts of fallen friends or enemies. They went back to their normal lives, and it would be many years before their contribution to the Allied victory was openly acknowledged. One

reason is that the government kept information about the Code Talkers secret until 1968, perhaps because they thought they might use them again in another war.

General Colin Powell at an exhibit honoring the Navajo Code Talkers at the Pentagon in Washington, D.C., 1992. *(Reproduced by permission of AP/Wide World Photos.)*

Honoring the Code Talkers

In 1969, the 4th Marine Division held a reunion for World War II veterans, and they invited the Code Talkers, along with Philip Johnston, to attend. They were presented with special bronze medallions depicting a Native American on a pony next to the Iwo Jima flag-raising scene. A representative of President Richard Nixon read a message honoring the Code Talkers for their role in the war. In 1971, the Code Talkers held their own reunion at Window Rock, Arizona, where they gave demonstrations of their skills to a thrilled audience of younger Navajos.

There has been more recognition for the Code Talkers in recent years. In 1981, President Ronald Reagan praised them for their "dedicated service, unique achievement, patriotism, resourcefulness, and courage." And in September 1992, thirty-five surviving Navajo Code Talkers attended the dedication of a special exhibit at the Pentagon (the headquarters of the Defense Department) in Washington, D.C. Put on permanent display were photographs, equipment, the original code, and explanations of how the code worked, so that for many years to come visitors would learn about the unique contributions the Navajo Code Talkers had made during World War II.

Where to Learn More

Books

Aaseng, Nathan. *Navajo Code Talkers.* New York: Walker and Company, 1992.

Kawano, Kenji. *Warriors: The Navajo Code Talkers.* Flagstaff, AZ: Northland Publishing Company, 1990.

Lagerquist, Syble. *Philip Johnston and the Navajo Codetalkers.* Council for Indian Education, 1996.

McClain, S. *Navajo Weapon.* Boulder, CO: Books Beyond Borders, 1994.

Paul, Doris A. *The Navajo Code Talkers.* Philadelphia, PA: Dorrance & Co., 1973.

Web sites

Knowles, Gerald. "America's Secret Weapon in Defeating the Japanese in World War II." *Passages West: The Navajo Code Talkers.* [Online] Available http://www.unink.com/passages/Monument-Valley/Ledgends/CodeTalkers.html (February 10, 1999).

Kukral, L.C. "The Navajo Code Talkers." Navy and Marine Corps World War II Commemorative Committee, Navy Office of Information. [Online] Available http://wae.com/webcat/navajos.htm (February 10, 1999).

J. Robert Oppenheimer

Born April 22, 1904
New York, New York
Died February 18, 1967
Princeton, New Jersey

American physicist

J. Robert Oppenheimer's brilliant research in the field of quantum mechanics (the study of the energy of atomic particles) led to his selection as the director of the weapons laboratory at Los Alamos, New Mexico. There, scientists from all over the world worked secretly to develop a powerful atomic bomb that, it was hoped, would end World War II. Oppenheimer was known not only for the important role he played in the Manhattan Project, but also for his work as a researcher and teacher. After the war, he advised the government on how best to use nuclear energy and weapons.

A bright and curious boy

Oppenheimer was born into a wealthy, cultured family. His father, Julius Oppenheimer, had emigrated from Germany as a young man and had built a successful textile importing company. His mother, Ella Friedman, was a painter who loved art and music. The family lived in a large apartment in New York City, but spent their summers on nearby Long Island.

J. Robert Oppenheimer headed the Manhattan Project—the successful effort by a group of scientists to build the first atomic bomb, which would bring the war to a swift close when used against the Japanese.

Portrait: J. Robert Oppenheimer. *(Reproduced by permission of The Library of Congress.)*

183

Oppenheimer's great intelligence and curiosity were obvious early in his life. By the time he was eleven he had put together a huge rock collection and became the youngest member ever admitted to the New York Mineralogical Society; at twelve, he presented a paper to the society. Oppenheimer attended the liberal, academically challenging Ethical Culture School in New York City. After graduating he went to Europe for the summer, but there he contracted dysentery (a severe intestinal illness) and had to spend the next year recovering.

A young star in the world of physics

In 1922, Oppenheimer entered Harvard University, where, he later said (as quoted in *Current Biography*) he "lived in the [library] stacks, just raided the place intellectually." He studied a wide range of subjects—including science and foreign languages—but he was most drawn to physics, and that became his major. Oppenheimer graduated *summa cum laude* (with highest honors) in only three years.

Oppenheimer graduated from college at a very exciting time in the field of physics, when many discoveries were being made. He decided to go to Europe to continue his study of theoretical physics. He started at the Cavendish Laboratory at Cambridge University in England. In his first paper as a graduate student, Oppenheimer explained aspects of the behavior of the molecule (the smallest part of a substance that has all the properties of that substance and is made up of one or more atoms). In 1926, Oppenheimer moved to the University of Göttingen in Germany, where he worked with a famous physicist, Max Born, to develop the "Born-Oppenheimer Theory" of molecular activity.

Oppenheimer earned his doctorate in 1927, and went on to conduct more research in Leiden, Holland, and Zurich, Switzerland. In Switzerland he worked closely with another famous scientist, Wolfgang Pauli. During these years of study, Oppenheimer showed how quickly he could grasp and analyze ideas and how well he could draw connections between theories and detect problems.

A popular, inspiring teacher

On his return from Europe, ten universities offered Oppenheimer teaching positions. In 1928 he accepted two of them, the University of California at Berkeley and the California Institute of Technology (Cal Tech) at Pasadena. For the next thirteen years he divided his time between these two schools, doing his own research as well as teaching. During this period he established Berkeley as a major American center for the study of quantum physics (the study of the energy of atomic particles).

Oppenheimer also gained a reputation as an excellent teacher. His classes moved at a rapid pace, as he stood at the blackboard with his ever-present cigarette in one hand and a piece of chalk in the other. He sparked many students' interest in theoretical physics, and some of them admired him so much that they imitated his mannerisms (such as his habit, developed during his time in Germany, of saying "Ja! Ja! Ja!" to encourage discussion) and followed him from one campus to another, sometimes repeating courses they'd already taken.

Although Oppenheimer continued to have a wide range of interests, including the other sciences, literature, and art, he lived a sheltered life (he had no telephone, did not read newspapers, and did not even vote) until the middle of the 1930s. Then some developments in the world, such as the hard economic times many people were experiencing and the rise of harsh dictators around the world, began to catch his notice. He became involved with several groups working for social reform, including some that had ties to the Communist Party. Oppenheimer, however, never became a Communist.

The world moves toward war

As World War II loomed, science made discoveries that would change the face of warfare. In 1934, Italian physicist Enrico Fermi had devised a way to bombard uranium (a radioactive metallic element) with neutrons (a particle from the nucleus or center of an atom) to create a reaction called nuclear fission. Many scientists believed that if a large enough amount of uranium—called a "critical mass"—could be used, a chain reaction would occur, instantly setting off a huge explosion of energy. Various physics laboratories were studying the possibility of using this reaction in a military weapon—an atomic bomb.

After the United States had entered World War II on December 7, 1941, Allied intelligence operations (spying activ-

A World-Famous Physicist Joins the Manhattan Project

One of the most famous scientists to take in the Manhattan Project was the Italian physicist Enrico Fermi, who had defected (to abandon one's country to become a citizen of a new country) to the United States after winning the Nobel Prize in 1938.

Born in Rome, Italy on September 29, 1901, Fermi grew into a talented, bright teenager who learned more about physics while he was still in high school than many university graduate students. He earned his Ph.D. in physics in Italy when he was only 21, then went on to study at the German universities of Göttingen and Leiden. In 1924 he came back to Italy and became a professor at the University of Florence.

While teaching in Florence, Fermi wrote an important paper about the actions of subatomic particles. Now recognized as a leader in physics, Fermi was named to the newly created chair of theoretical physics at the University of Rome, where he worked over the next six years with a number of leading physicists and brilliant students.

During the early 1930s, while studying the atomic nucleus, Fermi discovered a new kind of particle called a "neutrino" and a new kind of force called "weak force." Later he experimented with bombarding atoms in various chemical elements with neutrons, showing that this process could produce radioactive forms (unstable atoms that give off particles and energy). Later he discovered that if a uranium atom was bombarded with neutrons it would split, producing a reaction called nuclear fission that releases huge amounts of energy.

In 1938 Fermi was awarded the Nobel Prize for his work with neutron bombardment, and after accepting his award in Sweden he and his family didn't return to Italy but went to the United States. His own country's Fascist dictator Benito Mussolini (1883–1945; see entry) was an ally of Germany's dictator Adolf Hitler, who had begun harsh measures against Jews, and Fermi's wife was Jewish. Fermi now became a professor of physics at Columbia University in New York City.

ities of the countries fighting together against Germany, Japan, and Italy, including the United States, Great Britain, and the Soviet Union) learned that the Germans were also working on an atomic bomb. President Franklin D. Roosevelt (1882–1945; see entry) decided that the United States must immediately start its own atomic research program, which would be called the Manhattan Project.

Enrico Fermi. *(Reproduced by permission of Los Alamos National Laboratory.)*

In August 1939 President Franklin D. Roosevelt (1882–1945; see entry) received a letter from Hungarian-American physicist Leo Szilard and world-renowned physicist Albert Einstein warning that nuclear weapons (which would make use of the powerful energy released by nuclear fission) were going to be developed and used by Germany. Roosevelt's response was to set up the Manhattan Project so that American scientists could explore the possibility of making an atomic bomb.

Working in his lab under Columbia's squash courts on December 2, 1942, Fermi produced the world's first self-sustaining nuclear chain reaction. He continued his work on nuclear fission at a Chicago laboratory for two years, but in 1944 he and his wife (both new citizens of the United States) moved to Los Alamos, New Mexico, so that Fermi could join the scientists working under the direction of Robert Oppenheimer.

Fermi was put in charge of his own division, which was assigned to resolve any special problems that might arise as work on the first atomic bombs continued. The bombs were finally tested and dropped on Japan, effectively ending the war in Asia. Fermi returned to the University of Chicago, where he remained as a professor and researcher for the rest of his life. He received the Civilian Medal of Merit in 1946 for his work on the Manhattan Project. After his death in 1954, the U.S. Atomic Energy Commission named Fermi the first recipient of its Enrico Fermi Award.

The Manhattan Project takes off

Oppenheimer was recruited for the program not because he was particularly interested in it but because he was widely recognized as a brilliant, pioneering physicist. He took part in some of the first meetings to discuss the possible use of an atomic bomb, and in early 1942 he was asked to direct research on the bomb at Berkeley. Soon the government put

Oppenheimer, third from left, with other scientists working on the Manhattan Project, 1945. (Photograph by Popperfoto. Reproduced by permission of Archive Photos.)

the project under the control of the U.S. Army, and Colonel (later General) Leslie Groves was put in charge.

Development of the bomb took place at a number of laboratories in different places. Oppenheimer recommended that a single lab be set up, where scientists could work more closely and in secret. It was Groves who decided that Oppenheimer—despite his lack of administrative and management experience—should direct the lab; he told his doubtful colleagues, "we (are) not going to find a better man."

Oppenheimer suggested that the laboratory be built at Los Alamos, New Mexico, near an area where he had often vacationed. The area was geographically isolated and transportation was difficult, but this would help ensure the secrecy the project required. Oppenheimer supervised the construction of the huge complex (which, by the end of World War II, housed 5,000 workers) and the collection of equipment needed for research. He had to put together a team of leading scientists, all with different, sometimes difficult personalities, and get them to work together in harmony. And he had to convince them to bring their families to Los Alamos and stay until the war was over.

Oppenheimer accomplished all these things, establishing at Los Alamos an atmosphere of hard work and a free exchange of information. He also opened up his own home as an informal social center, where he and his wife, Katherine (whom he had married in 1940), often entertained the laboratory's scientists and staff.

Creating and testing an atomic bomb
The biggest problem the Los Alamos physicists had to solve was how to achieve critical mass—how to bring two pieces of uranium together quickly enough to create a chain reaction and produce an explosion. Another stumbling block was the length of time it took to refine uranium to the required purity; this process took place in two factories in Oak Ridge, Tennessee, and Hanford, Washington, but production was moving more slowly than expected.

By the summer of 1945, the technical problems had finally been resolved, and the atomic bomb was ready for testing. The test took place on July 16 on the Alamogordo Bombing Range. At 5:30 A.M. the bomb was detonated, setting off a flood of white light and a loud roaring noise, and causing a ball of fire to raise an immense cloud of sand and debris 40,000 feet into the air.

"The Shatterer of Worlds"
Watching the tremendous explosion from five miles away, Oppenheimer was reminded of two lines from the

Bhagavad-Gita, the Hindu sacred text that he had read in its original Sanskrit (one of eight languages he could read). One line referred to the "radiance of a thousand suns," and the other said, "I am become death, the Shatterer of Worlds." Like others present at the test, Oppenheimer's feelings were a mixture of pride in the success of their efforts, terror at the bomb's immense destructive power, and anxiety about what it meant for the future.

By this time, Germany had already surrendered and the war in Europe was over. But it seemed that Japan, despite major losses and very bleak prospects, would continue no matter the odds. Oppenheimer met with three other scientists (Ernest Lawrence, Enrico Fermi, and Arthur Compton) to discuss whether the United States should use the atomic bomb against Japan. The only alternative to the bomb, the U.S. government asserted, was to invade Japan, which would cost many American lives. On the other hand, the bomb could be dropped on a military target but would undoubtedly kill many Japanese civilians.

Although Oppenheimer would later regret his decision (claiming that the killing of civilians could and should have been avoided), he and the other scientists recommended that the United States use the atomic bomb against Japan. The final decision was made by President Harry S. Truman (1884–1975; see entry), who gave the plan his approval.

On August 6, 1945, the first bomb, nicknamed "Little Boy," was dropped on Hiroshima. Instantly, the city was destroyed: from 78,000 to 80,000 people were killed and 60,000 buildings were demolished. Over the next weeks and months, thousands more people would die of the sickness caused by the radioactive particles released by the explosion. On August 9, a second bomb ("Fat Man") was dropped on Nagasaki, killing between 25,000 and 40,000 people that day and many more later, as radiation sickness again took its toll. Japan surrendered on August 14, ending World War II.

Advisor on atomic energy and weapons

The existence of the atomic bomb had been kept secret until the Hiroshima bombing. News of the bomb made Oppenheimer famous as the so-called "Father of the A-Bomb."

secretary of war Henry Stimson claimed that "the development of the bomb has been largely due to his genius and the inspiration and leadership he has given to his associates." Yet Oppenheimer himself had very serious concerns about the bomb, and wanted to make sure it was properly controlled and used only to prevent wars.

After the war, Oppenheimer was asked to advise the government on how to control and manage atomic energy and weapons. In 1947 he was appointed to serve on the General Advisory Committee of the Atomic Energy Commission, which had been established the previous year when it was decided that atomic energy should be under civilian, rather than military, control. Oppenheimer served in this position until 1952.

Building a research center

In 1947, Oppenheimer became the director of the Institute for Advanced Study at Princeton University, overseeing its development into a first-rate physics research center. Under his leadership the institute's population grew, attracting many young scientists who enjoyed the lively atmosphere in which new ideas were discussed and tested. In describing the institute's work, Oppenheimer commented, "What we do not know we try to explain to each other."

During this period, Oppenheimer wrote and lectured on atomic energy, and also on the relationship between the scientist and society. His interest in how to make science understandable to those with little background in it was the topic of his 1954 book, *Science and the Common Understanding*.

Security clearance withdrawn

Despite the praise Oppenheimer received for his job as director of the Manhattan Project, he had made some enemies during his career. His opposition to the H-bomb (a much more powerful weapon than the atomic bomb that uses hydrogen instead of uranium or plutonium) had angered the scientists who backed it, especially its developer, Robert Teller. Oppenheimer believed the United States should focus not on building a bigger bomb but on arms treaties. The United States and the Soviet Union were, he said, like "two scorpions in a bottle, each capable of killing the other but only at the risk of its own life."

During the mid-1950s, anti-Communist (communism is the political system that features communal or group ownership of property) fever was sweeping the country. Senator Joseph McCarthy and others crusaded to rid the government of those they considered Communist sympathizers. In 1954, Oppenheimer was informed that his security clearance was being withdrawn. He asked for a hearing so that he could defend himself. At the three-week hearing, Oppenheimer's past connections with communist-related groups were brought up to discredit him, and his failure to support the H-bomb program was criticized. The final result was that even though he was undoubtedly a "loyal citizen," his security clearance would still be canceled.

The scientific community was outraged by what had happened to Oppenheimer, and they openly supported and praised him. Although he never again worked for the government, he continued his work at Princeton. In 1963, the Atomic Energy Commission gave Oppenheimer the important Enrico Fermi Award, which came with a $50,000 prize. Presented to him by President Johnson, the award was seen by many as the government's way of making amends with Oppenheimer. Four years later, he died of cancer at age sixty-two.

Where to Learn More

Books

Driemen, J.E. *Atomic Dawn: A Biography of Robert Oppenheimer.* Minneapolis, MN: Dillon Press, 1989.

Goodchild, Peter. *J. Robert Oppenheimer: Shatterer of Worlds.* New York: Fromm International, 1985.

Kunetka, James W. *Oppenheimer: The Years of Risk.* Englewood Cliffs, NJ: Prentice-Hall, 1982.

Larsen, Rebecca. *Oppenheimer and the Atomic Bomb.* New York: Franklin Watts, 1988.

Periodicals

"Brotherhood of the Bomb: Two Flinty Physicists Struggle Over Their Terrifying Legacy." *U.S. News & World Report* Special Report: Masters of Discovery: The Great Inventions of the 20th Century (August 17, 1998): 64.

George S. Patton

Born November 11, 1885
Pasadena, California
Died December 21, 1945
Heidelberg, Germany

American general

An inspiring and controversial American general, George S. Patton led Allied troops in several victorious campaigns, especially the invasion of France that followed the D-Day landings.

Recognized as one of the greatest wartime generals of all time, George S. Patton was a colorful figure remembered as much for his vulgar language and ivory-handled pistol as for his battlefield brilliance. Those who knew Patton well understood that he hid the softer, refined side of his nature under the bluster and swagger he felt were necessary to a soldier's image. Patton's aggressive style of fighting and his ability to inspire soldiers to perform beyond expectations contributed greatly to the Allied victory over Germany. In fact, he was the Allied general most admired and feared by the Germans.

A privileged childhood

Born into a wealthy family in California, Patton was descended from a long line of soldiers and achievers, and he always felt that their spirits were watching and judging what he did. One of his ancestors had fought for the rebel hero, Bonnie Prince Charlie, who led a revolt in Scotland in 1746, and others had served with the Confederate Army in the Civil War (1861–1865). Patton's grandfather, Benjamin Davis Wilson, had been mayor of Los Angeles and later established the suc-

Portrait: George S. Patton.
(Reproduced by permission of The Library of Congress.)

193

cessful Lake Vineyard. Patton's father gave up his job as district attorney of Los Angeles to run the family winery.

Although he learned to talk at an early age and had a vivid imagination, Patton suffered from a learning disability that made reading and writing extremely difficult for him. His family wanted to shelter him from ridicule, so he was educated at home by his doting Aunt Nannie. She read to him constantly, choosing myths and folk tales as well as passages from the Bible and even military history. The young Patton loved to act out the great battles of history, and his claims of having been present at these conflicts were so convincing that his family thought he had some kind of supernatural gift.

Patton started attending school when he was twelve. His classmates made fun of him because he still couldn't read or write. Nonetheless he managed to progress through a combination of strong determination and a good memory. It was at this time that Patton began to hide his insecurities beneath a tough, swaggering image. He was an adventurous boy who enjoyed riding, shooting, fishing, and hunting; in fact, he was so adventurous that he took a lot of risks and had many accidents.

Success at West Point

When he was only seventeen years old, Patton met Beatrice Ayer. Like Patton, she liked sports and was from a wealthy family. The couple married eight years later, even though Beatrice's father didn't want his daughter to marry a military man. Patton told him, "It is as natural for me to be a soldier as it is to breathe."

It's not too surprising, then, that Patton called the U.S. Military Academy at West Point, New York, "that holy place." He wanted desperately to attend West Point but feared he would fail the admission test. Then he discovered that if he went to the Virginia Military Institute (VMI) in Virginia for a year, he could get into West Point without taking the test.

Patton entered VMI in 1903 and transferred to West Point the next year. His father was so worried that Patton would flunk out of the academy that he made sure someone from the family lived close to West Point throughout the six years Patton attended. The first year, he failed math and had to repeat a whole year of classes. He was shocked and ashamed, but was determined to succeed.

At West Point, Patton was known as a strong leader and a good athlete who believed that a soldier should strictly follow behavior and dress codes—a belief he would continue to hold throughout his life. He looked forward to some day taking part in a war, for, he wrote, "it is in war alone that I am fitted to do anything of importance."

His early career

Patton graduated from West Point in 1909 and was assigned to serve at Fort Sheridan, Illinois, and later at Fort Myer, Virginia. Meanwhile he was enjoying such sophisticated hobbies as playing polo, fencing, buying thoroughbred horses, and ballroom dancing. He competed in the 1912 Olympics in Stockholm, Sweden, placing fifth in the military pentathlon (pistol shooting, fencing, swimming, steeplechase riding, and a 500-meter run).

Patton was an excellent swordsman, and when he went to Fort Riley, Kansas, in 1912 to study at the army's Mounted Service School he also got a job as a fencing instructor. He held the title of Master of the Sword and was the army's top fencing expert. This pursuit helped him to project a swashbuckling persona that belied the sensitive side of his personality.

In 1916, Patton joined a Texas cavalry regiment under the command of General John J. Pershing for an expedition into Mexico. The purpose of the expedition was to punish the rebel leader Pancho Villa, who had recently raided an American town. Patton took part in a Wild West-type gun battle and thoroughly enjoyed this adventure.

World War I and beyond

After World War I (1914–1918; a war that started as a conflict between Austria-Hungary and Serbia and escalated into a global war involving thirty-two countries) began Patton again joined up with General Pershing's forces, this time in France. But he was far from the fighting, so he quit Pershing's

"The Soldier's General": Omar Bradley

Although he was General George Patton's fellow commander and one of his closest colleagues, General Omar Bradley couldn't have been more different in personality and approach to his troops. Patton swaggered and swore and slapped soldiers who complained of suffering from "battle fatigue." Bradley was a calm, quiet man and a cautious commander whose consideration for individual lives earned him the respect and gratitude of those who served under him.

Bradley had a deep understanding of the average G.I.'s viewpoint, who, he said, "trudges into battle knowing that statistics are stacked against his survival. He fights without promise of either reward or relief. Behind every river, there's another hill—and behind that hill, another river....Sooner or later, unless victory comes, the chase must end on the litter [used to transport the wounded] or in the grave."

Born into a poor family in Clark, Missouri, on February 12, 1893, Bradley graduated from the U.S. Military Academy at West Point, New York, in 1915. He became the first member of his West Point class to earn a general's star. Bradley served an assignment in the United States during World War I. In 1920, he became a math instructor at West Point, after which he served a tour of duty in Hawaii, and then taught tactics for four years at the army's Infantry School at Fort Benning, Georgia. The Infantry School's director at the time was then-Lieutenant Colonel George Marshall (1880–1959; see entry), who would later serve as army chief of staff during World War II and who entered Bradley into his "black book" full of names of promising young officers.

Bradley graduated from the Army War College in 1934 and taught again at West Point in 1937. In 1938, Bradley was transferred to Washington, D.C., to serve on the Army General Staff under Marshall. He became its assistant secretary in July 1939, but in 1941 he moved to the Infantry School to serve as commandant. There Bradley was promoted to the rank of brigadier general. He earned another star (making him a major general) soon after

staff and joined the U.S. Tank Corps. In 1918, Patton was promoted to lieutenant colonel and put in charge of the Tank Corps, taking part in the St. Mihiel and Meuse-Argonne battles before being wounded. Although he was disappointed to be out of the fighting for the rest of the war, Patton received the Distinguished Service Medal and the Distinguished Service Cross for his courageous performance.

the U.S. entered World War II, and was put in command of the army's 82nd and 28th Divisions. In 1943 Bradley was sent to North Africa in 1943 to serve as "eyes and ears" for General Dwight D. Eisenhower (1890–1969; see entry), who wanted his old West Point classmate to recommend ways to improve training.

Bradley took over for Patton as commander of the 2nd Corps in Tunisia when Patton left to prepare for the invasion of Sicily. Bradley led the 2nd Corps to Sicily in the summer of 1943, after which he went to England to help plan Operation Overlord, the Allied invasion of France. Appointed commander in chief of the American ground forces for the invasion, he led the First Army when they landed on the beaches of Normandy in northern France in June 1944.

Two months later Bradley took over command of the Allied 12th Army Group, which played a major role in the push across western Europe and eventual defeat of Germany. After the war, Bradley stayed for a while with the occupation army in Germany before returning to the United States and becoming, in June 1945, the head of the Veterans Administration. In this position his job was to help soldiers make the transition into civilian life and get the medical, educational, and housing benefits they were owed. In 1948 Bradley succeeded Eisenhower as chief of staff of the army (the army's highest position), earning two more general's stars over the next two years.

Bradley became the first chairman of the newly created Joint Chiefs of Staff (a group made up of the heads of each of the branches of the armed forces) in August 1949 and was reappointed in August 1951. He retired from the army in 1953 after forty-two years of service. Bradley then entered the business world as chairman of the board of the Bulova Watch Company, published his memoirs (A Soldier's Story, 1951), and headed a presidential committee on veterans' benefits. He died in New York City on April 8, 1981.

In the years between the two world wars, Patton held a variety of staff positions and received additional training. He graduated from the Command and General Staff School in 1924 and from the Army War College in 1932. He continued his study of military history and of tank warfare (one of his favorite subjects), wrote articles, pursued his favorite hobbies, and kept physically fit. But he was bored.

"Old Blood and Guts"

The Germans relieved Patton's boredom in 1939 by invading Poland and triggering the start of World War II. France and Britain declared war on Germany. Eventually, many other countries would become involved in the conflict, including the United States. In 1940 Patton was made a general and given command of a tank division; he wrote to a friend: "All that is now needed is a nice juicy war." Speaking to a group of officers at Fort Benning, Georgia, Patton reinforced his tough image by remarking that "war will be won by blood and guts alone." Over the next several years, the men who served under Patton would often refer to him as "Old Blood and Guts."

In February 1942—two months after the United States entered World War II—Patton was given command of the 1st Armored Corps. This group participated in the successful invasion of North Africa (called Operation Torch) that took place in November. Fresh from that success, Patton took over as commander of the 2nd Corps in Tunisia, which had just suffered a discouraging defeat and was not performing well. He is credited with reviving the sagging spirits of the men and helping them improve their fighting ability.

Patton believed in aggressive warfare, which is characterized by rapid movement and the element of surprise. His approach to the conduct of his soldiers was equally aggressive. An example is this segment of a speech he gave his junior officers at the start of Operation Torch: "Now if you have any doubts as to what you're to do, I can put it very simply. The idea is to move ahead. You usually will know where the front is by the sound of gunfire, and that's the direction you should proceed. Now suppose you lose a hand or an ear is shot off, or perhaps a piece of your nose, and you think you should walk back to get first aid. If I see you, it will be the last goddamned walk you'll ever take."

Patton also enforced a strict dress code, insisting that his men appear polished and buttoned at all times, that they shave daily despite water rationing, and that they wear their neckties into battle.

Success and controversy in Sicily

Promoted to lieutenant general and given command of the U.S. 7th Army, Patton went to Sicily in July 1943 to lead the Allied invasion of the German-occupied island off the coast of Italy . With help from the British 8th Army, Patton's forces cleared Sicily of Axis (Italian and German) forces in only thirty-eight days. Patton's daring and effective maneuvers made headlines, and he became a popular hero—at least until what may have been the most controversial episode in his career.

Patton was visiting wounded men at a military hospital when several soldiers told him that they suffered not from injuries but from combat fatigue; "It's my nerves, sir!" one said. "I just can't stand the shelling anymore!" Enraged that anyone would spend time in a hospital for such a complaint, Patton called the soldier a "yellow bastard" and slapped him with his hand or glove, adding that there was no such thing as battle fatigue, only "goddamned cowards."

This incident generated much negative publicity, even though Patton later claimed that he was just trying to shock the men into recovery. Patton's superior officer, General Dwight D. Eisenhower (1890–1969; see entry), seriously considered relieving him of his command, but knew he was too valuable a general to lose. So Eisenhower ordered Patton to apologize to the men involved as well as to everyone who had been present, which Patton willingly did. For the next few months, he was on his best behavior.

The Normandy invasion

The Allies were busy planning their invasion of France, which would begin with a landing of more than 150,000 troops on the beaches of Normandy in northern France. Aware of the Germans' great regard for Patton's skills, the Allied leadership played a trick on the Germans. They decided to use Patton as a decoy, calling him to London to "command" the First U.S. Army Group (FUSAG), which did not actually exist. The army placed equipment that was not being used on the British shores across the English Channel from Pas de Calais in France, to make the Germans think the Allies were planning to attack from there. In reality the invasion came from further west.

Patton talking with American soldiers in Europe.
(Reproduced by permission of AP/Wide World Photos.)

The Allied invasion began on June 6, 1944, and six days later, Patton's command of the 3rd Army—a force that was very real indeed—was sent into action. In August Patton's men began their massive sweep across France, which took them from Normandy through Brittany and northern France to the town of Bastogne, which they liberated in December.

The Germans made a desperate last stand later in December at the Battle of the Bulge, which took place in the Ardennes region of Belgium. Attempting to gain some ground, the Germans had managed to split the Allied forces in two, creating a "bulge" in the front line. In response, Patton performed what General Omar Bradley (1893–1981) called "one of the most astonishing feats of generalship of our campaign in the west." Patton shifted his army with incredible speed and complex movements into position to defeat the Germans.

The 3rd Army then headed toward the Rhine River, crossing one day ahead of British general Bernard Montgomery (1887–1976; see entry), who had long been Patton's chief rival. They crossed southern Germany but, much to Patton's chagrin, had to stop at the border of Czechoslovakia, which the Russians had been slated to invade. The Germans were finally defeated, and the war soon ended.

Not suited for governing

Immediately following the end of the war, Patton was assigned to serve as the military governor of the German province of Bavaria, a job that did not suit his interests and abilities. A witness at the time wrote: "Instead of killing Germans, what he knows best, Patton is asked to govern them, what he knows least. It won't work." Patton was soon criticized for being too soft on former Nazis, allowing them to retain their government jobs. He made a number of anti-Semitic (anti-Jewish) or otherwise embarrassing statements, such as one in which he compared Germans joining the Nazi Party to Americans deciding whether to become Democrats or Republicans.

The result of the controversy was Patton's transfer on October 7, 1945, from the 3rd Army to the smaller, less significant 15th Army Group. Patton was depressed, convinced that—just as he had said as a young man—he was only useful in war. On December 9, while on his way to hunt pheasant near Mannheim, Germany, Patton was seriously injured in a car accident. On the way to the military hospital in Heidelberg, he remarked, "This is a helluva way to die." He died twelve days later.

Patton was buried alongside other fallen soldiers of his beloved 3rd Army, in a military cemetery in Luxembourg, Belgium.

Where to Learn More

Books

Ambrose, Stephen E. *Citizen Soldiers: The U.S. Army from the Normandy Beaches to the Bulge to the Surrender of Germany.* New York: Simon and Schuster, 1997.

Blumenson, Martin. *Patton: The Man Behind the Legend.* New York: William Morrow, 1985.

D'Este, Carlo. *Patton: A Genius for War.* New York: Harper Collins, 1995.

Devaney, John. *"Blood and Guts": The True Story of General George S. Patton, USA.* New York: J. Messner, 1982.

Patton, George S. *War as I Knew It.* Boston: Houghton, 1947.

Peifer, Charles. *Soldier of Destiny: A Biography of George Patton.* Minneapolis, MN: Dillon Press, 1989

Web sites

Pogue, Forrest C. "George S. Patton, Jr." [Online] Available http://www.grolier.com/wwii/wwii_patton.html (December 3, 1998).

Ernie Pyle

Born August 3, 1900
Dana, Indiana
Died April 18, 1945
Ie Shima, Japan

American journalist

Even before World War II made him famous around the world, Ernie Pyle had attracted a strong following in the United States with his newspaper columns focused on the lives of ordinary Americans. His talent for showing readers the remarkable aspects of life served him well when he went overseas to record the experiences of American troops. He earned their respect by living just as they did, and he gained million of readers with his descriptive writings about the war. Later critics complained that Pyle and other World War II correspondents whitewashed the realities of the war, never fully revealing its shocking brutalities. But Pyle's admirers claim that in fact he helped Americans to survive the war and to give it more meaning and purpose. When people called World War II the "Good War" (meaning the war that was justified and worth fighting) as they would for generations to come, they were referring to the war Pyle had shown them. According to his biographer, James Tobin, he was "America's eyewitness to the 20th century's supreme ordeal."

Ernie Pyle was America's favorite war correspondent during World War II. He earned the soldiers' respect by living just as they did, and he gained million of readers with his gracefully written newspaper columns about the war.

Portrait: Ernie Pyle.
(Reproduced by permission of Archive Photos.)

"The South End of a Horse ..."

Pyle was born on a farm near the small town of Dana, Indiana. His father, Will Pyle, was a quiet, kind man who had turned to farming when he couldn't make enough money as a carpenter, his true profession. The real leader of the family was Pyle's mother, Maria (who was called Marie). She was very hardworking, energetic, and blunt, and she treated her only child, Ernest, with a mixture of tough discipline and tenderness. Another important member of the family was Pyle's Aunt Mary (his mother's sister), who was also a very strong-willed, energetic woman.

An intelligent boy whose mother fussed over him, Pyle grew up feeling inferior to the "town boys" with whom he went to school. He was not at all interested in farm work (later he wrote that "anything was better than looking at the south end of a horse going north") and kept a scrapbook of postcards from other places, dreaming of leaving Dana.

In 1917 the United States entered World War I (1914–18), and Pyle was gravely disappointed that he was too young to join the army. He entered Indiana University in Bloomington in 1919. Although he majored in economics, Pyle had a keen interest in journalism and served as a reporter and editor on the university's newspaper, the *Daily Student*. In the middle of his senior year, Pyle dropped out of college to take a job as reporter at the *Daily Herald* in LaPorte, Indiana.

A talented young reporter

Pyle did well enough at the *Herald* to be noticed by an editor from the Scripps-Howard newspaper company who was looking for talented young writers. He offered Pyle a job at the *Washington Daily News* in Washington, D.C. Thrilled at the prospect of moving to a big city and making $2.50 a week more, Pyle took the job. He quickly gained praise for his clearly written stories and also for his skill in editing the work of other reporters.

In 1923, Pyle met Geraldine "Jerry" Siebolds, an intelligent, charming, unconventional young woman from Minnesota. The couple married in 1925 and a year later started off on a long trip across the United States, camping most of the time. They ended up in New York City, where they spent a dismal year living in a tiny basement apartment while Pyle worked as a copyeditor for several newspapers. Then the new editor of the *Washington Daily News,* Lee Miller (who would remain Pyle's good friend and colleague until the end of his life), lured Pyle back to Washington with an offer to work at the paper.

The thrill of aviation

During the 1920s, aviation was a relatively young and very exciting field, with daring pilots performing thrilling feats in the air and airline travel gaining popularity. In March 1928 Pyle convinced his editors that an aviation column would interest many readers, and he was assigned to write it.

He spent the next four years visiting airfields around Washington, D.C., interviewing pilots, mechanics, and other industry people, reporting on such issues as passenger safety, airplane design, and new airports. In these columns—which were very well received by the public, as Pyle had predicted—Pyle developed the loose, highly descriptive, and personable style that would mark his World War II writings.

Pyle enjoyed his work as an aviation columnist, and he was not particularly thrilled to be offered a job as managing editor of the *Washington Daily News.* Nevertheless, he accepted the offer, and spent the next three years unhappily working at a desk. Meanwhile, Jerry began having emotional problems and was struggling with alcoholism, both of which would continue to plague her for years to come.

Becoming a roving reporter

After taking a three-week vacation in the southwestern United States, Pyle wrote about his experiences in a special eleven-article series. This gave him the idea of becoming a kind of "roving" reporter who would travel around the United States and write stories about the different places he visited and people he met. A high-level editor at Scripps-Howard who had admired Pyle's southwestern stories gave him permission to try his idea. Soon he and Jerry packed a few belongings into a Dodge convertible coupe and began their adventure.

Pyle spent the next seven years (from 1935 to early 1942) wandering across the United States, visiting all forty-eight states plus Alaska and Hawaii (which were not yet states), Canada, and Central and South America. Along the way he stopped often to talk to thousands of people from all walks of life, from mayors to cowboys to farmers to store clerks and many, many others. Writing about what he saw and heard in columns that were published in over forty newspapers, Pyle created what Tobin called a "forgotten but magnificent mosaic of the American scene in the Great Depression" (the period of economic hardship that lasted from the late 1929 until 1939).

Pyle attracted a considerable following of readers who liked the friendly, self-deprecating voice that spoke through his writing, like the voice of a compassionate friend who understood what the lives of ordinary people were really like. Pyle's physical appearance—he was a short, skinny, balding man with a fringe of reddish, graying hair and a kind, mild face—made him even more likable. He never preached or put on airs, and he often talked about his own family members in his columns, referring to his wife, for example, as "That Girl Who Rides With Me." His descriptions of what he saw (especially landscapes) were especially vivid and gracefully written.

The coming of war

During those seven years, the Pyles were constantly on the road, and even though they enjoyed much of it, the wandering took its toll. Pyle himself grew physically tired and was often ill, while Jerry grew even more depressed and isolated and abused pills and alcohol. Finally the Pyles decided to build a house in Albuquerque, New Mexico, and settle down.

Meanwhile, by the end of 1939 war was already raging in Europe, where troops under the command of Germany's dictator, Adolf Hitler (1889–1945; see entry) had invaded Poland and France. The war was often in Pyle's thoughts, and when Germany began its bombing raids on London, Pyle decided to cross the ocean and see these important events for himself. He arrived in London on December 9, 1940, planning to share his experiences with the American people through columns to be sent from overseas.

Helping Americans "see" the war

On December 29, Pyle witnessed one of the worst bombing raids of the war. German planes set London's skyline

Up Front with Bill Mauldin

While Ernie Pyle used words to help Americans back home imagine how soldiers lived and what they thought, Bill Mauldin drew cartoons that also brought their wartime experiences to life. His two most famous characters, Willie and Joe, provided a peek into the realities of army life and combat in World War II.

Born in 1921 in Arizona, Mauldin was already a budding cartoonist when, at age eighteen, he joined his state's National Guard unit, which became part of the 45th Infantry Division. He saw combat in Sicily (an island off the southern coast of Italy) and was part of the fighting at the bloody battle at Anzio beach in Italy, as well as other frontlines.

Mauldin became known as someone who could capture in pictures and captions the true feelings and experiences of ordinary soldiers. Even though he often made fun of the "brass" (commanding officers), they decided his drawings were good for morale (made the soldiers feel better about their situation). In 1943 Mauldin got a job as cartoonist for the army newspaper *Stars and Stripes*.

He continued to travel with the troops, portraying them through the characters of Willie and Joe. They started out as fairly neat, clean-shaven young men but appeared more bedraggled, tired, dirty, and unshaven as the months passed and the Allies fought hard battles against the Germans.

Criticized for making American soldiers look so messy, Mauldin claimed, "I draw our guys like that because that's the way they are." After so much fighting and death, he said, "they've aged ten or fifteen years." Ernie Pyle also defended Mauldin: as a caption for a photo of a ragged, weary soldier, he wrote, "So you at home think cartoonist Bill Mauldin's 'GI Joe' doesn't look that way. Well, he does, and here's proof."

Mauldin's cartoons were collected in a book, *Up Front,* in which he explained his attitude toward the men depicted in his work: "I'm convinced that the infantry is the group in the army which gives more and gets less than anybody else. I draw pictures for and about the dogfaces [a common nickname for GIs] because I know what their life is like....They don't get fancy pay, they know their food is the worst in the army because you can't whip up lemon pies or even hot soup at the front, and they know how much of the burden they bear."

After the war, Mauldin returned to civilian life and became a political cartoonist.

ablaze. Instead of moving to a bomb shelter, Pyle watched from a hotel balcony and later wrote a vivid description of the "most hateful, most beautiful single scene I have ever known." He also expressed his admiration for the bravery and determination of the British people, suggesting that Americans should support their efforts against the Germans.

In those years before television could bring pictures of far-off events, Pyle's columns helped them "see" what was happening in England. His readership grew, and when he returned to the United States in March 1941 he was surprised by all the new fans who recognized and greeted him enthusiastically. His columns were even published in a book, *Ernie Pyle in England* (1941).

Pyle's plans for a trip to Asia were scuttled by the Japanese attack on the U.S. naval base at Pearl Harbor (December 7, 1941), which was followed quickly by President Franklin D. Roosevelt's (1882–1945; see entry) declaration of war against Japan. A few days later Germany and Italy, who had signed a pact with Japan, declared war on the United States. America became fully involved in World War II. Pyle tried to enlist in the U.S. Navy, but was too small to meet the physical requirements. In April, he and Jerry were divorced, and in June 1942 she entered a hospital for treatment of her physical and emotional ailments. With nothing more to keep him in the United States, Pyle decided to spend six months touring the war zones.

With the troops in North Africa

Pyle went first to Great Britain, where U.S. troops were preparing for the battles that would soon follow. He roamed from camp to camp, talking to the soldiers and recording the details of their daily routine as they waited for the fighting to begin. It finally did begin in November, when, in an invasion nicknamed Operation Torch, American forces landed in North Africa to join the British army, which was already fighting the Germans' very experienced, very efficient Afrika Korps.

Pyle soon followed, joining American troops in Tunisia. Instead of living among officers or staying far away from the action, he remained close to the G.I.s (the enlisted infantry men; G.I. stands for government issue, which was stamped on all of the enlisted men's gear). Like them, Pyle slept on the ground, ate in a mess tent, wore dirty clothes and went without hot baths. The troops appreciated Pyle's efforts to see the war from their viewpoint and to share their discomforts, and they responded warmly to him. The columns Pyle sent home to American readers were full of small details about what the soldiers were doing, thinking, and feeling—details that American readers were eager to hear.

Pyle accompanied the men into combat, often putting himself in great danger as they met the Germans in fierce desert battles. Pyle's columns focused entirely on "the goddamned infantry, as they like to call themselves." With riveting descriptions and graceful writing, he told of their transformation from ordinary men into warriors.

The top war correspondent

Back home, Pyle had gained recognition as America's top war correspondent. Between November 1942 and April 1943 his readership increased from 3.3 to 9 million as his column appeared in 122 newspapers. He received a huge number of letters from readers who thought of him as a personal friend: they sent him gifts and cookies, and asked him to look up particular soldiers (he used his column to explain, with regret, that it was impossible for him to do this). Pyle's Africa columns were collected in a book called *Here Is Your War* (1943).

The invasion of Sicily

Once the Allies (the countries fighting Germany, Italy, and Japan) had taken North Africa from the Germans, they were ready to conquer Italy, which had aligned itself with the Axis nations (Germany and Japan). It was decided that the invasion should begin in Sicily, a large island located off Italy's southern coast. Pyle went along on the invasion again. This time he traveled on the battleship USS *Biscayne*. He joined General George S. Patton's (1885–1945; see entry) 7th Army as they fought their way north toward the town of Messina, and he witnessed some of the most intense, bloodiest fighting of the war.

Overwhelmed by the death and chaos that surrounded him, Pyle suffered from the same kind of "battlefield fever" (sometimes called battle fatigue) that many soldiers experienced when the reality of war became too much to bear. He felt both physically and emotionally exhausted. When the Sicily campaign was over—and the Allies had again emerged victorious—Pyle decided to go home and recuperate.

The famous man from Indiana

Pyle had been warned that he would return to the United States to find himself famous, but he was still unprepared for the attention he received after landing in New York. He was besieged with people who wanted to meet him, ask him about the war, or offer him jobs and speaking engagements. He wrote that "no statesman ... or general or admiral or movie star ever got a quicker or more complete bath of fame than this thin man from Indiana."

Pyle had even made it to Hollywood, for work had started on a film, *The Story of G.I. Joe,* that was to be based on *Here Is Your War.* He had no desire to stay around and watch the filming, though. He had already decided to return to Europe. Pyle stopped in Washington, D.C., on his way overseas, and while he was there he was summoned to the White House for tea with the First Lady, Eleanor Roosevelt (see sidebar on p. 236). Despite Pyle's embarrassment about having to wear his one, very shabby suit to the meeting, he had a long, pleasant chat with Mrs. Roosevelt.

Creating the heroic image

Soon Pyle was on his way to Italy, where he would spend five months with American troops struggling under terrible conditions—including heavy rain, bone-chilling cold, and fierce resistance from German and Italian soldiers. This experience only deepened Pyle's admiration for those he called "the kids up there," who "live and die so miserably and ... do it with such determined acceptance."

Pyle is credited with doing much to create a heroic image of the American soldier in World War II, described by Tobin as "the long-suffering G.I. who triumphed over death through dogged perseverance." One of the most famous columns he wrote during this period told the story of a young soldier who went into a dangerous area to retrieve the body of his popular company commander, Captain Henry Waskow. In simple, graceful language, Pyle relates how individual soldiers came to say their good-byes to the fallen Waskow.

By February 25, the troops had reached the town of Anzio, where the casualties (deaths and injuries) were especially high. On March 17, the house in which Pyle was staying was shelled and the room he'd been sleeping in (he had gotten up to look out the window just before the shell hit) collapsed, but he escaped injury. In April, Pyle went to London where the Allies were planning "Operation Overlord," the invasion of Normandy, France, which would become known as D-Day. There, he learned that he had won the Pulitzer Prize (an important award given to journalists).

Witnessing the Normandy invasion

Pyle was invited to travel to Normandy with General Omar Bradley on the command ship Augusta, which meant he'd witness the arrival of the first troops on the beaches of northern France, but from a relatively safe position among the top army officers. Instead, Pyle decided to go aboard an LST (landing ship, tank) with regular soldiers.

The massive invasion began on June 6, and Pyle went ashore the next day. Unsure how to describe the scene to his readers, he took a long walk on the beach. In his columns, he mentioned how difficult and bloody it had been for the Allies to take the beach, but he focused mostly on what he had seen during his walk, such as bodies floating in the calm water, wrecked equipment, and piles of personal gear (including toothbrushes, Bibles, and photographs) which had belonged to soldiers killed in the fighting.

For a few weeks Pyle remained in the thick of the fighting as the Allied troops fought their way deeper and deeper into France. When he began to experience battle fatigue again, he left the front to report on other army units. Meanwhile, back home, Pyle appeared on the front cover of the July 17, 1944 issue of *Time* magazine. After witnessing the Allied assault near the town of St.-Lo, France—and being caught there in very heavy bombing—as well as the liberation of Paris on August 25, Pyle decided to return to the United States for a rest and then head for the Pacific, where the Allies were still fighting the Japanese.

Pyle, working on a column in Normandy, France. *(Reproduced by permission of AP/Wide World Photos)*

Off to the Pacific

At that time, it was estimated that Pyle had approximately forty million devoted readers around the world. On his return to the United States, he was courted by various newspaper companies but remained loyal to Scripps-Howard. He also turned down several offers to have his columns broadcast on radio. Pyle and his wife had been remarried (by long distance) while he was in North Africa, and he returned to their house in Albuquerque. Although at first it seemed as if Jerry was much improved, Pyle's hectic visit and plans to leave again upset her greatly. She made a suicide attempt, and had to enter the hospital again. Though worried about Jerry, Pyle left for the Pacific in January 1945.

After a short stay in Honolulu, Hawaii, Pyle flew to Guam and then on to Saipan (both islands in the Marianas chain in the South Pacific). There he spent some leisurely days with a young relative, Jack Bales (an airplane radio operator), and other pilots who were conducting regular bombing raids on Japan. Pyle also went for a cruise on a light aircraft carrier, the USS *Cabot*. In his columns, he wrote that the life of troops in the South Pacific seemed much easier than that of soldiers in Europe—the weather was pleasant and living conditions comfortable, everything moved at a slower pace, and there was little to see.

For the first time, Pyle's writings drew negative criticism, especially from enlisted men who claimed he had spent all his time with officers and had not tried to see or portray the grittier realities of the war in the Pacific. Pyle promised that he would try harder to do so.

"I'm not coming back..."

The Allies planned to invade the Japanese island of Okinawa, and Pyle decided that he would go along with the marines when they landed. "I'm not coming back from this one," he told a friend. Pyle traveled to Okinawa aboard the ship *Panamint* and stepped ashore on April 1. Since most of the fighting was taking place further inland, the beach was quiet.

On April 17, Pyle decided to go to Ie Shima, a tiny island that the marines had invaded the previous day. He spent the night on the island, and the next morning he climbed into a jeep with several other men to drive inland. They had been driving for a short time when they heard the sound of a Japanese machine gun, so they all jumped out of the jeep and into a ditch. When Pyle raised his head, the Japanese sniper fired again, shooting him in the left temple and killing him instantly.

Pyle's many friends and admirers—including the millions who had gotten to know him through his columns—were stunned by his death. Only six days earlier President Roosevelt had died and the new president, Harry S. Truman (1884–1975; see entry), said, "The nation is quickly saddened again by the death of Ernie Pyle."

His body was initially buried on Ie Shima, but it was later moved to lie among army and navy dead in the National Memorial Cemetery of the Pacific in Punchbowl Crater in Honolulu. On Ie Shima, soldiers placed a plaque that reads "At this spot, the 77th Infantry Division Lost a Buddy, Ernie Pyle, 18 April 1945."

Where to Learn More

Books

Miller, Lee G. *The Story of Ernie Pyle*. Westport, CT: Greenwood Press, 1950.

Nichols, David, ed. *Ernie's War: The Best of Ernie Pyle's World War II Dispatches*. New York: Random House, 1986.

O'Connor, Barbara. *The Soldier's Voice: The Story of Ernie Pyle*. Minneapolis, MN: Carolrhoda Books, 1996.

Tobin, James. *Ernie Pyle's War: America's Eyewitness to World War II*. New York: The Free Press, 1997.

Wilson, Ellen Janet Cameron. *Ernie Pyle, Boy from Back Home*. Indianapolis, IN: Bobbs-Merrill, 1962.

Web sites

"Ernie Pyle." *Access Indiana Teaching & Learning Center*. [Online] Available http://tlc.ai.org/pyle.htm (March 4, 1999).

Jeannette Rankin

Born June 11, 1880
Missoula, Montana
Died May 18, 1973
Carmel, California

American politician, feminist, and pacifist

The first woman in U.S. history to serve in Congress, Jeannette Rankin was elected at a time when most American women were not even allowed to vote. Throughout her life she was a strong advocate for women's rights, leading the campaigns for women's suffrage (the right to vote) as well as for social reforms to help working and poor people. Rankin was also a strict pacifist (someone who does not believe in using violence to solve disputes), and this belief damaged her political career when she voted against U.S. entry into both World War I and World War II. In fact, Rankin ignored the overwhelming tide of public opinion to become the only member of Congress to vote "no" on President Franklin D. Roosevelt's (1882–1945; see entry) resolution to enter World War II. An energetic, relentless fighter for causes she believed in, even if they were unpopular, Rankin voted her conscience despite the consequences.

A frontier childhood

Rankin was the oldest of seven children born to John Rankin, a wealthy rancher and land developer who had immigrated to Montana from Canada, and Olive Pickering Rankin,

"As a woman I can't go to war, and I refuse to send anyone else."

Portrait: Jeannette Rankin.
(Reproduced by permission of Archive Photos.)

a schoolteacher. When Rankin was born, Montana was still a territory (it would become a state in 1889) and Missoula was very much a frontier town where one was likely to see Native Americans wearing their traditional clothing. An adventurous, intelligent girl, Rankin didn't like school much but was a quick learner. She enjoyed riding horses as well as designing and sewing her own dresses.

When the University of Montana opened in Missoula in 1898, Rankin was one of its first students. She graduated four years later with a degree in biology but still unsure about what she would do with her life. She became an elementary schoolteacher for a short time—one of few career options available to women at the beginning of the twentieth century—but found the classroom too limiting. She also served as an apprentice to a seamstress and took a correspondence course in furniture making, but these pursuits did not satisfy her either.

Becoming aware of social problems

In 1904, Rankin left Montana for the first time, traveling to Boston to visit her beloved brother Wellington, who was a student at Harvard University. Shocked by the poverty and miserable conditions of people living in the slums of Boston, she started reading the works of various social reformers to learn how these problems could be lessened. Rankin decided that she would become a social worker and try to help people improve their lives.

Returning to the West Coast, Rankin began working in a San Francisco settlement house (a kind of community-service center located in an impoverished inner-city neighborhood). In 1908 she left this job to attend the New York School of Philanthropy (which later became the Columbia University School of Social Work). About a year later, Rankin moved to Seattle, where she did some social work while studying economics, public speaking, and sociology at the University of Washington.

Fighting for women's suffrage

At this time the women's suffrage movement was gaining more and more followers, and Rankin joined the fight to give women the right to vote. She signed up with Washington's state suffrage organization, and when its leaders discovered her talents as an organizer and public speaker, they sent her around the state to work on the campaign. In November 1910, Washington voters approved the amendment guaranteeing women's suffrage. Meanwhile, Rankin had gained valuable experience organizing local groups and coordinating campaign activities.

She would put these new skills to use only three months later, when she returned to Montana to lead the women's suffrage movement there. Rankin organized the Equal Franchise Society to push for the amendment giving women the right to vote in that state, and became the first woman ever to address the Montana state legislature when she made a speech in favor of women's suffrage. Although the amendment failed to pass on this first try, Rankin had helped to establish a strong women's rights movement in Montana, and the state's women did finally gain the right to vote in 1914.

A successful campaign

Meanwhile, Rankin served as legislative secretary of the National American Woman Suffrage Association and promoted the cause in several other states, including New York, California, and Ohio. During a long vacation in New Zealand (where women already had the right to vote), Rankin decided that she could put her beliefs into action by running for the U.S. Congress. Her brother Wellington agreed and supported her decision.

Rankin's experience in social reform and campaigning helped her as she prepared to run for office as a Republican in a mostly Democratic state. Her platform (a statement of a party's beliefs or positions on issues) included national women's suffrage, child protection law, the ban on alcohol known as prohibition (she kept quiet on this issue, though, to avoid opposition from Montana's liquor companies), and pacifism (nonviolence). Rankin won the Republican nomination over seven male candidates, partly because many female Democrats crossed party lines to vote for her. During the campaign that followed, Rankin traveled all over Montana. When the votes were counted, Rankin had won one of only two seats in the House of Representatives—the only Republican winner in Montana's election.

Rankin became the first woman elected to the U.S. Congress, an impressive feat in view of the fact that at the time most American women did not even have the right to vote. Rankin intended to use her office as a forum to speak out for women's rights and the others issues she supported, but World War I (1914–18) would change her plans.

As Congress opened its session on April 2, 1917, Rankin was escorted to the Capitol by a group of excited supporters, including the prominent feminist leader Carrie Chapman Catt. There were many cheers for Rankin as she walked down the aisle of the House chamber. But only four days later, the mood in Congress changed when President Woodrow Wilson proposed that the United States declare war against Germany.

Taking an unpopular stand

Relations between the United States and Germany had been going downhill for several years, and Germany—already at war with Great Britain and France—had recently sunk some American merchant ships at sea. Although for several years most Americans had favored isolationism (staying out of the affairs and conflicts of other countries), many now felt that Germany had gone too far.

Although the prospect of war had not been an issue in Rankin's campaign, she had never made her pacifism a secret. She did not believe the United States should go to war, and she thought most of her fellow Montana residents agreed with her.

At a special session on April 6, the Senate approved Wilson's resolution When it came to the House for a debate and vote, Rankin's brother urged her to vote in favor of the resolution. So did her suffragist friends, who worried that Rankin might hurt their cause if she voted against it. Nevertheless, when it was her turn to vote, Rankin stated, "I want to stand by my country, but I cannot vote for war." The resolution passed, and later in the day President Wilson declared war against Germany.

In a later statement explaining her position, Rankin commented that "It was easy to stand against the pressure of the militarists, but very difficult to go against friends and dear ones who felt that I was making a needless sacrifice by voting against the war, since my vote would not be a decisive one." Even though approximately fifty male members of Congress had also voted against the resolution, Rankin received the most attention. She was accused of acting "just like a woman," and there were calls for her resignation; some suffrage groups even canceled her speaking engagements.

A dedicated member of Congress

Despite her opposition to the fighting, Rankin sold Liberty Bonds to support the war effort. She voted in favor of the draft (which requires qualified young men to serve in the military) but against the Espionage Act, which cast suspicion on foreign residents of the United States and also made it dangerous to disagree with government policy.

During her two years in office Rankin also introduced a bill to make women independent citizens, apart from their husbands. She promoted government-sponsored aid for mothers and children and helped bring about better working conditions for employees of the Bureau of Engraving and Printing. She also worked to resolve the problems of Montana's copper miners (including trying to settle a strike).

In 1918 Rankin decided to run for the Senate. When she failed to get the Republican nomination, she ran as the candidate of the liberal National Party. She was defeated by the Democratic candidate, who had the support of the powerful Anaconda Copper Company.

Working for peace, at home and abroad

Over the next twenty years, Rankin threw all of her energy into a variety of social reform efforts. In 1919 she became involved with a variety of international groups that were working to promote women's rights and world peace. In 1923, she bought a farm in Athens, Georgia, and became a part-time resident of that state, founding the Georgia Peace Society in 1928. She advocated peace on the international level through her support of the International Court of Justice, the General Disarmament Conference, and the London Naval Conference.

Toward the end of the 1930s, the world seemed headed toward another war. By 1939, Great Britain and France were

already at war with Germany, and the United States was supplying them with supplies and weapons. Many felt it was only a matter of time before the United States would be drawn into the conflict. Nevertheless, Rankin remained a strong pacifist, and in 1940 the citizens of Montana again elected her to the House of Representatives. Running on an antiwar platform, Rankin had conducted a very effective campaign—visiting, for example, fifty-two of the fifty-five high schools in her district—and had won a big victory.

Voting "no" a second time

Despite the nation's generally isolationist mood, more people were becoming aware of the dangers of fascism (a political system that elevates the central government above citizens and is often run by the military), which was spreading across Europe. On December 7, 1941, the Japanese launched a devastating attack on the U.S. naval base at Pearl Harbor, Hawaii, killing thousands of people and destroying battleships, air-planes, and other equipment. The American public was shocked and outraged at the attack. The next day, President Roosevelt brought before Congress a proposal to declare war on Japan.

Just as she had done more than twenty years earlier, Rankin took an unpopular stand and voted against the resolution. "As a woman I can't go to war," she said, "and I refuse to send anyone else." The only member of Congress to vote no, Rankin caused a great furor: she was booed and cursed and had to be escorted by police back to her office, where she remained, under guard, for the rest of the day. In the weeks that followed, she received a huge amount of hate mail.

Remaining involved in social issues

Needless to say, Rankin was not reelected. Once again she returned to social reform work, setting up a "cooperative homestead" (in which residents live and work together cooperatively) for women in Georgia. Interested in and inspired by Indian leader and pacifist Mohatma Mohandas Gandhi, the advocate of peaceful resistance who led his country to independence in 1947, Rankin visited India seven times between 1946 and 1971. In 1962, ignoring the atmosphere of suspicion and hostility between the United States and the Soviet Union, she traveled to Moscow as an observer at the World Peace Congress.

During the 1960s, the United States became involved in a conflict in Vietnam (where Communist North Vietnam fought to take over South Vietnam, which was supported by the United States). Strongly opposed to the war, Rankin took an active role in the protest movement that gathered strength toward the end of the decade. On January 15, 1968, at age eighty-eight, she led a procession of 5,000 women (who called themselves the Jeannette Rankin Brigade) to the U.S. Capitol; she was one of fifteen women allowed inside to meet with lawmakers to express their opposition to U.S. involvement in Vietnam.

In 1972, the National Organization for Women (NOW) honored Rankin as the first member of their Susan B. Anthony Hall of Fame, which highlights the achievements of American women. Even in her early nineties, Rankin remained active in public life, pushing, for example, for changes in the way presidents are elected. She also supported the work of consumer advocate Ralph Nader. She was even considering another run for Congress, but her failing health prevented her from doing so. She died in her sleep on May 18, 1973, just before her ninety-third birthday. In 1985, a bronze statue of Rankin was placed in the U.S. Capitol.

Where to Learn More

Books

Block, Judy Rachel. *The First Woman in Congress: Jeannette Rankin.* New York: C.P.I., 1978.

Giles, Kevin. *Flight of the Dove: The Story of Jeannette Rankin.* Beaverton, OR: Touchstone Press, 1980.

Josephson, Hannah. *First Lady in Congress: Jeannette Rankin.* Indianapolis, IN: Bobbs-Merrill, 1974.

Morin, Isabel. *Women of the U.S. Congress.* Minneapolis, MN: Oliver Press, 1994.

Videos

Regele, Susan, writer, Ronald Bayley, producer, and Nancy Landgren, director. *Jeannette Rankin: The Woman Who Voted No.* Video Recording. PBS Video, 1984.

Erwin Rommel

Born November 15, 1891
Heidenheim, Germany
Died October 14, 1944
near Herrlingen, Germany

German field marshal known as the "Desert Fox"

E rwin Rommel is known for leading Germany's Afrika Korps to victory in the deserts of North Africa. His ability to keep the enemy off balance, using surprise attacks and quick movements, earned him the nickname "Desert Fox." He was admired by friends and enemies alike; for example, British prime minister Winston Churchill told the House of Commons (England's legislative body) that Rommel was "a very daring and skillful opponent and, may I say across the havoc of war, a great general." By the end of World War II, Rommel had fallen out of favor with Germany's leader, Adolf Hitler (1889–1945; see entry), when he told him that Germany could not defeat the Allies (Great Britain, the United States, the Soviet Union, and the other countries fighting against Germany, Italy, and Japan.)

An impressive young soldier

Rommel was the second of four children born to middle-class parents, Erwin (a schoolteacher) and Helene Rommel, in Heidenheim in southern Germany. As a boy he was small and well behaved, with fair hair, blue eyes, and a quiet, dreamy

"A very daring and skillful opponent and, may I say across the havoc of war, a great general."

Winston Churchill

Portrait: Erwin Rommel.
(Reproduced by permission of The Library of Congress.)

223

manner. As a teenager he became more active and practical, spending much of his time on his bicycle or skis and studying his favorite subject, mathematics.

The young Rommel was interested in airplanes and gliders; in fact, he would have liked to study engineering and learn how to build them, but his father wanted him to enter the military. In July 1910, he entered the 124th Wurtemberg Infantry Regiment as a cadet, and two years later he was commissioned as a lieutenant. In 1914, he married Lucie Mollin, whom he had met several years earlier.

As a soldier in World War I (in which Germany, Austria-Hungary, and the Ottoman Empire fought against Great Britain, France, the Soviet Union, the United States, Belgium, Serbia, and many other countries from 1914 to 1918), Rommel impressed his superior officers through his boldness, courage, and determination as well as his ability to act quickly and decisively. He served in Romania, France, and Italy and in 1917 led the capture of Monte Matajur, near the Italian city of Caporetto. For his bravery the 27-year-old Rommel received the Pour le Merite or Iron Cross, the highest award in the German military, usually given only to much older and more experienced officers.

Germany's defeat in World War I plunged the country into a period of economic hardship. Rommel decided to stay in the army, even though the Versailles Treaty—the agreement which forced Germany to take various steps to make up for starting the war—had greatly reduced its role in Germany society. By 1921 he was serving as a company commander with a regiment based near Stuttgart, and his son Manfred had been born.

Attracts Hitler's attention

Next Rommel became an instructor at the Infantry School in Dresden. The lectures he gave during his four years there were collected and published as a book, *Infantry Attacks*. The lectures featured vivid descriptions based on Rommel's own war experiences. The Swiss army used the book to train its troops, and it was also read and admired by Adolf Hitler , who was then rising through the ranks of German politics as leader of the National Socialist German Workers' Party, known as the Nazi Party.

In 1933, Hitler took complete control of the German government. He outlawed all other political parties and became dictator of Germany, and soon began his program of strict control over all citizens and even harsher treatment of Jews and other people the Nazis considered their enemies. Hitler's plans included invading the countries around Germany.

Rommel was a lieutenant colonel in 1935 when he became an instructor at the Potsdam War Academy, where for a short period he helped to train the young boys of the Hitler Youth clubs. This assignment ended, however, when Rommel had a disagreement with the very strict Nazi officer in charge of the program.

Leading the German Army into France

In 1938, Germany conquered Czechoslovakia, using a very successful form of warfare called the *blitzkrieg*: troops in vehicles (usually tanks) would make quick, surprise attacks while planes dropped bombs on the enemy. Hitler wanted to show the Czechs what a strong leader he was, so he made plans to personally visit the capital city, Prague, in October. Rommel was chosen to command the group providing security for Hitler during his trip to Czechoslovakia, and he again impressed "der Führer" (Hitler's title, which means "the leader"). Germany had also recently taken over Austria, and in November Rommel became commandant of the Austrian war academy in Wiener Neustadt.

Less than a year later, German troops pushed across the Polish border, and with this invasion—which caused Great Britain and France to declare war against Germany—World War II began. Rommel was promoted to major general and given the command of Hitler's field headquarters in Poland.

During this period, Rommel greatly admired Hitler. He thought Hitler was an idealistic, devoted patriot who only wanted to make Germany stronger. Rommel did not realize until later how much Hitler hated Jews and how far he would go to destroy them.

As Germany prepared to attack France, Rommel was given command of the 7th Panzer (Tank) Division, which he led into France from Belgium. Rommel's troops were known as the "Ghost" or "Phantom" division because they moved at such terrific speed that they always seemed to appear out of nowhere. Rommel devised many bold, clever moves and played an important role in the successful takeover of France, for which he was awarded the Knight's Cross medal.

In command of the Afrika Korps

After the victory in France, Rommel was appointed to lead the Afrika Korps, the German force that would fight the British army in North Africa, where troops from Italy (Germany's ally in World War II) were struggling to hold their own. Beginning in 1941, Rommel commanded the Afrika Korps in a series of battles against the British 8th Army, and again the blitzkrieg proved an effective form of warfare. The Germans were able to push the British from Libya all the way to the Egyptian border—a distance of about 1,500 miles—bringing them close to the Suez Canal, an important strategic goal because it would allow them to more easily bring in supplies to the area.

It was the element of surprise he so often used and his clever maneuvers that earned Rommel the nickname "Desert Fox" as well as the admiration of both friends and enemies. In fact, one British general who admitted that Rommel was a "master of innovation" had to warn his own officers about admiring the German general too much—he was the enemy after all. Rommel's good reputation with Allied troops also had something to do with the fact that prisoners of the Afrika Korps were treated well, unlike those in other parts of the world. His own soldiers appreciated his habit of commanding battles from the middle of the action, rather than from a safe, distant spot, even though it meant that he was sometimes away from headquarters when important decisions had to be made.

The youngest field marshal

As news of Afrika Korps victories reached Germany, Rommel became a great hero in his own country. Hitler publicized Rommel's accomplishments because he realized how valuable such a popular figure could be in promoting the war effort. And Rommel was a good choice for a war hero because he had no political ambitions of his own and would never challenge Hitler's power. In June 1942, Rommel was made a

field marshal, the highest rank in the Germany army, becoming the youngest officer ever to achieve it; he commented, however, that he would have preferred instead to be sent another division of troops to help him fight the British.

As 1942 progressed, the British began to improve their position and performance in North Africa, partly due to the dynamic leadership of General Bernard Montgomery (1887–

Rommel (pointing) led the Afrika Korps in many successful battles against the British 8th Army in North Africa.

(Reproduced by permission of Archive Photos.)

1976; see entry). Rommel was unable to get the supplies, equipment, and troops he needed to take the Suez Canal, and Afrika Korps started losing its battles against the British 8th Army. One of the biggest defeats occurred at El Alamein, located a few hundred miles west of Cairo, Egypt; as a result of the battle, Rommel's troops were driven back 2,000 miles across the desert to Tunisia. With the March 1943 loss at Medenine against American troops led by General Dwight D. Eisenhower (1890–1969; see entry), the Germans had to accept defeat in North Africa. Meanwhile, Rommel had developed stomach and other health problems and had already left to seek medical treatment in Germany.

Preparing for the Allied invasion

After recovering from an illness, Rommel was sent to northern Italy to help Germany's ally Benito Mussolini (1883–1945; see entry), Italy's dictator. The Allies had invaded Sicily (a large island off the coast of Italy) and then the Italian mainland. As they pushed their way north, Italian partisans (forces fighting against the Axis from within Italy) overthrew Mussolini and arrested him. The Germans saved him from the partisans and set him up as leader of Northern Italy, which was still controlled by the Axis.

By the end of 1943 it was thought that the Allies would soon launch an invasion of Europe. In response to this Rommel, who had been put in command of all German troops from the Netherlands to the Loire River in northern France, went to France in 1944 to prepare for the possible invasion.

Rommel believed that the best strategy was to fight and beat the Allies as soon as they landed, while others thought that more troops should be placed inland to catch the Allied forces as they moved into the French countryside. In the end neither strategy was really chosen: Hitler insisted on a kind of compromise, which did not prove very effective. Rommel was able to set up a few defenses on and around the beaches where they thought the Allies might try to invade. Rommel used defenses such as underwater explosive devices and "Rommel's asparagus"—stakes driven in the ground and draped with barbed wire and mines to prevent Allied boats and airplanes from landing safely.

The Plot to Kill Hitler

As the war went on and it appeared that Nazi Germany could not beat the Allies, many of Adolf Hitler's former supporters began to think the country would be better off without him. One of these was Nicholas von Stauffenberg, who had served as a staff officer in the German invasions of Poland, the Netherlands, and France. Born into a wealthy family, Stauffenberg was a devout Catholic, and he was horrified by the Nazi brutalities he witnessed. He joined two other officers who were plotting to assassinate (kill) Hitler.

In April 1943, Stauffenberg was serving with a tank division in North Africa when the car in which he was traveling came under fire. He was seriously wounded, losing his left eye, his right hand, and two fingers on his left hand. While recovering in a German hospital, he decided that Hitler must be killed soon. He told his wife, "I feel I must do something now to save Germany. We General Staff officers must all accept our share of the responsibility."

Stauffenberg and his co-conspirators planned the assassination for July 20, 1944. Hitler was having a military conference at one of his headquarters, called Wolf's Lair, and Stauffenberg had been asked to attend. When Stauffenberg arrived, he was carrying a bomb in his briefcase. A captured British time bomb, it was fitted with a device that would produce an explosion a certain period of time after it was triggered.

Stauffenberg armed the bomb just before entering the conference room. He asked to be seated close to Hitler, which did not seem unusual since he had poor hearing. He put down his briefcase about six feet from Hitler, then said he had to make a phone call and left the room. He was in his car, headed for the airport, when he heard the bomb explode.

Stauffenberg did not know that just after he had left, someone had moved his briefcase away from Hitler. The explosion killed four men but only slightly injured Hitler. After he reached his Berlin headquarters, Stauffenberg learned that Hitler was not dead. He tried to convince other army officers to join the plot anyway and overthrow Hitler, but they refused.

Stauffenberg and several others were soon arrested and taken to Hitler's military headquarters. In a courtyard lit only by a truck's headlights, they were killed by firing squad. Before the shots were fired, Stauffenberg reportedly shouted, "Long live our sacred Germany!"

Hitler refuses to accept defeat

On June 6, 1944, the massive Allied invasion known as D-Day occurred when about 150,000 Allied troops landed on the beaches of Normandy in northern France. After the successful landing, Rommel realized that Germany could not win the war. It was around this time that he also learned of the concentration camps, the prisons where millions of Jews were being confined and murdered. Rommel met with Hitler and urged him to close the camps and take other measures to improve Germany's chances, but Hitler refused to listen. Rommel felt disillusioned and bitter. On July 15 he sent Hitler a message stating that this "unequal struggle is at an end," but he received no reply.

On July 17, Rommel was traveling along a French road when his car was machine-gunned by a British warplane. The driver was killed and Rommel received a skull fracture. He was unconscious for a week and was flown home to Germany to recover.

Meanwhile, a group of German officers who were unhappy with Hitler's leadership had made a plan to assassinate him. While Hitler was meeting with other leaders, one of the plotters left a bomb close to him and then left the room. The bomb was pushed to a different part of the room, so that when it exploded it killed some other men present but not Hitler. Some of those who had planned the attack were quickly found and executed, while investigators kept looking for others.

"I have come to say goodbye"

Because Rommel had openly stated his poor opinion of Hitler (claiming, for instance, that Hitler was insane, and that Germany should surrender to the Allies), he was suspected of being involved in the bomb plot, even though he was lying unconscious in a hospital bed at the time. Indeed, Rommel may have known about the plot but he was probably not actively involved in it; he had said that he thought Hitler should be arrested and brought to trial, not assassinated.

In any case, Rommel was summoned to Nazi headquarters in Berlin on October 7, 1944. Convinced that his life was in danger, Rommel stayed home. But on October 14, two generals arrived at his house and asked to speak to him privately. Afterward, Rommel went into the room where his wife and son were waiting and told them, "I have come to say goodbye. In a quarter of an hour I will be dead." The generals had delivered a message from Hitler that Rommel was to make a choice: he could commit suicide, or come before the Nazi "people's court" to face charges of being involved in the assassination plot. If he chose suicide, Rommel's family would not be harmed, but this would not be the case if he decided to go to trial.

The generals had brought with them a vial of poison that they claimed would kill him within seconds. Rommel drove off in their car with them. Fifteen minutes later, his wife Lucie received a phone call telling her that her husband had died of a heart attack. In fact, of course, he had taken the poison and died.

Hitler was worried about how the public would react to the real facts of Rommel's death, so it was announced that he had died of his war wounds. Rommel was given a grand state funeral, with fine speeches and stirring music—an event that his wife found almost unbearable. In fact, she refused Hitler's offer to set up a memorial to her husband, knowing that this would be a false tribute from the man who had ordered Rommel's death.

Where to Learn More

Books

Blanco, Richard L. *Rommel, the Desert Warrior: The Afrika Korps in World War II*. New York: J. Messner, 1982.

Douglas-Home, Charles. *Rommel*. New York: Weidenfeld and Nicolson, 1974.

Fraser, David. *Knight's Cross*. New York: HarperCollins, 1993.

Irving, David. *The Trail of the Fox: A Search for the True Field Marshal Rommel*. New York: Macmillan, 1977.

Mitcham, Samuel W., Jr. *Triumphant Fox: Erwin Rommel and the Rise of the Afrika Korps*. New York: Stein and Day, 1984.

Pimlott, John, ed. *Rommel: In His Own Words*. London: Greenhill Books, 1994.

Young, Desmond. *Rommel*. London: Collins, 1950.

Franklin D. Roosevelt

Born January 30, 1882
Hyde Park, New York
Died April 12, 1945
Warm Springs, Georgia

32nd president of the United States (1932-1945)

Franklin D. Roosevelt led the United States through two of its most difficult periods, the Great Depression and World War II.

Portrait: Franklin D. Roosevelt. *(Reproduced by permission of the Franklin D. Roosevelt Library.)*

Considered one of America's greatest leaders, Franklin D. Roosevelt was the only president to be elected to four terms in office. Both beloved and controversial, he took charge at a turbulent time in American history. The Great Depression (1929–39) caused widespread suffering as many people lost their jobs, homes, and businesses and some people wondered whether the United States could survive as a democracy. Roosevelt's solution was a set of programs and reforms he called the "New Deal," many of which have survived to the present day. Not all of them were successful, but Roosevelt's energy and optimism gave many Americans the strength they needed to carry on. In the same determined way, he led his country through World War II and helped its citizens to feel that the sacrifices made and many lives lost were not in vain.

A child of privilege

Roosevelt came from a very privileged background. Born on his wealthy family's estate in Hyde Park, New York, he was the only child of Sara Delano and James Roosevelt. He was a distant cousin of Theodore Roosevelt, who was to serve as president from 1901 to 1909. He remained close to his devoted, domineering mother all his life, but his father (who was twenty-six years older than his mother) was often ill and somewhat distant.

Roosevelt's childhood was sheltered but happy. As a young boy he did not attend school but was taught at home by a tutor, and he often traveled to Europe with his parents. He was bright and energetic and loved sports and outdoor activities.

At fourteen, Roosevelt went to the exclusive Groton School in Massachusetts, an academy founded by Rector Endicott Peabody that encouraged its young male students to fulfill their responsibilities to society. Roosevelt took seriously the school's philosophy of public service.

A young husband and lawyer

In 1900 Roosevelt entered Harvard University, where he studied history and government. His academic performance was not spectacular but he had an active social life and took part in many outside activities, including serving as editor in chief of the *Harvard Crimson*, the university's undergraduate newspaper. It was during his years at Harvard that Roosevelt developed his leadership abilities and strong political beliefs.

During his senior year, Roosevelt became engaged to his distant cousin Eleanor, who was the niece of Teddy Roosevelt. His mother did not approve of the match and tried to change his mind, but nevertheless the couple married on March 17, 1905, with Eleanor's famous uncle walking her down the aisle. Over the years the couple would have six children (one of whom died as a baby) and Eleanor would prove to be both a supportive partner to her husband and a dynamic leader in her own right.

After graduating from Harvard, Roosevelt attended New York's Columbia University Law School. In 1907 he joined a New York law firm, but he did not especially like the work. He decided to run for the New York Senate, and in 1910 became the first Democrat senator elected in New York in fifty years. As senator, Roosevelt worked hard to end the corruption that had overtaken much of New York's government.

An education in politics

Roosevelt supported the Democratic candidate, Woodrow Wilson, in the election of 1912 (even though he was running against Teddy Roosevelt). After Wilson's victory, Roosevelt was appointed assistant secretary of the navy. Roosevelt served in this position until after World War I, gaining valuable experience in how to work with a variety of people and opinions and how to deal with Congress.

At the 1920 Democratic convention Roosevelt was nominated to be the vice presidential candidate with James M. Cox as the presidential nominee. Cox and Roosevelt lost the election to Republican Warren G. Harding, but the campaign had taught Roosevelt much about running for office and public speaking. When it was over, he returned to New York to practice law.

Polio changes his life

A year later an event occurred that dramatically changed Roosevelt's life. While vacationing at his family's summer home on Campobello Island near New Brunswick, Canada, Roosevelt came down with polio, a serious disease that causes paralysis. As a result, Roosevelt could no longer move his legs; his back, arms, and hands were also affected.

At first Roosevelt was deeply depressed by his illness, but eventually he regained his positive outlook. His mother told him he should retire, but Eleanor encouraged him to continue in public life. He began a program of vigorous exercise and overcame the partial paralysis of his back, arms, and hands, and after some time he was even able to walk occasionally with the help of canes and braces. Although his legs grew very thin and weak from lack of use, his arms became very strong.

For the rest of his life, Roosevelt would spend most of his time in a wheelchair. The public remained largely unaware of this fact because the press rarely mentioned it and only published photographs that showed Roosevelt standing or sitting at a desk. Roosevelt's condition benefited him in some ways, because it helped him to develop greater patience and self-control, and it made him more aware of and sympathetic to the problems suffered by other people. Roosevelt was often admired for the courageous manner he dealt with his physical challenges. When, for instance, he made his way to the podium to give a speech at the 1924 Democratic convention, supported by his sixteen-year-old son James, he received a standing ovation from the audience.

Governor of New York

With Eleanor's help, Roosevelt remained knowledgeable and politically connected during this tough time, and he remained deeply interested in social problems. In 1928 he was elected governor of New York in a close election. The next year, the stock market crashed (most stocks lost their value, and investors lost their money), and the years of economic hardship known as the Great Depression had begun.

Faced with a high unemployment rate in his state, Roosevelt set up a system of direct relief for workers who had lost their jobs. His popularity soared and he was reelected in 1930, gaining a nationwide reputation as a leader with bold new ideas.

A new deal for the American people

During those rough first years of the Great Depression, Roosevelt was mentioned as a possible presidential candidate, and in 1932 he was nominated by the Democrats. He broke a longstanding tradition by flying to the convention to accept the nomination in person. In his acceptance speech he told the delegates, "I pledge you, I pledge myself to a new deal for the American people," a new deal that would include both direct relief and reform measures to prevent future economic depressions.

During the campaign that followed, Roosevelt appeared in thirty-eight states, dispelling any concerns over his physical health. He won a huge victory over President Herbert Hoover (whom many Americans blamed for the country's problems) and was inaugurated on March 4, 1933.

Even before he was sworn in, Roosevelt began working on the nation's problems, which were perhaps the worst it had ever faced. About fifteen million workers (one-quarter of the workforce) were unemployed. Many banks had closed, wiping

"First Lady Of The World" Eleanor Roosevelt

Before Franklin D. Roosevelt, the United States had never had a president who served for four terms. Similarly, the United States never had a First Lady like Roosevelt's wife Eleanor. She changed the way the nation viewed the role of the president's spouse.

Born into a wealthy family in 1884 in New York City, Eleanor was the niece of Theodore Roosevelt, who was president of the United States from 1901 to 1909. She was an awkward, shy girl who felt especially lonely after the deaths of both her parents before she was ten years old.

At age eighteen, like all rich young women of her set, she had to enter society and begin attending parties and dances. This was painful for such a shy girl, but she did often get to see her fifth cousin, Franklin Delano Roosevelt, who was a student at Harvard University. The two fell in love and were married on March 17, 1905. Their first child was born a year later, and over the next nine years they had five more children (one died as a baby).

When Franklin became a New York state senator, Eleanor took up the role of the senator's wife. She felt uncomfortable at first but soon adapted to her new position, though her shyness returned somewhat when the couple moved to Washington, D.C., after Franklin was named assistant secretary of the navy.

In the summer of 1921, Franklin contracted polio, which paralyzed his legs and endangered his political career. Political advisor Louis Howe advised Eleanor to become more active in public life so that her husband would not be forgotten while he recovered. She became an active member of the state's Democratic Party and was soon one of its leaders. In a few years Franklin was ready to resume his career, but in the meantime her own career was also blossoming.

Eleanor's growing interest in the problems of the unemployed and other disadvantaged people led to such activities as writing newspaper articles, starting and teaching at a special school for poor children, and helping to set up a furniture

out the savings people had worked their whole lives to collect. A huge number of people were homeless, and charities could not feed or house most of them. Young people lacked the money to attend or finish college, and many of them took to the roads to look for work. In the past, the government would not have been responsible for solving these problems, but Roosevelt believed that government *had to* help.

factory to give jobless people work. When Franklin was elected governor of New York, Eleanor began to travel all over the state and reported back to him on how people were living and what they were thinking.

Franklin was elected to his first term as president in 1932, and Eleanor began building a reputation as the most active, outspoken First Lady in American history. One of the topics Eleanor felt most strongly about was civil rights. She continually encouraged her husband to consider equal opportunities for African Americans in his New Deal programs. In 1939, she resigned her membership in the Daughters of the American Revolution (DAR) organization when they refused to allow African American singer Marian Anderson to appear at Constitution Hall in Philadelphia; Eleanor also arranged for Anderson to sing at the Lincoln Memorial in Washington.

Eleanor also used her influence to push for more equality for women, and to encourage women to fight for their rights. One way she did so was to create a White House Women's Press Corps and to make a rule that only women reporters could attend her press conferences, which meant that newspapers had to hire at least one woman.

Having seen the devastating effects of World War I Eleanor was a staunch promoter of international peace. During World War II, she made several goodwill tours as her husband's representative in England, the South Pacific, and the Caribbean.

After the death of her husband in 1945, Eleanor continued to play a very public role in American life. She was chosen to serve as part of the first U.S. delegation to the new United Nations, in which position President Harry Truman called her the "First Lady of the World." Eleanor was instrumental in writing the UN's Declaration on Human Rights and took part in the formation of UNICEF (the UN's fund for children). She continued to write articles and books and remained involved in Democratic politics. Eleanor died in 1962.

Trying new solutions

In his inaugural address, Roosevelt promised Americans that the country would recover from these terrible times. He pledged that he would experiment with new solutions to solve the problems of society, and he urged people to keep calm and to be courageous: "The only thing we have to fear," he told them, "is fear itself."

Thus Roosevelt immediately started demonstrating his ability to inspire confidence in others, to share with them his own hope and optimism. His willingness to give the federal government a bigger role in American life made him different from previous presidents, and his warm personality, energy, self-confidence, and positive approach to life made people like and trust him. He gained the support of a wide range of citizens, including farmers, labor union members, both poor and middle-class city-dwellers, and African Americans (who switched their loyalty from the Republicans—the party of President Abraham Lincoln—to support Roosevelt).

An excellent communicator

Roosevelt was popular partly because of his excellent communication skills. He believed in having a good relationship with the press, so he held two press conferences a week and always made the transcripts of what he'd said available to the public.

But one of his most important accomplishments was his understanding of the power of radio and the central role it played in American homes. Every week, Roosevelt delivered a radio broadcast called a "Fireside Chat," in which he spoke to his listeners in an informal, relaxed way—addressing them as "My friends" and making them feel that he was talking to each of them directly while discussing important issues.

100 days of change

Roosevelt's first term as president began with a special, 100-day session of Congress that passed an unusually high number of measures. First Roosevelt declared a "bank holiday" that temporarily closed all banks (which provided relief for banks and panicked investors); then he pushed through a law that allowed only the most sound banks to reopen, so that people felt secure about their money.

To combat the unemployment problem, Roosevelt felt people would keep their self-respect if they were offered jobs rather than money. With that in mind he sponsored such programs as the Civilian Conservation Corps, which put 2.5 million young men to work in parks and forests; the National Youth Administration, which gave part-time work to two million high school and college students; and the Works Progress Administration, which employed eight million people in the building of roads, schools, dams, and other projects.

Other major programs started during Roosevelt's first term included the Agricultural Adjustment Act, which helped farmers increase their income by reducing surpluses and raising prices; the Tennessee Valley Authority, through which dams were built to control floods and produce low-cost electricity; and the Federal Deposit Insurance Corporation, which protected bank deposits up to $5,000.

A more difficult second term

In 1936 Roosevelt ran for president again and won in a landslide, gaining 61 percent of the popular vote over Governor Alf Landon of Kansas. At the beginning of his second term, he was criticized for trying to reorganize the Supreme Court (which had opposed a number of his New Deal proposals). But soon after his reelection the Supreme Court approved some important programs, including the National Labor Relations (Wagner) Act, which guaranteed workers the right to join unions; the Social Security Act, offering citizens protection from poverty in old age, sickness, and unemployment; and the Fair Labor Standards Act, which established a minimum wage for workers.

During Roosevelt's second term as president, business leaders and Republicans criticized his policies, claiming that they were wasteful and that they gave government too large a role in people's lives. Roosevelt's popularity was also hurt when he cut government spending, causing another economic downturn and the loss of about two million jobs. Nevertheless, his supporters continued to credit him not only with making real improvements but with helping Americans to stay calm when, all over the world, hard times were leading to the rise of dictators (absolute rulers).

Dictators gain power

Roosevelt was well aware that leaders like Adolf Hitler (1889–1945; see entry) of Germany, Benito Mussolini (1883–1945; see entry) of Italy, and Hideki Tojo (1884–1948; see entry) of Japan were gaining power by restricting their people's freedoms. He believed that the United States should get involved in trying to control these dictators because they threatened the survival of democracy everywhere. At this point in history, however, the majority of the American people did not agree with him. They had experienced World War I (1914–1918) and had come out of it as isolationists: they did not want to become involved in the problems of other countries.

In September 1939 Germany invaded Poland; Great Britain and France responded by declaring war on Germany. The next year, Roosevelt was reelected (becoming the first American president to serve three terms), but by a slimmer margin than in previous elections. Meanwhile, his desire to help the Allies (the name for the countries fighting against Germany; at the beginning of the war this included Great Britain and France) in their war against the Nazis had only increased, even though public opinion still favored isolationism.

The arsenal of democracy

France was quickly defeated by the Germans in May 1940, leaving Great Britain to face the Germans alone.

Pledging to make the United States the "great arsenal of democracy" (by which he meant the provider of weapons and other equipment the Allies would use to defend their countries), Roosevelt got Congress to approve an exchange program by which the United States gave Great Britain fifty destroyers (ships equipped with high-powered guns) in return for the use of British naval bases close to the United States.

As Great Britain withstood months of heavy bombing raids by the Germans, Roosevelt kept working to provide support for them. He pushed through a law setting up a Lend-Lease Program, through which supplies and weapons sent to those fighting against the Axis nations (Germany, Italy, and eventually Japan) could be paid for after the war. Roosevelt met with British prime minister Winston Churchill (1874–1965; see entry) in August 1941 to sign the Atlantic Charter. In this agreement Great Britain and the United States expressed their common opposition to tyranny and their commitment to setting up an international peace keeping organization.

Japan attacks Pearl Harbor

Meanwhile, in the Pacific region, Japan had attacked China as well as other areas of Asia that had been controlled by Great Britain and France. To force the Japanese to stop their aggressive actions, Roosevelt put a halt to trade with Japan. This led to Japan's decision to launch a devastating surprise attack on the U.S. naval base at Pearl Harbor, Hawaii. The attack occurred early on the morning of December 7, 1941, sinking or damaging battleships and killing more than 2,500 people.

Americans were shocked and angered by the surprise attack. The next day, calling December 7 "a day which will live in infamy," Roosevelt declared war on Japan. In 1940 Germany, Japan, and Italy had signed the Tripartite Pact, in which they agreed to defend each other if any of them went to war. A few days after the United States declared war on Japan, Germany and Italy declared war on the United States. Just as Roosevelt had inspired the American people to have faith and determination to overcome the Great Depression, he now called upon them to resist military aggression and dictatorship.

Preparing the nation for war

During the early months of the war, Roosevelt put together an extraordinary team of generals and admirals to lead the U.S. war effort, while he presided over the most important strategic decisions. He began to gear the U.S. economy toward preparing for war, starting up a number of agencies to handle such tasks as processing recruits (those who had volunteered or been drafted to serve) into the armed forces or producing the weapons and tanks the military would need. Other important steps he took during the first few years of the war included setting up the Manhattan Project to research the possibility of building an atomic bomb (see J. Robert Oppenheimer entry) and persuading twenty-six countries to join the organization to be named the United Nations.

Although Roosevelt and his military commanders thought the Allies should first invade Europe and attack Germany on its own soil, they were finally persuaded by the British to attack first in North Africa, where British troops had been battling Germany's Afrika Korps under the able command of

Field Marshal Erwin Rommel (1891–1944; see entry). They also invaded Sicily (an island off the Italian mainland) and Italy. In the Pacific theater (where only about 15 percent of Allied resources would be sent), the Allied forces also fought their way up through the region's many island chains toward Japan.

Victories in Europe, and a massive invasion

As the Allies carried on their successful military campaign in Europe, defeating the Germans in North Africa, Sicily, and Italy, the Soviet Union struggled mightily against the German invaders in their own country. Germany had invaded the Soviet Union in June 1941. The Soviets lost about twenty million lives in the fighting but managed to keep the German forces from overtaking the whole country. Soviet leader Joseph Stalin (1879–1953; see entry)—a controversial figure due to his brutal policies against his own people— joined Roosevelt and Churchill at several major conferences throughout the war. At Casablanca in early 1943, Roosevelt and his colleagues declared that they would accept only "unconditional surrender" by the Axis nations; and at Quebec in August 1943 they planned a massive invasion of France to take place the next spring.

After six months of preparation under the direction of General Dwight D. Eisenhower (1890–1969; see entry), the invasion that had been nicknamed "Operation Overlord" took place. On June 6, 1944, about 150,000 Allied troops landed on the heavily defended beaches of the Normandy region of northern France. By the time a month had passed, about a million soldiers were pushing on across France toward Germany, stopped only briefly by a German counteroffensive (called the Battle of the Bulge) in December in the Ardennes region. In March 1945, they crossed the Rhine River into Germany, and by May the Germans were forced to surrender.

A short fourth term

In November 1944, Roosevelt had been elected to a fourth term. By now the massive spending of the wartime period had wiped out the Great Depression, and many of Roosevelt's New Deal reforms had been eliminated. Most Americans appreciated Roosevelt's strong leadership during the crisis of World War II. Some critics claim that he had made some serious mistakes including actually allowing the attack on Pearl Harbor to occur, relocating Japanese Americans to internment camps, not ordering that the military be desegregated, and not doing enough to help Jewish refugees.

In February 1945 Roosevelt traveled to a conference of Allied leaders held at Yalta in the Soviet Union. With Churchill and Stalin, he discussed plans to bring the war to a close and how Europe would be rebuilt after the war. Some would later fault Roosevelt for trusting Stalin too much and allowing the Soviet Union too much control of Eastern Europe. At the time, though, Roosevelt thought this was necessary in order to ensure that the Soviet Union would continue to fight for the Allies.

After his return from Yalta, Roosevelt went to Warm Springs, Georgia, where he owned a small home and where he had established a foundation to help other polio victims. He often went to Warm Springs for rest and recovery; for some time, he had been in poor health with heart problems and other ailments. On April 12, 1945, Roosevelt died from a cerebral hemorrhage (bleeding of the brain). Later the same day, Vice President Harry S. Truman (1884–1972; see entry) was sworn in as the nation's thirty-third president. It would be up to Truman to lead the nation out of war and into peacetime.

"Let us move forward ..."

Thousands of Americans gathered to watch as Roosevelt's body was taken north by train. He was buried on the grounds of his estate at Hyde Park, under a stone that bore only his name and years of birth and death. The last words he dictated on the day before his death are, perhaps, more expressive of his lifelong philosophy: "The only real limit to our realization of tomorrow will be our doubts of today. Let us move forward with strong and active faith."

Where to Learn More

Books

Davis, Kenneth S. *FDR: Into the Storm, 1937–1940*. New York: Random House, 1993.

Freedman, Russell. *Franklin Delano Roosevelt*. New York: Clarion Books, 1990.

Freidel, Frank Burt. *Franklin Delano Roosevelt: A Rendezvous with Destiny*. Boston: Little, Brown, 1972.

Goodwin, Doris Kearns. *No Ordinary Time: Franklin and Eleanor Roosevelt: The Home Front in World War II*. New York: Simon & Schuster, 1994.

Heinrichs, Waldo H. *Franklin Delano Roosevelt and the American Entry Into World War II*. Oxford: Oxford University Press, 1988.

Morgan, Ted. *FDR: A Biography*. New York: Simon & Schuster, 1985.

Potts, Steve. *Franklin D. Roosevelt: A Photo-Illustrated Biography*. Mankato, MN: Bridgestone Books, 1996.

Joseph Stalin

Born December 21, 1879
Gori, Georgia, Russia
Died March 5, 1953
Moscow, Russia

Dictator of the Soviet Union from 1928 to 1953

Joseph Stalin became the leader of the Soviet Union after the death of Vladimir Lenin, who had led the revolution that removed the Russian czar (an all-powerful, hereditary ruler like a king) from power and put the Communist Party in charge of the country in 1917. Under Stalin, the Soviet Union became one of the world's major powers, but his was a reign of terror as millions of people who displeased Stalin in various ways were executed or sent to labor camps called "gulags." During World War II, Stalin rallied the Russian people to defeat the Germans and they did so, but at a terrible cost—about twenty-five million Russians lost their lives in the war.

Joseph Stalin led his country to repel a German invasion and join Allied forces during World War II.

A boy called "Soso"

Stalin was born Iosef (Joseph) Vissarionovich Dzhugashvili in Gori, in the country of Georgia, which was then part of Russia's empire in western Asia. He was the only one of four children in his family who did not die as a baby. Stalin's father, Vissarion, was a shoemaker and an alcoholic who died from wounds he received in a fight. His mother, Yekaterina, took in washing and sewing and hired out as a

Portrait: Joseph Stalin.
(Reproduced by permission of UPI/Corbis-Bettmann.)

245

housekeeper to support her son, whom she nursed through several serious childhood illnesses, including smallpox.

Called "Soso" as a boy, Stalin spoke only the Georgian language until he was eight. At that age he started school, where he learned Russian (the common language of the Russian empire) and studied religion, geography, and other subjects. Although she could not read or write herself, Stalin's very religious mother had grand ambitions for her son; in particular, she wanted him to become a priest, and perhaps eventually a bishop.

Learning about Marxism

In 1894 Stalin won a scholarship to the theological seminary in Tbilisi (the largest city in Georgia). He earned good grades the first year, but during the second year he rebelled against the school's strict rules. He smuggled banned books into the school, and once refused to bow to a school official. It was during these years that Stalin learned about Marxism (the theory of Karl Marx that calls for the working class to revolt and create a classless society). Stalin began reading works by Marxist writers, especially Vladimir Lenin, who would later lead Russia's revolution.

In 1899 Stalin was expelled from the seminary (even after her son became the leader of the Soviet Union, his mother considered him a failure for not entering the priesthood). He continued to dream of revolution, and began calling himself "Koba" (which means "The Indomitable") after a hero from Georgian folk tales.

Stalin got a job as a bookkeeper at the Tbilisi observatory, and there he met members of a group called the Social Democrats, who used the observatory as a meeting place. These people were communists (believers in a political system in which all citizens own property as a group rather than individually), which was illegal in Russia at the time. Stalin joined the group, and when his employers discovered this he lost his job.

A full-time revolutionary

Unemployed, Stalin became an active member of the Social Democratic Party's militant wing and devoted all of his time to revolutionary activities, which mostly involved trying to convince industrial workers to support the group. In 1894 he married a peasant girl, Yekaterina Svanidze, but after only three happy years—and the birth of a son, Jacob—she died. Arrested in 1902 for his revolutionary activities, Stalin was sent to Siberia (a huge, desolate part of northern Russia where people were often sent as punishment for crimes) but escaped two years later and returned to Georgia.

In 1905 Stalin attended a political meeting in Finland, and there he met Vladimir Lenin for the first time. The Social Democratic Party had split into two parts: the Mensheviks, who believed in gradual change and compromise; and the extremist Bolsheviks, led by Lenin, who called for immediate revolution. Lenin could see that Stalin was a loyal party member who was good at organizing and at solving practical problems, and he put Stalin to work raising money for the Bolsheviks by robbing banks and government money transports—Lenin did so quietly, however, since this was an activity of which some Bolsheviks might not have approved.

After performing such tasks for some time Stalin was in danger of arrest, so he was expelled from his local party, and he disappeared. He soon resurfaced in Baku, Azerbaijan (located near the Caspian Sea), where he tried to convince the area's oil workers to join the Bolsheviks. Constantly in and out of trouble with the police, Stalin spent several periods of exile in Siberia.

Trusted by Lenin

In 1912 Lenin cut his ties with the Social Democrats and formed his own party. Knowing how invaluable Stalin's ruthlessness and intelligence were, Lenin nominated him to his party's central committee. But Stalin was soon arrested again, and this time he stayed in Siberia for a longer period. He did not return, in fact, until March 1917, when the Russian revolution toppled the czar's (all-powerful ruler) regime. By this time he was calling himself Stalin, which comes from the Russian word "stal" which means steel.

At this period, Russia was made up of a collection of individual republics that would, in 1924, together become the Soviet Union. Meanwhile, however, the country was ruled by a provisional (temporary) government made up of several different political parties that had worked together to overthrow the czar. In April, Lenin returned to Russia from Switzerland, where he had been living in exile, and announced his dissatisfaction with the new government. After issuing a demand for peace, bread (meaning adequate food), and land for the Russian people, Lenin and his followers organized a revolutionary committee and began urging urban workers, rural people, and members of the military to back them.

Over the next few months, the members of the revolutionary committee—who were now calling themselves Communists as well as Bolsheviks—gradually gained influence, so that by October they were able to stage a bloodless takeover of the provisional government. The Communist Party now ruled Russia, with Lenin as its top leader.

Lenin now named Stalin Commissar of Nationalities, putting him in charge of placing Communists among all the many ethnic groups in Russia so that the party's power would increase. Meanwhile, Stalin also attracted his own supporters among the most powerful Communist leaders. During these years Stalin was proving himself to be a strong leader who could make tough decisions and stick with them; he was not considered an intellectual leader, but was determined to get what he wanted.

Between 1918 and 1921, the Communists and their "Red Army" fought a civil war with those who still resisted their dominance: called the "Whites," these opponents included some who fought for a return to a czarist regime and some who wanted a more democratic government. Stalin served as a military commander during this conflict. In 1919, when Lenin set up agencies to perform various government tasks, Stalin was made Commissar of the Workers and Peasants Inspectorate. He became a member of the party secretariat or "Politboro." Stalin also took a second wife, Nadezhda Alliluyeva, the sixteen-year-old daughter of an old friend. The couple had two children, Vasili and Svetlana, born in 1919 and 1925. In 1932, Nadezhda would kill herself, leaving a note that expressed disapproval of Stalin as a man and leader.

Building his own power

Lenin made it clear that he continued to value Stalin when, in 1922, he made him the general secretary of the Central Committee of the Communist Party. This was an important position, because Stalin had the power to give key party jobs to people who were loyal to him. In that way, he was able to staff the party's higher levels with many of his supporters.

In May 1922 Lenin had a stroke and his health grew worse and worse. At the same time, he began to express fear about the amount of power that Stalin and others had built for themselves. But Lenin was losing influence in the party, as some members accused him of forgetting some of the ideals around which the Communist Party had been founded.

After Lenin's death in January 1924, the country was at first led jointly by five men: Stalin, Leon Trotsky (the head of the Red Army), Lev Kamenev and Grigori Zinoviev (Moscow and Leningrad party chiefs), and Nikolai Bukharin (the party's theorist). Each of these men would have liked to be Russia's top ruler, but it was Stalin who emerged on top. He did so by carefully building an image of himself as humble, calm, efficient, and fatherly and by pitting his opponents against each other.

A plan to advance the Soviet Union

First Stalin plotted with Kamenev and Zinoviev to remove Trotsky from power (he went into exile in Mexico, where he was eventually killed by Stalin's agents). Then Stalin and Bukharin worked together to get rid of Kamenev and Zinoviev. Finally Stalin turned against Bukharin. In less than ten years, Stalin was the only one of these original five leaders left alive, thanks to his own ruthless pursuit of power.

Stalin now had complete control of the Soviet Union, which he ran with the help of a strong, brutal police force. His main objective was to develop his country's industry and agriculture, and in 1928 he proposed the "Five-Year Plan" (which was followed by other five-year plans) to quickly reach the goals he had set. "We are 50 to 100 years behind the advanced countries," Stalin told his people. "We must cover this distance in ten years. Either we do this or they will crush us."

Across the Soviet Union, construction began on factories, dams, and other major projects, and within five years the country was producing steel, machine tools, tractors, and other industrial products. Meanwhile, farmers were forced to give up their small family farms and move onto state-owned,

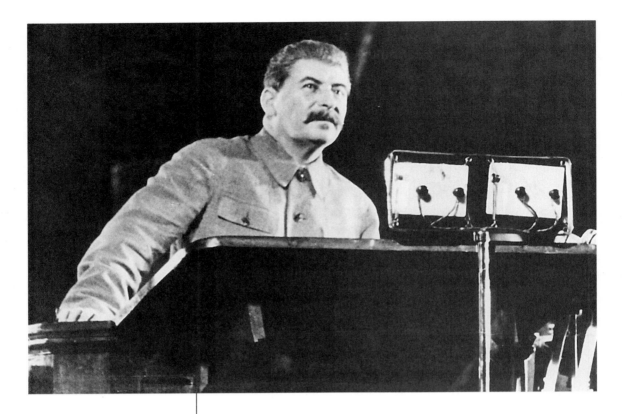

In 1928, Stalin presented his "Five-Year Plan" to make the Soviet Union a world power.
(Reproduced by permission of UPI/Corbis-Bettmann.)

collective farms; Stalin did not believe that the government could effectively control smaller farms.

Change brings suffering to the Russian people

These changes were hard on the Russian people. Factory workers made only enough money for basic necessities, and food and goods were sometimes hard to find. People had to get special permission to change jobs, and special passports to travel. Some farmers did not want to give up their farms, and they were labeled "kulaks" (tightwads) and killed or sent to the "gulags"—the network of labor camps set up for those accused of crimes against the state. Other farmers starved when the government punished them by taking their grain. People were afraid to express themselves freely (especially if they disagreed with the government), because they knew the penalty would be swift and harsh.

By the late 1930s, most of Soviet agriculture had been collectivized, but some of the rules were changed so that people were allowed to keep their own houses and tools and grow private gardens for their own use.

A time of terror

Meanwhile, Stalin was creating a public image of himself as a great hero. Cities, towns, villages, and even the tallest mountain in Russia were named after him, and he was mentioned in the national anthem. Yet he was more and more fearful of enemies and suspicious of everyone around him. In the mid-1930s he began a series of purges (a practice of getting rid of people by killing them or sending them to prison). It is estimated that from seventeen to twenty-five million people were sent to the gulags during Stalin's reign; about a million were executed, while about seven million died in the gulags.

One purge that Stalin would later have a reason to regret was that of the Soviet armed forces, when most of the country's marshals, generals, and admirals were killed. These officers would be sorely missed in only a few years, when Russia entered World War II.

Surprised by German invasion

During the 1930s, Adolf Hitler had cemented his place as dictator (a ruler with absolute power) of Germany and was leading his army in conquests of various nearby countries such as Czechoslovakia and Poland. The Soviet Union was also interested in expanding its territories. In August 1939 Stalin signed an agreement with Hitler in which Russia and Germany divided the countries of Eastern Europe between them and promised not to attack each other. Lithuania, Latvia, and Estonia were forced to join the Soviet Union and, after a short war of resistance, so was Finland.

Although he had been warned by some of his advisors that Hitler would not honor his agreement with the Soviet Union, Stalin was shocked when, in June 1941, the German army invaded Russia. For about two weeks he seemed stunned and unable to do anything; he said, "Everything which Lenin created we have lost forever!" But then Stalin recovered, taking personal command of the Soviet armed forces.

A Great Russian General

The general in charge of the Soviet Union's important victories against the Germans at Moscow, Leningrad, Stalingrad, and Kursk was Goergi Zhukov, who is considered one of World War II's greatest generals.

Zhukov was born into a poor family in 1896 in Strelkovka, a small village located about 60 miles from Moscow. As a young boy he worked as a furrier's apprentice, but in 1915 he joined the Russian army. During the revolution and civil war that established Russia as a Communist country, Zhukov joined the new Red Army, serving as a squadron commander until 1920. During the 1920s he attended schools for military commanders while rising through the ranks.

Over the course of the 1930s, Zhukov somehow managed to avoid being killed in Stalin's purge of the Soviet military leadership. He made his mark in 1939 when he went to Upper Mongolia (now part of China) where the Japanese were conducting an undeclared war along their border with that region. He commanded the Soviet First Army Group in its victory against the Japanese Sixth Army at the Khalkhin-Gol River, and was promoted to the rank of general in May 1940.

In February 1941 Zhukov was made chief of the Soviet General Staff and deputy commissioner for defense. After the Germans invaded the Soviet Union, Zhukov began to show the leadership qualities that would make him one of the best of all World War II generals. He led the defense of Leningrad in the summer and fall of 1941, then returned to Moscow in December to defend the city against German attack. Successful in that effort, he went on to coordinate the Soviet victories at Stalingrad in 1942 and 1943 and Kursk in July and August 1943. In August 1942 Zhukov was made deputy supreme

On July 3, 1941, he addressed the Soviet people in a radio broadcast (the first time most of them had heard their leader's voice) and called on them to resist the enemy with all their might. The Soviet Union had entered World War II on the side of the Allies (the United States, Great Britain, and other countries fighting against Germany, Italy, and Japan.)

Fighting back and winning

The Germans quickly moved through the country until they reached the outskirts of two of its biggest cities, commander in chief of the Red Army and Navy, which meant that he was second in command only to Stalin in terms of military authority.

With the end of the war in Europe in sight, Zhukov led his troops across Eastern Europe toward Germany, and in May 1945 they captured Berlin. Zhukov was at the head of the delegation that accepted Germany's unconditional surrender on May 8, 1945. Immediately after the war, Zhukov was in charge of the Soviet occupation of Germany, but he was removed from that job a year later by leader Joseph Stalin, who resented Zhukov's great popularity. Zhukov had won three Gold Medals as a "Hero of the Soviet Union" during the war and was probably the Soviet people's second-most respected figure after Stalin.

Stalin now pushed Zhukov off into positions commanding the Odessa and Ural military districts, far from the center of Soviet political life. But when Stalin died in 1953 Zhukov became deputy defense minister, and he was defense minister from 1955 to 1957. His close relationship with Communist Party leader Nikita Khruschev resulted in Zhukov's being made a member of the party's Central Committee. Only a few months later, however, Khruschev too began to fear Zhukov's popularity, and he was removed from public office.

Zhukov retired to his country home and began working on his memoirs, which were initially published only in censored form because Soviet leaders did not want his important role in the war to be publicized. The full version of Zhukov's memoirs appeared in 1989, 15 years after his death, and in 1995 a statue was built to honor his memory.

Moscow and Leningrad. They had confiscated about half of Russia's industry and agriculture, and about 40 percent of the population was under German control. In response, Stalin shifted many Soviet industries to the eastern part of the country where they would be safer from the Germans, arranged to borrow supplies and equipment from the other Allied countries, and built morale by stirring up the religious and patriotic feelings of the Soviet citizens. He even relaxed some of the restrictions he had imposed, letting people practice their traditional religion more openly and allowing more artistic expression.

Stalin believed in a "scorched earth" policy (which meant that it was better to destroy crops and property than to let the Germans take them) and refused to surrender any ground. With the Germans dug in for the winter around Moscow, Stalin ignored the brutally cold weather and called for a counterattack. The Red Army did gain some ground, but at a great cost in casualties (people dead or wounded).

More evidence of Stalin's extremism—and, some would say, his deep cruelty—was offered when, in July of 1942, he issued a rule that any Soviet soldier taken prisoner would be considered a traitor to Russia. In fact, Stalin's own son Vasili was captured by the Germans; Stalin responded by disowning him, later refusing an offer by the Germans to exchange Vasili for a captured German officer.

Stalin used the threat of severe punishment to intimidate not only ordinary citizens and foot soldiers but also higher officers and government officials. Nevertheless, most agreed that he ran the war effort well, planning strategies that worked, promoting good commanders, and representing his country at several important war conferences attended by the leaders of the Allied countries.

Victory brings admiration

In January 1943, the Red Army won another long, bloody, and important battle, this time to regain the city of Stalingrad (now Volgograd). That summer, they beat the Germans at Kursk, and from then on the Germans were constantly in retreat, pursued by Russian troops back toward the German border.

These victories boosted Stalin's image both at home and abroad. Allied troops referred to him as "Uncle Joe" and considered him a passionate enemy of Nazism, even though he had made agreements with the Nazis just before the war. In only a few years, the rest of the world would realize that Stalin was, in fact, an isolationist (someone who does not believe in becoming involved in other nation's affairs) with a deep distrust of the non-Communist countries.

Russia is rewarded with new territory

In April 1945 Russian troops were the first to enter the German capital, Berlin, where Hitler was hiding in an underground bunker. He killed himself on April 30, and the Germans quickly surrendered to the Allies. As the war drew to a close, Stalin used his newfound popularity—and the undeniable contribution the Russian people had made to the Allied victory—to gain rewards for Russia. In the end, the Soviet Union had control over most of Eastern Europe.

The same old brutality and paranoia

Despite hopes that the war's end would change the way Stalin governed, he soon went back to the same harsh measures. This marked the beginning of the "Cold War" between the Soviet Union and western countries (especially the United States), a conflict fought not with guns and bombs but with words, suspicion, and threats of aggression and which lasted until the 1980s.

Meanwhile, Stalin's paranoia continued, and he seemed to trust no one, not even his closest friends and family members. He had just started a new series of purges when, in March of 1953, he suffered a stroke and died of internal bleeding. Over the next few decades, the Soviet Union would face a long, slow recovery from the brutal, damaging years of Stalin's reign.

Where to Learn More

Books

Caulkins, Janet. *Joseph Stalin*. New York: Franklin Watts, 1990.

Conquest, Robert. *Stalin: Breaker of Nations*. New York: Viking Penguin, 1991.

Hoobler, Dorothy, and Thomas Hoobler. *Joseph Stalin*. New York: Chelsea House, 1985.

Kallen, Stuart A. *The Stalin Era: 1925–1953*. Edina, MN: Abdo & Daughters, 1992.

Marrin, Albert. *Stalin*. New York: Viking Kestrel, 1988.

Whitelaw, Nancy. *Joseph Stalin: From Peasant to Premier*. New York: Dillon Press, 1992.

Web sites

Simmonds, George W. "Joseph Stalin." [Online] Available http://www.grolier.com/wwii/wwii_stalin.html (February 24, 1999).

Edith Stein

Born October 12, 1891
Breslau, Germany (now Wroclaw, Poland)
Died August 9, 1942
Auschwitz, Poland

German Jew who converted to Catholicism
and became a nun

Killed in a concentration camp, Edith Stein caused a controversy fifty years later when Pope John Paul II made her a saint.

O n October 11, 1998, Edith Stein became the first Jewish person in modern times to achieve sainthood. The Roman Catholic Church gave her this honor because, they said, she had done so much to promote understanding between Christians and Jews and because she had died a martyr (someone who dies rather than renounce his or her religion) for both her heritage and her faith. A respected thinker and writer on philosophical issues and an atheist (person who does not believe in God) as a young woman, Stein converted to the Catholic religion when she was thirty years old. Twelve years later, she entered a convent as a nun. In 1942 she was executed at the Nazi concentration camp at Auschwitz, Poland. Stein's sainthood caused a controversy because many Jews felt that she had died not because of her Catholicism, but because she had been born a Jew. They feared that her canonization (being made a saint) would deflect attention away from the fact that most of the victims of the Holocaust (the period between 1933 and 1945 when Nazi Germany murdered millions of Jews, Gypsies, homosexuals, and others) were Jews and that the Catholic Church had remained silent about Nazi brutality during World War II.

An intelligent little girl

Stein was born into a Jewish family on Yom Kippur (the Jewish holiday that is the "Day of Atonement" or time to make up for past wrongdoing). The Steins lived in the town of Breslau in a part of Germany that later became part of Poland (changing the town's name to Wroclaw); at that time Breslau had one of the largest Jewish communities in Germany. Stein was the youngest of seven children—four of whom would later die in the concentration camps—born to Siegfried and Auguste Stein. Her father died when she was two years old, and her strong, capable mother took over the family lumber business.

Stein's intelligence was evident when she was very young: at six, she begged her mother to let her bypass kindergarten and start school immediately. She was also a kind, understanding person to whom, her sister Erna later wrote, "one could entrust one's troubles and secrets." Describing herself in her autobiography, *Life in a Jewish Family,* Stein wrote, "In my dreams I always foresaw a brilliant future for myself .... I was convinced that I was destined for something great...."

An atheist and a brilliant student

When she was fifteen, Stein gave up her Jewish faith, announcing that she was an atheist. She also dropped out of school for a short period, but after six months she told her mother she was going back and even planned to attend college. She entered the University of Breslau in 1911 and stayed for two years, then transferred to the University of Göttingen.

For a while Stein studied psychology, but she was dissatisfied with this subject and finally turned to philosophy. She became a student of a famous philosopher named Edmund Husserl, who was a leader in the field of phenomenology, a kind of philosophy that concerns the nature of thought and experience.

While she pursued her doctorate degree at Göttingen, Stein was a well-liked member of a circle of brilliant students, several of whom would later become famous philosophers. She had an especially close friendship with one of them, Hans Lipp, but their relationship never developed into a romance as their friends expected it would. During this period Stein enjoyed art, music, and literature as well as hikes and picnics with her friends.

World War I and after

When Germany entered World War I (1914–1918; a war that began as a conflict between Austria-Hungary and Serbia and escalated to include thirty-two countries), Stein volunteered to serve in a hospital run by the Red Cross. For six months in 1915 she worked at the Weisskirchen Epidemic Hospital in Moravia, nursing Austrian soldiers with infectious diseases, such as dysentery and cholera.

After the war Stein returned to Breslau and taught for eight months in her former high school. Then she went back to Göttingen to finish her doctoral thesis (major paper written to fulfill the requirements of the Ph.D.), which was on the problem of empathy or how a person can know anything about the inner life of another person. Stein was thrilled when Husserl asked her to be his assistant, and she served in this position for eighteen months, teaching Husserl's beginning students and putting his papers in order so that they could be published.

Two religious experiences

It was around this time that Stein had one of the most important experiences of her life. One of her best friends and professors from the Göttingen circle, Adolf Reinach, had been killed in 1917 in the war. Stein went to visit and console his widow, Anna Reinach. She was surprised to find that it was Anna who consoled her. During the war, both Reinachs had converted to Christianity, and Anna's strong religious faith allowed her to calmly accept her husband's death. Stein was deeply moved by her friend's faith. She decided that she too would become a Christian, but she was not yet sure which religious denomination (religious organization or church, such as Roman Catholic, Presbyterian, or Baptist) to join.

In 1918, having earned her Ph.D., Stein returned to Breslau, where she continued to write and publish articles about philosophy. She would have liked to become a professor but no German universities would hire a female philosophy professor. Three years later Stein had another important religious experience. While visiting a friend, she was left alone one evening when everyone else went out. To keep herself occupied, she started reading the autobiography of Theresa of Avila, a dynamic Catholic saint who lived from 1515 to 1582. Captivated by Theresa's words, Stein stayed up all night reading the book, and when she finished she said to herself, "This is the truth."

Becoming a Catholic

Despite the strong objections of her mother and many of her friends, who felt she'd turned her back on her own heritage, Stein was baptized into the Catholic religion on January 1, 1922. She wanted to enter a convent immediately, but a spiritual advisor she consulted advised her against that step, claiming it would be too difficult for her family to accept. Instead, she spent the next eleven years as a teacher and also continued to write and lecture. Even though she was not yet a nun, she privately took the same vows of chastity (not having sex), poverty, and obedience that nuns commonly take.

From 1923 to 1931 Stein worked at a teacher's college, where she helped high school girls and nuns prepare for teaching careers. Those who knew her during this period described her as a calm, gentle, and patient person who liked to laugh and often told funny stories. In 1932, Stein was hired to teach at the German Institute for Scientific Pedagogy in Munster.

Deciding to enter the convent

Stein's teaching career was cut short by the Nazis, who took control of Germany in the early 1930s. Led by the dictator (absolute ruler) Adolf Hitler (1889–1945; see entry), the Nazis had begun a series of harsh measures against Jews. In 1933, Jews were banned from holding public positions. Stein had to leave her job, and her writings could no longer be published.

For some time Stein had been feeling uncomfortable in the secular (nonreligious) world, and at that point she decided to enter the convent. This caused heartache among her family, who loved her but could not understand her choice. Stein's elderly mother was especially upset, knowing that she would probably never see her daughter again (the nuns were cloistered, which meant that they never left the convent and lived in a silent world of poverty and prayer). Asked why she was abandoning the Jewish people now, Stein replied that she was not rejecting her heritage, which she considered a great one, but that she could do Jews the most good by praying for them from within the convent.

Teresa Benedicta of the Cross

On October 14, 1933, Stein took the name Teresa Benedicta of the Cross and entered the Cologne Carmel (convent of the Carmelite order of nuns). Recognizing her gifts, her superiors gave her time to study and to write about religious and philosophical topics. She also worked on her autobiography, with which she hoped to honor her beloved mother and to show that the lives of Jews were different from negative images put forth by the Nazi Party.

Meanwhile, Stein was well aware of what was happening to Jews in the outside world. Like other German Jews, Stein was made to wear a yellow Star of David (a Jewish religious symbol) sewn to her clothing—in her case, a nun's habit (a long, flowing garment that covers all but the face and hands). She wrote a letter to Pope Pius XII, who was then the head of the Roman Catholic Church, asking him to publicly condemn the Nazis, but she received no reply.

Arrested by the Nazis

On November 9, 1938, the Nazis carried out their Kristallnacht (Crystal Night, also called the "Night of Broken Glass"), a terrible "pogrom" or attack on Jews. Homes, businesses, and synagogues were destroyed and as many as 40,000 Jews were sent to concentration camps. For her protection, Stein was sent to a convent in Echt, Holland. But her safety lasted less than three years.

On August 2, 1942, the Nazis entered the convent and arrested Stein and her sister Rosa, who had also converted to Catholicism. Stein reportedly said, "Come, let us go for our people" before she was taken away. She spent about a week in two transport camps in Holland before being sent to Auschwitz. She arrived on August 9 and was soon killed, like so many other Jews (and, on the same day, her own sister and about 700 Dutch Catholics), by poisonous gas piped into a sealed room crowded with unsuspecting people.

"A daughter of Israel"

At a ceremony held in the Cologne soccer stadium in May 1987, Pope John Paul II *beatified* Stein—he declared that she was a holy person, and should be admired and respected. The pope called her a "daughter of Israel who remained faithful" to both her Jewish heritage and her Catholic faith.

Rumors that Stein would eventually be made a saint stirred up much controversy. Some Jews were troubled by her conversion (changing) from Judaism to Christianity, especially at a time when it was so dangerous to be Jewish. Others did not like the idea of focusing on Stein's Catholicism when the real reason she'd died was because she was a Jew. The vast majority of Holocaust victims, they argued, were Jews, and Stein's sainthood might take attention away from that fact. Instead, the Catholic Church should be facing up to its own failure to condemn Nazism.

The Catholic Church responded by claiming that Stein and the other Catholics killed at the same time were probably murdered in revenge for a statement against Nazism that Holland's Catholic bishops had made a month earlier. When Stein was canonized, on October 11, 1998, the church's top official for Jewish-Catholic relations, Cardinal William Keller, made it clear that Stein's sainthood must not take attention away from the fact that the Jewish people were the true targets and victims of the Holocaust.

Honoring Stein, stated Keller, "does not lessen but rather strengthens our need to preserve and honor the memory of the Jewish victims."

Where to Learn More

Books

Herbstrith, Waltraud. *Edith Stein.* San Francisco: Harper and Row, 1985.

Oben, Freda Mary. *Edith Stein: Scholar, Feminist, Saint.* New York: Alba House, 1988.

Periodicals

Donohue, John W. "Edith Stein, Saint." *America* (June, 21 1997): 8.

Gordon, Mary. "Saint Edith?" *Tikkun* (March-April 1999): 17.

Jerome, Richard. "The Convert: Born a Jew, Edith Stein Is Tapped for Sainthood." *People Weekly* (May 19, 1997): 161.

Michael, Eleanor. "Saints and Nazi Skeletons." *History Today* (October 1998): 4.

Payne, Steven. "Edith Stein: A Fragmented Life." *America* (October 10, 1998): 11.

Penner, Martin. "A Martyr, But Whose?" *Time* (October 19, 1998): 16.

Dorothy Thompson

Born July 9, 1893
Lancaster, New York
Died January 30, 1961
Lisbon, Portugal

American journalist

Dorothy Thompson was one of the world's most famous reporters in the 1920s and 1930s, and one of the first women to reach the top of the journalism field. She wrote newspaper and magazine articles and made radio broadcasts, informing her audience about world events and some of the most important issues of the time—especially the rise of dictators (absolute rulers) like Germany's Adolf Hitler (1889–1945; see entry) and Italy's Benito Mussolini (1883–1945; see entry). Thompson helped people understand the causes and events of World War II, and hers was one of the earliest and strongest voices raised against Nazism, the brutal German political system that led to the deaths of millions of people.

A childhood both happy and sad

Thompson was born in Lancaster, a rural town in upstate (northern) New York. Her parents, Peter (a Methodist minister) and Margaret Thompson, were both kind and compassionate people. The family, which included two other children besides Dorothy, was poor but they shared what they had

Dorothy Thompson wrote about the rise of European dictatorships before World War II, and continued to report and comment on world events during the war.

with those in greater need. Thompson was a bright, sassy child who loved practical jokes.

Thompson was only seven when her mother died tragically, killed by strong herbs Dorothy's grandmother had given to Margaret in order to end a pregnancy she feared would be too great a burden on her daughter. Three years later, Peter Thompson married a woman named Eliza Abbott. Dorothy did not get along with her stepmother, and she also resented her father for not defending her. In 1908 she was sent to Chicago to live with her two aunts.

Discovering a talent for writing

This was a happy period in Thompson's life, for her aunts paid her a lot of attention and she did well in school. She attended the Lewis Institute, which combined high school courses with a two-year college program. She entered New York's Syracuse University as a junior in 1912, her tuition paid for by a scholarship for the children of Methodist ministers. Known as an intelligent, well-spoken young woman, Thompson graduated in 1914.

Thompson's first job after college was working for the women's suffrage (the right to vote) movement, which was gaining strength in many parts of the United States. For eight dollars a week, she worked at the New York State Women's Suffrage Party Headquarters. By 1917 (the year New York women did gain the right to vote), Thompson had proved herself a good writer and speaker and she was sent out to give lectures about suffrage.

These experiences stirred up Thompson's interest in becoming a writer and she began to compose articles on various political and women's issues, which were published in local newspapers. After an unhappy six months working as a copywriter for an advertising agency, and another short stint as a publicity director for a social reform agency, Thompson decided to travel to Russia in search of reporting opportunities.

A journalist's career begins

In 1920 Thompson boarded a boat headed for London. During the journey across the ocean, she met a group of zionists, people who were working to establish a Jewish state in the middle eastern country of Palestine (now Israel). Interested in their cause, she interviewed them and did some research on Zionism. Twelve days later, when Thompson reached London, she wrote an article on Zionism that was published by the International News Service. Her career as a journalist had begun.

Soon Thompson was a successful, busy reporter with many assignments, writing stories about the Irish independence movement and an Italian autoworkers strike, among other topics. She decided to drop her plan to go to Russia, since there was plenty to write about in Europe.

The next year, when Thompson was 28, she went to Vienna, Austria, to report on events in central Europe. It was an exciting and dangerous time in Europe, and she was right in the middle of it. World War I had just ended and most of the European countries were suffering from economic hard times, which was causing a lot of social unrest. She once almost made the mistake of wearing a fur coat into a mob of angry demonstrators who, she was warned, might think she was a rich person who didn't belong there (afterward she made the famous quote, "Never wear a fur coat to a revolution"). In 1921, she was shot at during a riot in Bulgaria.

A busy career and two marriages

By 1924, both the *Philadelphia Public Ledger* and the *New York Evening Post* had made Thompson their central European bureau chief. From her headquarters in Berlin, Germany, she covered events in that city as well as Vienna and Warsaw, Poland. She interviewed many famous people, including the great psychiatrist Sigmund Freud, and became rather famous herself.

In 1927, Thompson divorced her husband, a handsome Hungarian writer named Joseph Bard whom she had married five years earlier. She traveled to the Soviet Union and published a series of articles about that country that were published as a book, *The New Russia*, a year later. Also in 1928, Thompson married Sinclair Lewis, a major American novelist who had written *Babbitt* (1922), *Main Street* (1920), and other works.

Margaret Bourke-White: Photographs of War

A talented photographer who created "photo-essays" on many events and topics, Margaret Bourke-White helped people to see the war that journalists like Thompson were describing.

Bourke-White was born in 1904 in New York City and studied photography at Columbia University. She attended several midwestern universities and married and divorced before finally earning her bachelor's degree at Cornell University in 1927. At Cornell she took many photographs of natural settings, but later she became more interested in technology.

During the 1920s and 1930s, Bourke-White worked on celebrating, through photography, the beauty of machines and the products they made. In 1927 she established herself as a professional photographer in Cleveland, specializing in architectural and industrial subjects. She began working for a new magazine called *Fortune* and moved to New York to build a career in advertising.

Bourke-White traveled to the Soviet Union in 1930 and later published the photographs she took there in a book. She also chronicled the drought that had overtaken the "Dust Bowl" area of the American plains with photos that showed the great human tragedy of this natural disaster. In the late 1930s Bourke-White worked with writer Erskine Caldwell to portray the hardships endured by poor people in the southern United States.

Bourke-White was in Moscow with Caldwell (whom she had married several years earlier) when, in 1941, the Germans attacked the city. The only foreign correspondent in Moscow at the time, Bourke-White photographed the event while Caldwell wrote about it. After the United States entered World War II (December 1941) Bourke-White became an official Army Air Corps photographer whose work was used both by the military and by *Life* magazine.

Although she was not allowed to fly with the American pilots when they moved from England into action in North Africa, she went there instead on a ship that was torpedoed along the way. In January 1943 she was finally allowed to go along on a bombing mission in Tunisia.

When the Allies invaded Italy later that year, Bourke-White photographed the bloody combat in the Cassino Valley, and as the war drew to a close she traveled with General George Patton's (1885–1945; see entry) Third Army into Germany. Bourke-White took many photographs inside the Nazi concentration camps as they were liberated, creating such unforgettable images as "The Living Dead of Buchenwald."

After the war Bourke-White continued to work for *Life*, photographing such subjects as India's leader Mohandas Gandhi, life in South Africa, and guerrilla fighters in the Korean War. She died of Parkinson's disease in 1971.

Thompson and Lewis were very much in love when they began their marriage. They bought a 300-acre farm in Vermont that they named Twin Farms, because it had two houses, so that both writers had private space to continue to pursue their successful writing careers. Thompson grew very attached to her stepson, eleven-year-old Wells Lewis.

A troubled family life

After only a few years, however, Thompson's marriage was in trouble. Lewis had lost some of his popularity as a novelist, and he had become an alcoholic. He resented the time Thompson spent with her close women friends, and accused her of caring more about her career than her family.

The couple hoped that two events of 1930—the birth of their son Michael and Lewis's winning the Nobel Prize for literature—would solve their problems, but this was not to be. Instead, both parents neglected their sons, Lewis by withdrawing into himself and Thompson by spending long periods away from home on reporting assignments. In 1931 she and her husband separated.

An interview with Hitler

In December 1931 Thompson went to Germany to interview Adolf Hitler for *Cosmopolitan Magazine*. At that time, Hitler was the leader of the anti-Semitic (anti-Jewish) Nazi Party, which was gaining popularity in Germany. Thompson found Hitler an unpleasant, unimpressive person, and she predicted that he would never achieve the power he desired.

While she was in Germany, Thompson did take note of the German people's support for Hitler and the Nazis, as she watched the Nazi soldiers called "storm troopers" march by shouting "Perish the Jews!" She was alarmed by the red, white, and black Nazi flags bearing swastikas (the symbol of the Nazi party) flying from many houses. She also came upon a Hitler Youth camp, where about 6,000 young boys were being trained to fight for the Nazi cause.

In several articles and a book (*I Saw Hitler!* [1932]) Thompson kept attacking the Nazis and made fun of their quest for power; these writings increased her fame even more and she was much in demand for lectures. But by 1933, Hitler had taken control of Germany, proving Thompson wrong about his chance for success. She was embarrassed and dismayed by this turn of events.

Kicked out of Germany

Thompson remained in Germany and continued to condemn the Nazis, begging the rest of the world to do the same and thus somehow prevent them from gaining more power. Angered by Thompson, Hitler finally got revenge. On August 25, 1934, he sent a Gestapo (the secret state police of Nazi Germany) agent to her hotel room with an order giving her twenty-four hours to leave the country. Thompson left quickly and got a warm welcome home from her fellow journalists and admirers, who praised her for her courage in criticizing Hitler for as long as she had. She was the first of many foreign journalists to be expelled (forced out of the country) by Hitler.

Fame and respect grows

Suddenly famous as the enemy of dictators like Hitler and an expert in international affairs, Thompson went on a lecture tour around the country. Two articles published in *Foreign Affairs* magazine gave her a reputation as a serious political commentator. Lewis was also inspired by his wife's work, and wrote a novel called *It Can't Happen Here* (1935) about the possibility of a dictator taking over the American government.

In 1936, Thompson's popularity as a speaker led to her being hired as a radio commentator for NBC (the National Broadcasting Company), a job she held throughout World War II. She also began writing a column, "On the Record," for the *New York Herald Tribune* that also appeared in 170 newspapers and was read by an estimated eight to ten million people every day. In 1937, she started writing a column in the monthly *Ladies Home Journal* magazine.

As the 1930s drew to a close, people everywhere worried as war seemed close to breaking out in Europe. Every Monday evening, five million listeners gathered around their radios to hear what Thompson would say about what was happening in the world. Although she reported the news, she also made it clear in her personal commentaries that she was passionately opposed to Nazism.

Concerned about refugees

World War II officially began with Hitler's invasion of Poland in September 1939, when both Great Britain and France declared war on Germany. Now a flood of refugees (people forced to leave their homes because of war or other events) began pouring out of Europe, and Thompson's concern for them led her to open her own home to some. She was nicknamed Cassandra, after the character from Greek myth who stands on the walls of Troy to predict that war is coming. Thompson also wrote articles urging governments to take the refugees' plight seriously and do something to help.

Thompson was called on to advise President Franklin D. Roosevelt (1882–1945; see entry) in 1940. She continued to lecture and write, taking great care to make her work easily read and understood by all the worried, confused people who were eager for news of the war in Europe.

Broadcasting into Germany

The day after Japan bombed the American naval base at Pearl Harbor, Hawaii (December 7, 1941), the United States entered World War II. Thompson's contribution to the war effort included broadcasting into Germany by short-wave radio. Hoping to reach a wide variety of Germans and inspire them to rebel against Hitler, she pleaded for an end to the fighting. She also continued to show concern for refugees, working as a member of the Emergency Rescue Committee.

In 1942, Thompson was divorced from Lewis. That same year, a movie called *Woman of the Year* was released. It featured a journalist heroine, played by Katherine Hepburn, who was loosely based on Thompson. Thompson found the movie unrealistic because it ends with the character giving up her career, which Thompson claimed she would never do. In 1943, Thompson married Maxim Kopf, an Austrian-born artist with an easygoing personality. They remained happily married until his death in 1958.

Saddened by the war

Soon after Germans surrendered in May 1945, Thompson went to Europe to visit some wartorn areas, including the concentration camp at Dachau, Poland, and the heavily bombed city of Dresden, Germany. Thompson had lost some good friends, as well as her beloved stepson, to the war, and she returned feeling very sad and tired. She was already back in the United States when the dropping of atomic bombs on two Japanese cities in August 1945 brought the war in the Pacific to a close.

Having witnessed so much destruction, Thompson was no longer as idealistic (believing that one's ideas of how things should be can be fulfilled) as she had been before the war. She even wrote an obituary (death notice) for the earth: "It died because its inhabitants, being endowed with brains to penetrate the secret of all matter, preferred to perish rather than use them any further."

Still writing after the war

Thompson continued to write her newspaper column for two years after the war, and also published several books. She became deeply interested in the struggle between citizens of the new state of Israel and the Arabs who had been uprooted by its creation. Thompson's pro-Arab stance angered some of her former admirers, who accused her of being anti-Semitic. She responded that she was opposed not to Jews but to the violence some Jews used against Arabs.

During the 1950s, other issues that concerned Thompson included the influence of television on young people; in particular, she was one of the first to note the amount of violence on television. She also encouraged women to stand up for their rights, and she warned about the dangers of nuclear weapons. Thompson's last newspaper column appeared in 1958, but she continued to write her column for *Ladies Home Journal* until the end of her life.

While on vacation in Lisbon, Portugal, in 1961, Thompson was alone in her hotel room when she died of a heart attack. She was buried next to her third husband, beneath a stone that reads: "Dorothy Thompson Kopf—Writer."

Where to Learn More

Books

Jakes, John. *Great Women Reporters*. New York: Putnam, 1969.

Kurth, Peter. *American Cassandra: The Life of Dorothy Thompson*. Boston, Toronto, and London: Little, Brown and Company, 1990.

Sanders, Marion K. *Dorothy Thompson: A Legend in Her Time*. Boston: Houghton Mifflin, 1973.

Whitelaw, Nancy. *They Wrote Their Own Headlines: American Women Journalists*. Greensboro, NC: M. Reynolds, 1994.

Web sites

"Dorothy Thompson." [Online] Available http://www.ilstu.edu/~separry/dorothy.htm (March 25, 1999).

Hideki Tojo

Born December 30, 1884
Tokyo, Japan
Died December 23, 1948
Tokyo, Japan

Japanese military and political leader

As Prime Minister of Japan from 1941 to 1945, Hideki Tojo led his country into an unsuccessful war against the Allied nations (the United States, Great Britain, France, and the Soviet Union).

Portrait: Hideki Tojo.
(Reproduced by permission of AP/Wide World Photos.)

In the years leading up to World War II, Japan began to aggressively expand its empire into nearby Asian countries, especially China. This expansion concerned the leaders other nations, and they began to view Tojo, the Japanese prime minister and the leading symbol of the country's militarism. Tojo was seen as an all-powerful dictator similar to Germany's Adolf Hitler (1889–1945; see entry) or Italy's Benito Mussolini (1883–1945; see entries). Although Tojo played a major role in Japan's wartime affairs, his power and ambitions were actually not as great as Hitler's or Mussolini's. He has been described as an uncomplicated, hardworking man intensely dedicated to his profession. His fatal error was in not realizing that the United States and its allies could win a long-term, large-scale war.

The Kamisori (razor)

Tojo was born into a family known for producing many *samurais* or warriors. His father, Eikyo Tojo, was an army general who fought in Japan's war with Russia. In school, Tojo was an energetic, competitive, self-confident boy; fellow students nicknamed him "Fighting Tojo." He graduated from the

Japanese Military Academy in 1915 and entered the army. He spent a few years in Europe, including a stint in Switzerland and one as assistant military attaché (advisor to the embassy) in Berlin, Germany. Returning to Japan, Tojo became an instructor in Japan's war college.

During the late 1920s and early 1930s, Tojo rose through the ranks of the military, gaining a reputation as a decisive, hardworking, very efficient officer whose nickname was kamisori (the razor). He became a member of the Control Group, which was made up of army officers who thought the military should have more control; moreover, they also believed that Japan could solve its economic and population problems by expanding its borders into China and other parts of southeast Asia. The Control Group felt that the Western countries (especially the United States) were hostile toward Japan and that Japan would have to aggressively defend its own interests.

By 1933 Tojo had reached the rank of major general, and in 1935 he became the head of military police for the Kwangtung Army (the branch of Japan's army that was in China). He took a strong "law and order" stance, enforcing rules strictly. From 1937 to 1938 he was appointed chief of staff of the Kwangtung Army, and he proved his leadership abilities in combat when fighting broke out between the Chinese and the Japanese in the summer of 1937.

The fighting between Japan and China was very brutal. The Japanese completely destroyed many of the cities and villages that they invaded. The Chinese forces fought hard to prevent the Japanese from taking Shanghai, defending it for four months, from August to November, before the Japanese were able to take the city. The worst example of Japan's brutality is the reported destruction of China's capital city of Nanking. Irish Chang, author of *The Rape of Nanking,* reports that here, in December 1937, Japanese soldiers murdered nearly 100,000 Chinese prisoners of war and raped, tortured, and killed hundreds of thousands of Chinese civilians.

Pushing Japan further toward war

In May 1938 Tojo was called back to Tokyo to serve in the government of Prime Minister Fumimaro Konoye. He took

Doolittle Leads Revenge Attack

In the months after the December 7, 1941, surprise attack on the U.S. naval base at Pearl Harbor, Hawaii, American military commanders worked on a plan to take revenge on the Japanese. By April 1942 their plan was ready: bomber planes led by General James Doolittle would carry out a raid on Tokyo, the capital of Japan.

The plan called for sixteen bombers to take off from the deck of the aircraft carrier *Hornet,* which sailed from San Francisco on April 2, 1942. They hoped to make a surprise attack. On April 18 the aircraft carrier was spotted by a Japanese patrol boat, so the planes had to take off immediately. They arrived at Tokyo in the middle of the day, instead of at night as they had planned, and began dropping bombs on this city as well as Osaka, Nagoya, and Kobe.

After the attack, the planes flew to the Chinese mainland, but because of the change in timing the airfield was not ready to receive them and the pilots had to make crash landings or bail out of their planes. Twelve of the eighty-two men who had taken part in the raid were killed.

Although the raid did not have a huge effect on the outcome of the war, it boosted American spirits. For his role in the action Doolittle received the Congressional Medal of Honor and a promotion to brigadier general.

an aggressive stance, claiming that Japan would have to go to war (against both China and the Soviet Union) to reach its goals and that Japan's weak economy could only be improved if the military became stronger. Tojo left this position in December 1938 to become inspector general of army aviation.

By July 1941, when Tojo was appointed minister of war, Japan was still fighting China and had also invaded Korea. The United States government protested these actions strongly and even stopped selling U.S. goods to Japan, thus increasing Japan's economic hardships. Some moderate leaders wanted to withdraw troops from China and negotiate with the United States, but Tojo opposed them. He drew up new plans for more aggression, and he approved the Tripartite Pact—an agreement that made Japan an ally of Germany and Italy—because he felt it would put Japan in a stronger position.

A prime minister with a "clean slate"

When Konoye resigned in October 1941, Tojo took over the job of prime minister, while remaining head of the departments of war, education, commerce, and industry. Tojo insisted that he begin his new job with a "clean slate," meaning that he did not have to honor any earlier promises to negotiate with the United States. Although the military was now in control of the country and Tojo was its top leader, he was not a dictator, because he still had to answer to a "Supreme Command" made up of civilian and military leaders. He was also supposed to be under the emperor's command, but in fact Emperor Hirohito (1901–1989; see entry) did not have much real power.

On December 7, 1941—even as some Japanese diplomats were in Washington, D.C., meeting with U.S. leaders—Japan launched a surprise attack on the U.S. naval base at Pearl Harbor, Hawaii. Thousands of people were killed and many ships and airplanes were destroyed. The next day, President Franklin D. Roosevelt (1882–1945; see entry) declared war on Japan. Meanwhile, Tojo broadcast a radio message to the Japanese people, warning them that "to annihilate this enemy and to establish a stable new order in east Asia, the nation must necessarily anticipate a long war."

Japan loses the war

What Tojo did not anticipate was the strength of the Allied forces and their determination to win the war. Although the Japanese forces achieved some success at the beginning (including invasions of the Philippines and Singapore), their fortunes began to decline as the war continued and they lost several important battles. Nevertheless, Tojo rejected the idea of a negotiated peace treaty. He thought Japan should continue to fight. But in July 1945, U.S. troops defeated the Japanese on Saipan (part of the Marianas island chain in the South Pacific) putting American bomber planes in range of the main Japanese islands.

Tojo now came under great pressure to leave the government, and on July 18 he resigned. Harshly criticized by the public, who blamed him for Japan's problems, he and his wife retired to private life. In early August the Allies dropped atomic

bombs on two Japanese cities, Hiroshima and Nagasaki, and the war soon came to an end. Shortly thereafter the Japanese agreed to an unconditional surrender.

Tried and executed for war crimes

General Douglas MacArthur (1880–1964; see entry) was chosen to lead Japan's occupation government and help the nation prepare for economic recovery and transition to a democratic society. MacArthur arrived in Tokyo in September and immediately called for the arrest of all those who were thought to have committed war crimes (violations of the laws or customs of war), especially top military leaders. When Tojo learned that American soldiers had arrived at his home to arrest him, he shot himself in the chest. The wound did not kill him, however, and American doctors saved his life.

Tojo was held in prison until May 1946, when his trial before the International Military Tribunal began. During the two-year trial, Tojo took the blame for his country's actions during the war, but claimed that it had all been done for Japan's survival. The trial found that Tojo had "major responsibility for Japan's criminal attacks on her neighbors," and he was sentenced to death. He was hanged on December 23, 1948, one of seven Japanese war criminals executed for their parts in World War II. In his final statement, Tojo expressed regret for the many horrible acts committed by Japanese forces.

Where to Learn More

Books

Butow, Robert J. C. *Tojo and the Coming of the War.* Stanford, CT: Stanford University Press, 1961.

Browne, Courtney. *Tojo: The Last Banzai.* New York: De Capo Press, 1998.

Chang, Iris. *The Rape of Nanking.* New York: Basic Books, 1997.

Hoyt, Edwin P. *Warlord.* Lanham, MD: Scarborough House, 1993.

Harry S. Truman

Born May 8, 1884
Lamar, Missouri
Died December 26, 1972
Kansas City, Missouri

33rd president of the United States

Harry S. Truman is remembered as one of few American presidents who had a real knowledge of and feeling for the ordinary citizens of his country. Known as an honest, hard-working man with a lot of common sense, he was serving as vice president when, in April of 1945, President Franklin D. Roosevelt (1882–1945; see entry) died in office. Truman took over the presidency at a crucial time, with World War II almost over and Americans feeling both euphoric about the Allied victory and anxious about the economy and other issues. Over the next seven years, Truman would make some difficult decisions—especially the one that led to dropping two atomic bombs on Japan—and lead the United States through important changes in foreign and domestic policy.

A Missouri boyhood

Truman was born in a small farming town located about 120 miles south of Kansas City, Missouri. His father was a farmer who also bought and sold horses and mules. In 1890, after the births of two more children, the family moved to the larger town of Independence. It was here, when he was six

Portrait: Harry S. Truman.
(Reproduced by permission of The Library of Congress.)

years old, that Truman first met Elizabeth (Bess) Wallace, who would one day become his wife.

As a young boy Truman contracted diphtheria and nearly died. He also had very poor eyesight, and because he had to wear strong, expensive eyeglasses, he was not allowed to play sports. Instead, he spent a lot of his time reading and became interested in American history. In 1901, Truman graduated from high school. He applied to the U.S. Military Academy at West Point, New York, but was rejected due to his poor eyesight.

A hardworking young man

Lacking money to pay for college, Truman went to Kansas City to work. He spent the next four years in various clerical jobs—in a newspaper's mailroom, for a railroad, and in two banks. Even though his monthly salary had increased from $35 to $120, Truman was unhappy, and in 1906 he moved to a family-owned farm near Grandview (about twenty miles from Independence), where he would stay for the next eleven years.

This was an important period in Truman's life, as he managed his 600 acres of land and performed much of the farm work himself. It was on the farm that he began his life-long habit of rising at 5:00 or 5:30 in the morning, even as president, when he had often been up very late the previous evening. This was also a lonely time for Truman, but soon he began courting Bess Wallace.

"Captain Harry"

When the United States entered World War I in April, 1917, Truman's National Guard unit was sent into action as the 129th Field Artillery, attached to the 35th Division from Missouri and Kansas. Truman arrived overseas in April of 1918 and was immediately promoted to captain.

In July he became the commander of Battery D, which had a reputation of being full of unruly, difficult soldiers. Truman tamed them, using a mixture of firmness and friendliness. Affectionately known as "Captain Harry," he led his troops in the battles at St. Mihiel and Meuse Argonne in France. Years later, after he was sworn in as president, members of the battery marched on both sides of his car during the inaugural parade.

Businessman and politician

After the war Truman returned to Missouri, and married Bess in June 1919. That November, he opened a men's clothing store with a friend from the military, Edward Jacobs, but the store was not successful and went bankrupt in 1922. Through another war buddy, Truman met Thomas J. Pendergast, the Democratic boss (a political leader whose power is often established or maintained through dishonest means) of Kansas City. Pendergast was impressed by Truman because he was honest. Needing such a man on the Democratic ticket to bolster his own reputation, he persuaded Truman to run for office.

In 1923, Truman was elected eastern judge (a position that was actually that of county commissioner, rather than a judge who sits in court) for Jackson County. To make up for his lack of legal experience, Truman studied law at night for two years at the Kansas City Law School. In February 1924 the Trumans' daughter (and only child), Mary Margaret, was born. That same year Truman was voted out of office, but in 1926 he ran for the job of presiding judge and was again elected. He served two four-year terms in this office, and was in charge of a $60 million budget for public works.

Two terms as senator

Encouraged by his political victories, Truman ran successfully for the U.S. Senate in 1934. During his first term as a senator, he was a quiet backer of President Roosevelt's New Deal (a program that featured many new laws and policies promoting social welfare and reform) and worked on transportation issues. Although an effective politician, Truman didn't get much attention from his fellow senators or from the president. Some said his old association with Pendergast (who was convicted on income tax evasion in 1938) made other Democrats want to avoid him.

It was during Truman's second term in the Senate that he was praised as an energetic and hardworking leader who stood up for ordinary Americans. His most important role was as chairman of a committee to investigate military spending. The committee uncovered a great deal of wastefulness and reportedly saved the American taxpayers $15 billion. This issue was especially important to Americans after Pearl Harbor was bombed (December 7, 1941) and the United States entered World War II, which brought an even greater need for wise spending and efficient production.

What the Atomic Bombs Did to Nagasaki and Hiroshima

On August 6, 1945 at 8:15 A.M., a B-29 Superfortress bomber plane called the *Enola Gay* flew over the city of Hiroshima, Japan, and Major Thomas W. Ferebee released the atomic bomb nicknamed "Little Boy." Most people ignored the air raid sirens when they saw only two planes approaching. Life was going on as usual—with many people outside on streets and children on playgrounds—when the atomic bomb exploded.

Survivors later reported seeing a blinding flash followed by a descent into terror and pain. Tens of thousands of people died instantly, while those who had not been killed but were close enough to sustain injuries were severely burned. People ran and stumbled amidst the rubble of the tremendous explosion, many with their skin charred or shredded away from their bodies, some missing limbs or facial features, as they searched desperately for relief, for water, and for missing family members.

It is estimated that about 130,000 to 140,000 people were killed at Hiroshima, including those killed instantly (about 80,000) as well as those who died later from burns or the sickness caused by the radiation released by the explosion. Another 25,000 or so died three days later when another atomic bomb—this one called "Fat Man"—landed on the city of Nagasaki, following the Japanese government's failure to surrender after the first attack. Although the Nagasaki bomb was bigger, it did not prove as deadly because the city's natural terrain protected it somewhat from the impact of the explosion.

In the decades following World War II, the approximately 350,000 survivors of the atomic bombs formed a special group in Japanese society. Called *hibakusha,* they suffered not only from physical pain and disfiguring scars but from being ridiculed and shunned by others. Studies have also shown that the radiation to which the hibakusha were exposed has had longlasting effects, including increased rates of cancer, liver and heart disease, and mental retardation in babies born to survivors.

From VP to president in eighty-two days

By 1944, Truman had proven himself a strong leader on a national level. When President Roosevelt ran for reelection in 1944, advisors recommended that he choose Truman as his running mate. The man who was then serving as vice president, Henry Wallace, was not popular and Democratic leaders wanted to find a vice presidential candidate who would make a good president if Roosevelt (who was ailing) should die in office.

At the time of the Democratic convention, Truman was supporting someone else as vice presidential candidate and had no interest in the job himself. But then he overheard a frustrated Roosevelt direct an advisor to "tell [Truman] that if he wants to break up the Democratic party in the middle of a war, that's his responsibility." So Truman accepted the nomination, and was elected with Roosevelt later that year.

Truman had served only eighty-two days as vice president when, on April 12, 1945, he was called to the White House and informed by the president's wife, Eleanor Roosevelt (see sidebar on p.236), that Roosevelt had died. Truman took the oath of office at 7:09 that evening, becoming the 33rd president of the United States. The next day, he told a group of reporters that he felt as if "the moon, the stars, and all the planets had fallen" on him, and he asked them to pray for him. This humble comment was widely quoted and helped make Truman seem like an ordinary man who had unexpectedly been called to play an extraordinary role.

A momentous decision

Truman had taken over the presidency at a crucial time in the nation's history, and he was immediately faced with some important tasks. On May 8—his 61st birthday—he announced the German surrender, an occasion of great public rejoicing that became known as VE (Victory in Europe) Day. In June, he signed the charter that brought the United Nations (an organization with members from all over the world who agree to cooperate with each other and promote global peace) into existence.

The most awesome responsibility facing Truman, however, was the decision about whether or not to try to end the war in Asia by dropping the atomic bomb on Japan. The U.S government had already spent $2.6 billion on the bomb, which had been developed by scientists working at Los Alamos, New Mexico (see J. Robert Oppenheimer entry). If the bomb was not used, the Allies would have to invade Japan, and military experts predicted that between 250,000 and 500,000

Did Truman Make The Right Decision?

Before the bomb was dropped, the true extent of its power was known only to a few scientists and leaders, and no one could guess what its long-term effects would be. Soon after he became president in April 1945, Harry S. Truman had to decide whether or not to drop an atomic bomb on Japan. He decided that bombing Japan was the right thing to do, but since then the question has been hotly debated. Some feel that the Allies had to drop the bomb in order to end the war, while others claim it was not the only solution. If you had been Truman, what would you have done?

After Germany surrendered (May 1945), Allied leaders had to decide how to bring the war in Asia to a close. In fact, Japan had no chance of winning now; its cities were in ruins after months of bombing and its economy was a shambles. Yet the Japanese still refused to surrender, and its leaders encouraged their people to fight to the bitter end. Japanese troops were highly disciplined, and they believed that surrender would bring disgrace. During the recent battle for the island of Okinawa, for example, over 100,000 Japanese soldiers had died while only 11,000 surrendered, and more than 100,000 civilians had been killed.

Allied leaders believed that an invasion of Japan's main islands would cause many casualties (deaths and injuries) on both sides. In fact, President Truman had been told that as many as 500,000 to one million Allied soldiers might die (later estimates put that figure at around 70,000). During the war, Japan had gained a bad reputation not only for the surprise attack on Pearl Harbor but because of its harsh treatment of political prisoners, and there was a widespread feeling that Japan deserved to be punished. It is also known that Japan was working on its own atomic bomb and might have used it against the United States.

Yet some military commanders claimed that neither dropping the bomb nor invading would be necessary, because Japan was about to collapse. Those who now condemn Truman's decision point out that the United States had already spent $2 billion on the development of the atomic bomb that would go to waste if it were not used. They even contend that the main reason the bombs (especially the second one) were dropped was to test their effects on human beings. Others claim that Truman wanted to keep the Soviet Union in line by demonstrating U.S. power.

Did the atomic bomb actually prevent far more deaths than it caused, or did it cause an event of unprecedented human suffering that could and should have been avoided? This question is still being argued.

Truman announcing the Japanese surrender to the press on August 14, 1945. *(Reproduced by permission of AP/Wide World Photos.)*

American soldiers would lose their lives. The Japanese were expected to be fierce defenders of their native land, who would fight to the death rather than accept capture or surrender.

Truman appointed an interim committee to weigh the alternatives. The committee recommended using the bomb on a major Japanese city without warning, even though many civilians (not just military personnel) would surely be killed.

Truman gave the order to go ahead, and bombs were dropped on Hiroshima on August 6 and Nagasaki on August 9. The bombs killed at least 100,000 people immediately, with many more falling ill and later dying from the sickness caused by the radiation released by the explosions. Whether Truman made the right choice has been debated ever since: many people feel that nothing could justify such a horrendous loss of innocent lives, while others claim that the action prevented the deaths of a much larger number of people.

"The buck stops here!"

When the Japanese signed a surrender treaty in September 1945, the war was officially over. Truman now faced a whole new host of difficult tasks, including returning the soldiers to normal life, closing down the various war agencies, managing the transition from wartime to peacetime economy, and dealing with inflation (rising prices on goods). He replaced the model of a gun on his desk with one of a plow, and also placed there a plaque that read, "The buck stops here!" That meant that as the person with final authority on so many matters, he took full responsibility for his own decisions.

Although he was a seasoned local politician, Truman lacked experience in foreign affairs. He learned fast, though, and during his first term he began to reverse America's usual tendency to stay out of other nations' affairs. He thought the United States should take an active role in keeping the whole world safe and free, and especially in keeping it free from communism (the political system in which all property is owned jointly, rather than by individuals; the Soviet Union was a strong Communist country at the time).

Taking an active role in the world

Truman opposed the spread of communism through three major programs: the Truman Doctrine, which gave billions of dollars to countries threatened by Communist takeover (in particular Turkey and Greece); the European Recovery Plan (known as the Marshall Plan), which offered economic aid to help European countries recover from the devastating effects of the war; and the North Atlantic Treaty Organization (NATO), which offered military assistance to protect countries from the Communist threat.

The fair deal

On issues closer to home, Truman continued to push for many of the New Deal programs that President Roosevelt had established, which Truman now called the "Fair Deal." These included federal controls on the economy, more civil rights laws, low-cost housing, a higher minimum wage, and repeal of the Taft-Hartley Act (which put tight restrictions on labor unions). He called for more financial aid for education, and access to health insurance for all Americans. But the time was not ripe for many of Truman's ideas, even though they would become popular several decades later. Just after the war, people wanted to relax, not worry about social problems. In addition, the Republican-controlled Congress blocked many of Truman's plans. Republicans are generally opposed to programs and laws, such as those Truman was proposing, that increase the size of the federal government and give it more control over business and the economy.

A surprising victory

When it came time for the 1948 election, many thought Truman had little chance of winning. He was opposed not only by Republican candidate Thomas Dewey but also by a group called the "Dixiecrats," led by South Carolina governor J. Strom Thurmond, who were against Truman's policies in favor of equal rights for African Americans (especially his 1948 Executive Order 9981 that called for integration of the armed forces); and by the Progressive Party, led by Henry Wallace.

Determined to win the presidency on his own merits, Truman began a high-energy "whistle-stop" campaign (referring to the sound of the campaign train pulling into a station) during which he traveled 22,000 miles and made 271 speeches. Campaigning under the slogan, "Give 'em hell Harry!" and criticizing what he called the "Do-Nothing 80th Congress," Truman took his message to factory workers in the cities and to farmers in the rural areas; he was also the first U.S. president to appear in Harlem, an African American community in New York City.

The morning after the election, no one was more surprised that Truman had won than the *Chicago Tribune,* which ran the headline "Dewey Defeats Truman!" In fact, Truman had beat Dewey by 2,000,000 votes.

The Korean War

The biggest foreign policy issue of Truman's second term was the Korean War (1950–1953), which began when Communist North Korea (backed by the Soviet Union and China) invaded South Korea. The United Nations Security Council voted to back South Korea, and as the leading member of the United Nations the United States sent troops to fight the North Koreans. But Truman did not declare war, choosing to refer to the conflict as a "police action." This left many Americans confused about what was happening in Korea and why the United States was involved.

A major controversy erupted when General Douglas MacArthur (1880–1964; see entry), the leader of the U.S. troops in Korea, publicly disagreed with U.S. policy in the conflict. Determined to show that in a democratic country the military must be under the control of a civilian government, Truman fired MacArthur. The Korean War ended in 1953, after Truman had left office, with a truce that left North and South Korea in an uneasy standoff.

Losing popularity

Meanwhile, back in the United States, both the Korean War and China's fall to communism in 1949 (when Nationalists led by Chiang Kai-Shek [1887–1975; see entry] were driven from the country) had raised serious concerns about the spread of communism. Republican leaders claimed that Communist sympathizers had infiltrated the U.S. government; in response Truman set up the Federal Employee Loyalty Program in 1947. He did not respond as well to charges that some parts of his own administration were corrupt, some of which proved to be true.

By 1952, Truman's popularity had dropped dramatically, and he decided not to run for president again. During the last few months of his presidency, he made labor unions as well as mill owners angry by dealing with a steel strike by having the government take over the mills. The Supreme Court agreed with the mill owners that a president did not have the power to take such an action. When election time came, Truman campaigned for the Democratic candidate, Illinois governor Adlai Stevenson, who was soundly beaten by the very popular former general, Dwight D. Eisenhower (1890–1969; see entry).

A quiet retirement

Truman returned to Independence to live in his nearly one-hundred-year-old house and to work on his memoirs (published in three volumes: *Year of Decisions,* [1955]; *Years of Trial and Hope,* [1956]; and *Mr. Citizen,* [1960]. The Harry S. Truman Library opened in Independence in 1957, and Truman worked there every day for nine years, until ill health slowed him down. About the library he said (as quoted in an article by Susanne Roschwalb and Gordon Smith in *USA Today*), "I want this to be a place where young people can come and learn what the office of the president is, what a great office it is no matter who happens to be in it at the time."

In his last years, Truman spent most of his time reading history, biographies, and books on the development of American government. He died in Kansas City at age eighty-eight and was buried on the grounds of the Truman Library.

Where to Learn More

Books

Daniels, Jonathan. *The Man of Independence.* Columbia: University of Missouri Press, 1998.

Ferrell, Robert H. *Harry S. Truman and the Modern American Presidency.* Boston: Little, Brown, 1983.

Kirkendall, Richard S. *Harry S. Truman Encyclopedia.* Boston: G. K. Hall, 1989.

McCullough, David. *Truman.* New York: Simon and Schuster, 1993.

Ross, Irwin. *The Loneliest Campaign: The Truman Victory of 1948.* Westport, CT: Greenwood Press, 1968.

Periodicals

Roschwalb, Susanne A. and Gordon L. Smith. "Harry S. Truman: America's Last Great Leader?" *USA Today* (January 1995): 86.

Index